WORLD IN THEIR HANDS

WORLD IN THEIR HANDS

THE STORY OF THE FIRST
WOMEN'S RUGBY WORLD CUP

MARTYN THOMAS

POLARIS
PUBLISHING

POLARIS PUBLISHING LTD
c/o Aberdein Considine
2nd Floor, Elder House
Multrees Walk
Edinburgh
EH1 3DX

Distributed by Birlinn Limited

www.polarispublishing.com

Text copyright © Martyn Thomas, 2022
Foreword © Sarah Hunter, 2022

ISBN: 9781913538934
eBook ISBN: 9781913538941

British Library Cataloguing-in-Publication Data
A catalogue record for this book is available on request from the British Library.

Designed and typeset by Polaris Publishing, Edinburgh
Printed in Great Britain by CPI Group (UK) Ltd, Croydon, CR0 4YY

CONTENTS

AUTHOR NOTE

THIS BOOK CENTRES on the inspiring stories of a group of pioneering women who refused to conform to society's expectations of them. Many of those who feature in these pages possess both an infectious love of rugby and a relentless drive to improve the lot of women who wish to play it. Kathy Flores, who tragically died in October 2021, was one of those women. Captain of the first ever USA women's national team, a member of the squad that competed in the first two Women's Rugby World Cups and coach of the Women's Eagles at the tournament in 2006 and 2010, there is not much she didn't achieve in her 40-plus years associated with the game. 'She basically was always trailblazing,' former USA prop Jamie Burke told me shortly after Kathy had passed away from colon cancer.

I had the privilege of speaking to Kathy for this book in May 2020. Her thoughts and opinions are quoted in the following pages in the present tense as they were spoken at the time. This is in keeping with the style of the book and is not intended to cause offence to anyone reading.

Surnames used in the book are, to the best of my knowledge, those that the person in question used at the time of the World Cup. Mary Forsyth, for example, is referred to throughout as Mary Forsyth, even when relaying an anecdote or story from a time when she would have been known by her maiden name, Schofield. Sue Dorrington is referred to as such throughout. Although her official surname was Wachholz-Dorrington in 1991, she went by Dorrington professionally, including in correspondence related to the organisation of the World Cup, and continues to do so today.

To my Dad, who is the reason I first picked up an oval ball, and to Romy, who I hope will grow up in a world that allows her to be whatever and whoever she wants to be.

FOREWORD

HAVING BEEN INTERVIEWED by Martyn Thomas on several occasions, it was great to see his journalistic skills used to shine a light on such a significant and important moment in the history of women's rugby and it is an honour to write this foreword. As a current Red Rose who has been lucky enough to have played in three World Cups to date and is hoping to be involved in a fourth, when the world of rugby heads to New Zealand for RWC 2021 playing in 2022, I have never had to give a second thought to having the opportunity to compete at the tournament. However, this has not always been the case and it was therefore compelling reading to understand not only the history of the game and how women struggled to be accepted within the sport but also how the first Women's Rugby World Cup came about.

After reading *World in Their Hands*, I feel rather ignorant that my understanding and knowledge of the history of the great sport that I have loved playing for over 25 years was so poor. Martyn's decision to take us back to the 19th century to give the reader an understanding of the history of both women's and men's rugby helps to showcase the landscape around the world which would inevitably pave the way for the first Women's World Cup.

I now have an appreciation of how the women's game struggled to be included and accepted across the world, which really does make me thankful for the era of the game I have been so lucky to play in. Having been part of an amateur era for much of my career, I can empathise with some of the struggles the women of the past went through. However, I have never had to be in fear of playing rugby or had to fight incredible battles to be allowed to play, and I am now so lucky to call myself a professional player – something that without these incredible women and men I might never have been able to do.

The first-hand accounts we hear throughout the book from Deborah Griffin, Alice Cooper, Sue Dorrington and Mary Forsyth really bring the story to life and gives a wonderful insight into what the organising committee went through from both a logistical point of view and an emotional one as well.

I believe that most players today take for granted being able to play in a World Cup. Not from a selection point of view but from the fact that there is one to play in and it is something that just happens every four years. I don't believe many would have any appreciation of how it began. Therefore, it is with great thanks that the players of today and future generations owe a debt to Griffin, Cooper, Dorrington and Forsyth for their perseverance, persistence and stubbornness to ensure that the first World Cup in 1991 took place. The ambition and risks that they took to ensure the tournament happened created a moment in history that changed the game forever.

We must also not forget those from across the world who went before Griffin, Cooper, Dorrington and Forsyth for everything they did in the fight for women to play rugby from Laurie O'Reilly to Henri Fléchon and Helen Matthews to Emily Valentine, Nita Webbe and everybody in between. Without these incredible, and at times brave, pioneers, the game would certainly not be where it is today and everyone within women's rugby can be eternally grateful.

I would highly recommend this book to any player past or present to understand the history of the amazing tournament we are extremely lucky to get an opportunity to play in every four years. Many, many players would have loved to but never had the opportunity.

Thank you, Martyn, for bringing this story to life.

Sarah Hunter
England captain

STATE OF THE UNION

IN LATE AUGUST 1990, an envelope dropped through the letter box of the North London flat Deborah Griffin shared with her husband Chris Brown. Griffin was 31 and around seven months pregnant with the couple's first child Victoria, who would be born a little over two months later. But as the correspondence flopped onto the floor on that summer morning, the expectant mother had little desire to wind down.

A successful accountant at a firm in the City of London, Griffin was also one of the most influential figures in Britain's burgeoning women's rugby scene. Since first picking up an oval ball as a student a dozen years previously, she had been at the forefront of the movement which had helped female participation blossom from a few university teams and one club side in Wales into an organised structure. Thanks to Griffin and others, a dedicated governing body now oversaw a league and cup system, as well as both regional and international representative sides.

In 1983, Griffin had been a founding member of the Women's Rugby Football Union (WRFU), which ran the women's game in England, Scotland and Wales and was looking to expand into Ireland. A year later, she helped set up England's first female club, Finchley WRFC, before, in 1986, leaving North West London with her teammates and moving south to Richmond to take advantage of better facilities and rights at the city's second oldest club.

During this time, Griffin held various roles within the WRFU, and her flat at 224A Camden Road had became a de facto PO Box for the organisation. Scores of letters and faxes would arrive from clubs and national bodies across the world enquiring about the progress of the women's game in the UK and Ireland and seeking advice on all manner of subjects, from setting up the game in their own locales to organising fixtures for future tours. More recently, the correspondence had almost exclusively been concerned with Griffin's latest and most ambitious project: the first Women's Rugby World Cup.

The WRFU had agreed to host a European Cup in 1991 following a relatively successful first edition in eastern France in 1988. By the end of 1989, however, enquiries had reached the organisation from teams beyond the Continent, first from two US club sides and then the national associations responsible for the women's game in the USA, Canada and New Zealand. Although these approaches were tentative, they were taken seriously enough that WRFU treasurer Kim Rowland sought the advice of the organisation's insurance brokers on staging a World Cup consisting of 'between five and six teams' during a meeting on 9 January 1990.

Four days later, Griffin outlined her proposals for the tournament for the first time, at a WRFU committee meeting in Loughborough. She insisted the document produced represented 'purely my own thoughts to get the ball rolling' as she urged her colleagues 'to start organising this ASAP'. But the outline of the inaugural Women's Rugby World Cup can be seen in those early plans. Her peers were so taken with them, in fact, that they installed her as chair of the organising committee and asked her to make her thoughts a reality.

Griffin was joined on the organising committee by three clubmates from Richmond: Alice Cooper, Sue Dorrington and Mary Forsyth. Dorrington and Forsyth had played alongside Griffin since their days at Finchley and brought considerable fundraising and financial expertise to the group. Cooper, who had taken up rugby shortly after the team moved to Richmond, was a regular contributor to *Rugby World & Post*, writing about the women's game. She would act as the World Cup's press officer.

By the beginning of August, having received encouraging feedback, if not official confirmation, from the majority of teams invited to take part, Griffin had written to the man effectively in charge of men's rugby union, Keith Rowlands, to alert him to their plans to hold a Women's Rugby World Cup the following April. Rowlands was the general secretary of the International Rugby Football Board (IRFB), having become the first paid administrator in the governing body's 102-year history on his appointment in 1988.

To purists, Rowlands' salary was the latest sign of the sport's inexorable slide into professionalism, as was the relaxation of the amateur code which he subsequently oversaw.[i] The general secretary was also a supporter of the men's Rugby World Cup (RWC), having voted in favour of the global tournament in 1985 as one of Wales' two IRFB representatives.

The men's event, which was first staged in Australia and New Zealand in 1987, had opened the game up to new commercial opportunities, and as a director of the 1991 tournament, due to be held in the UK, Ireland and France, Rowlands wanted to safeguard and expand those new revenue streams.

---

[i] On his sudden death in November 2006, Keith Rowlands' obituary in *The Times* stated that 'the Welshman ... was at the heart of the transition of rugby union from amateurism to professionalism'.

As Griffin thumbed the latest envelope to arrive through her door, she would have identified the likely sender by the Bristol postmark. But as she scanned the letter past the distinctive black, green and blue letterhead of the IRFB, she would have had no idea whether its contents would prove to be a gateway or a roadblock to her plans.

*****

Whatever message was contained within the envelope was unlikely to deter Griffin (or Cooper, Dorrington and Forsyth) from the mission of staging the inaugural women's World Cup, but the task would be made easier by having Rowlands' support. The WRFU (the body which oversaw the women's game in England, Scotland and Wales) had grown independently of the men's home unions and as such did not fall under the authority of the IRFB. In theory, that meant they could do what they wanted. In practice, though, Griffin would have known that even tacit approval from the men's game would ensure the quest for teams, venues and sponsors was less fraught.

Rowlands was himself evidence that the IRFB was beginning to modernise and prepare for a more professional age. But was the Board ready to embrace women's rugby? The headed paper on which he had written to Griffin featured, in the top-right corner, a rugby ball with a map of the world embossed on it. But if this small detail signified the game's desire to capture the hearts and minds of sportspeople across the globe, then it was at odds with the way in which it had operated for much of its first 100 years' existence.

Born out of a law dispute so fractious that the annual international between England and Scotland was not played in 1885, the IRFB came to life a year later following a meeting of the home unions in Dublin. England would not join until 1890, however, when they secured entry on terms deemed acceptable.[ii] This was an age when each nation played the game to slightly different rules, and disagreements over their implementation were common. Thus, the primary objective of the Board then, one that it retains today, was to act as the overall authority on the laws of the game.

As time moved on and the 19th century became the 20th, the IRFB began to concern itself with international fixtures and tours. These were largely confined to the outposts of the British Empire (Australia, New Zealand and South Africa), where it was believed that rugby could help instil the middle-class values of the mother country. Although each of the southern-hemisphere nations quickly proved themselves to be more than a match for the home unions, they were not deemed worthy of a place on the Board until 1949. It would take another 29 years for an eighth nation to be invited onto the IRFB, when France became its first non-English-speaking member.

It was not until the 1980s and the advent of the men's World Cup that the IRFB began to think and act like an international federation with responsibility to grow and develop the game outside the traditional nations. Until that point, it had generated no money and possessed no assets, headquarters or permanent staff. Not pivoting sooner has arguably made the task of expansion into new countries and territories harder in the ensuing decades. To understand why the IRFB operated as a closed shop for so long, you must go back to the very beginning, when the sport itself emerged into existence on the large, open playing field of Rugby School.

Although a code of football had been played on the Close at Rugby since at least the early 19th century, it was not until 1845 that anyone chose to write down a set of rules to govern the

---

[ii] England's Rugby Football Union refused to join the Board on an equal footing to the other home unions, arguing that it deserved a bigger say as it was home to the majority of clubs. Ultimately, England were given six votes, while Ireland, Scotland and Wales each had two.

game. Before that, disputes had been settled by team captains, and amendments to the accepted rules were passed down through the student body by word of mouth. Even after they had been committed to paper, the guidelines were guarded jealously by those who had been privileged to attend the public school.

The game formed an unofficial yet integral part of those schoolboys' education, one which was staunchly anti-effeminate. Rugby's famed headmaster Thomas Arnold, who arrived at the school in 1828, was no sportsman. He tolerated the playing of football only as a tool to steer the student body away from what he believed were the two biggest threats to a life of moral and religious rectitude: homosexuality and masturbation. The game as played at Rugby became tied to a notion of masculinity, the Close being considered a nursery for the next generation of leaders in business, government and war.

Like the vast majority of the population, women and girls were locked on the outside looking in, even as the game spread beyond Rugby. As it did, carried on trains to all corners of the UK in the minds of former pupils and the pages of *Tom Brown's School Days* and the Clarendon Commission report[iii], so the number of varying rules it was played to multiplied. In 1871, eight years after it was nearly subsumed within the embryonic Football Association (FA), a definitive attempt to codify the game was made when the Rugby Football Union (RFU) was founded. Three Old Rugbeians (A. Rutter, E.C. Holmes and L.J. Maton), lawyers by profession, were entrusted with drawing up rugby's first set of laws.

Each of the first five presidents of the RFU were former Rugby pupils, which only added to the nascent union's sense that it was the divine custodian of the game. Moreover, those men (many of playing age) had seen how their contemporaries from Eton,

---

[iii] A royal commission of 1861–64, the Clarendon Commission examined the governance and curriculum of nine public schools in England. Among other aspects, it praised Rugby's ethos of sporting competition.

Winchester and other public schools had been sidelined when Association football became a sport for the masses and were not willing to make the same mistake. Therefore, as the sport grew in the late 19th and early 20th centuries, it did so largely in the image of its middle-class custodians.

Rugby was promoted as 'the most ancient of British sports', a participation rather than spectator pastime which carried with it a certain social currency. It was a world in which the amateur ideal became sacrosanct and any developments made were viewed through the prism of Empire. International rugby became a private members' club, akin to those in which the IRFB regularly held its meetings, being run by and for the benefit of a small number of nations. Women did not feature in this sphere in any meaningful way, certainly not as potential players.

By the time Griffin began plotting the first women's World Cup, the picture had been altered irreversibly by events of the 1980s. There was still a degree of English exceptionalism (primarily when it came to the RFU stalling on passing on concessions to the IRFB's anti-professionalism regulations to its own players), but the Board had undoubtedly adopted a more global outlook. Nine nations were made full members of the IRFB ahead of the first men's World Cup in 1987, and a further 25 were admitted before the end of the decade.

That was not necessarily a positive move for the women tasked with organising their own global tournament, though. Unions in less traditional rugby-playing nations (such as Canada, the USA and Spain) had already taken on responsibility for female participation. That placed the women's committees of those unions under the jurisdiction of the IRFB. Would those countries need to seek board approval before committing to playing in the women's World Cup? If they did, would it be granted?

*****

It is unclear what the Rugby-educated Victorian presidents of the RFU would have made of women playing rugby, especially at Richmond. However, much like the notion that a team of Frenchmen could rock up at Rectory Field and beat England, it would no doubt have been heartily derided.[iv] That is not to say that women were completely absent from the Victorian rugby scene, as we will see, but their role was largely restricted to that of supporters. Blackheath's Rectory Field was one of many grounds round the country which had ladies' enclosures, and Arthur Guillemard, RFU president between 1878 and 1882, once rather mockingly suggested that 'Lady spectators' were in part to blame for the decision to ban the practice of hacking[v].

Rugby was, of course, a very different place by 1990. The idea that the Welsh state-educated son of a policeman would land the biggest job in rugby (and be paid for the privilege) would also have been anathema to those running the game at the end of the 19th century. However, Keith Rowlands epitomised how both the game and British society had changed over the intervening century, albeit at a gradual, sometimes glacial pace. Victorian gentlemen would certainly have acknowledged the 'pluck' he displayed as a commanding second row for London Welsh, Llanelli, Cardiff, Wales, the Barbarians and British and Irish Lions, even if they may have felt the number of clubs he amassed undignified. According to Syd Miller, the 6 ft 5 in, 17 stone lock had been the only Lion 'capable of matching the huge Springboks in physicality' during the 1962 tour of South Africa.

Rowlands' playing career was brought to an end by a broken leg, suffered against one of those former clubs, London Welsh,

---

[iv] Following the formation of the Football Association, it took six meetings to agree on a set of rules to govern the game. For much of that process there was hope concessions could be found to allow clubs playing under Rugby rules to join. However, when in the final meeting it became obvious that the new body would ban hacking, Blackheath's Francis Maule Campbell stormed out in disgust. He argued that doing so would 'do away with all the courage and pluck of the game, and I will be bound to bring over a lot of Frenchmen, who would beat you with a week's practice'.

[v] Hacking was the practice of bringing an opponent to ground by kicking his or her shins.

on New Year's Eve 1966. Eight weeks previously he had captained Cardiff to a famous win over Australia at the Arms Park, but as that door closed, another opened into the world of administration. On hanging up his boots, Rowlands entered the committee room at Cardiff, becoming chairman for the 1974/75 season. His profile rose as chairman of selectors during a particularly successful time for the Welsh Rugby Union, and he was appointed one of the body's two representatives on the IRFB in 1983.

Less than two years later, in March 1985, Rowlands played a key role as the sport underwent its most seismic change since the 'Big Split' which had ripped it in two[vi]. At the pivotal IRFB meeting in Paris that month, called to run the rule over a feasibility study into a potential men's Rugby World Cup, the Welshman voted in favour of the plans proposed by Australia and New Zealand. All four representatives from Ireland and Scotland had rejected the idea, as the Home Unions had done repeatedly over the previous century, but Rowlands and England's John Kendall-Carpenter were persuaded to split their respective nations' votes, thus ensuring the proposal was carried by ten votes to six.[vii]

Rowlands had staked his reputation on the World Cup being a success, serving on the organising committee of the inaugural tournament in Australia and New Zealand. It was a gamble which paid off handsomely. Rugby World Cup 1987 opened the game up to a raft of new commercial, broadcast and sponsorship opportunities, and the IRFB was keen to exploit those further when the tournament came to Europe four years later. In his role as director of the 1991 World Cup, Rowlands had been part of

---

[vi] On the 29th August, 1895 representatives of 21 clubs met at the George Hotel in Huddersfield and agreed to establish a Northern Rugby Football Union 'on the principle of payment for bona-fide broken-time only'. Battle lines were drawn as the group resigned en masse from the RFU, which hastily drew up a definition of professionalism and rules to outlaw it. Clubs and players found guilty of transgressing those laws were banned for life, but that could not stop a drain of teams from Lancashire and Yorkshire flowing to what would become rugby league.

[vii] The delegates from Australia, New Zealand, France and South Africa all voted in favour.

the negotiations which ended in October 1989 with ITV and Channel 4 signing a television deal worth around £3m. At the time, he said the tournament would be 'the biggest sporting event held in the UK since the soccer World Cup in 1966'. 'It is up to us to set standards for others to follow', he added, 'and we are in no way ashamed to seek sponsorship to strengthen the sport'.

Eight months later, commercial director Alan Callan predicted the men's tournament would generate £66m, including £41m in sponsorship and 'commercial spin-offs'. However, by the time Griffin's original letter dropped through Rowlands' letter box, those projections were beginning to look overly optimistic. With a little more than a year to go until the tournament kicked off, the men's World Cup had failed to sign a single deal with an event sponsor. Heinz would pay £1m to come on board before the end of 1990, but that sum was half what Callan and his company CPMA had promised for each of the eight packages available. Pressure on the IRFB and its organising committee (and therefore on Rowlands) was building, and it is not surprising that it would seek to safeguard its product from anything it thought could threaten or devalue it.

In his reply to Griffin, Rowlands did not warn her against staging a women's World Cup. He had no right to. As a non-affiliated body, the IRFB did not have any jurisdiction over what the WRFU did. 'However, I did obviously convey to John [Taylor, whose company would assist the hunt for sponsorship for the women's World Cup] my concern at an event which, without detail of timing or content, could act as a counter to the efforts of our event in 1991 in terms of media, sponsorship, public support and interest', Rowlands wrote. 'The very fact that this event came as a surprise to me gave me some concern.'

The IRFB secretary went on to ask Griffin to provide a 'broad outline' of her plans 'so that I can keep the organisers of Rugby World Cup informed and at the same time ensure that there is no real conflict of interest between us.' Rowlands signed off by praising the 'passion and respect for the spirit and traditions of our Game, held within women's rugby', but the tone of the correspondence could, and maybe should, have set off alarm bells within the Women's Rugby World Cup organising committee.

Griffin, Cooper, Dorrington and Forsyth were not looking for the kind of sums that the IRFB believed would swell its coffers, but the £100,000 they did hope to raise was no small beer. If companies were pausing for thought about sponsoring a tournament with a multi-million-pound broadcast deal in place, how would a competition due to be played largely at small provincial grounds with no guaranteed live coverage fare?

2

EARLY PIONEERS

SCOTLAND DID NOT send a team to the inaugural Women's Rugby World Cup, the tournament simply coming too soon in their development. That does not mean, though, that the country played no part in the history of the women's game. Far from it.

When proposals for the tournament began to be discussed in earnest at the start of 1990, there were only six women's teams north of the border, all associated with universities. Scotland would not contest a women's test for another three years, but those clubs were beginning to find their voice.

At a WRFU committee meeting in Loughborough on 13 January 1990, at which Deborah Griffin's initial plans for a European Cup were first distributed, the Scottish clubs announced their intention, via a letter from Ann Mackay, to form their own league. Up until that point, the six teams had competed as part of the northern section of the WRFU's Student Cup and came under the jurisdiction of the North of England committee. The cost of travel to matches and distances involved had, though, become prohibitive. Mackay, who was the Royal

(Dick) Veterinary College RFC captain, therefore wrote to the committee to inform them that the Scottish teams would be withdrawing from the Student Cup. She requested that they 'recognise the new Scottish League'.

Minutes from the meeting record that the 'committee agreed Scottish teams (all college sides at present) should have their own league'. Representatives of the six clubs were also invited to future meetings. It was the first step on the road to the formation not only of a national team but also the Scottish Women's Rugby Union in 1993. When the WRFU began to disband, to be replaced by individual unions representing England, Ireland, Scotland and Wales, it was the Scots who walked away first.

The saltire might have been absent as the World Cup got under way in South Wales in April 1991, but it is possible to trace the origin of the competition's story all the way back to Scotland. Hundreds of years before football enjoyed a renaissance at English public schools and was co-opted as a barometer of manliness and split into Association and Rugby rules, there is evidence to suggest that women in parts of Scotland were avid players. Certainly, on 21 August 1628, Mr John Lindsay, a Church of Scotland minister in the village of Carstairs, is recorded as being appalled by 'the break of the Sabbath by the insolent behaviour of men and women in footballing, dancing and Barley Breaks'.

Games of football had been played in the UK since at least the time of the Romans and became a popular pastime to celebrate festivals, such as Shrove Tuesday (or Fastern's E'en as it was known in Scotland). Matches were huge amorphous affairs which pitted sections of towns (e.g., those who lived on opposite sides of a river, or married men and bachelors) or villages against one another. The aim of these contests was simple: to gain possession of a round object, the football, and propel it, although usually not with the foot, towards a target. These goals might be miles apart, and therefore the fun could last from dawn until dusk without one being scored.

It was not uncommon for these matches to leave a trail of damaged property and broken limbs, and football therefore aroused the suspicion of the authorities. Playing of it was banned in London by Edward II in 1314, and several monarchs over the succeeding centuries issued similar proclamations. Under Henry VIII, it became a penal offence to keep a house or ground designated for football, but that did not do much to quell the sport's popularity. Indeed, 28 years after the incident in Carstairs, a minister in nearby Lamington wrote of 'one superstitious and abominable custom that has continued still in the parish, that men and women used promiscuously to play at foot-ball upon Fasting's even'.

It is in Scotland, too, that the first accounts of women playing against each other (rather than alongside men) are documented. On Tuesday 26 November 1889, the *Berwickshire News and General Advertiser* carried an article about a female football match in Coldstream on Ash Wednesday 1786. Under the subheading 'Petticoats Run Mad: or, The World Turned Topsy-turvey', the paper cites the Berwick Museum as its source of information for a match 'played with uncommon keenness' in which 'caps, handkerchiefs, petticoats, and every other article of female attire, suffered a general wreck in the hardy contest'. Darkness enveloped the players before a result could be determined, and so the women did the honourable thing and retired to an ale house.

Although the article suggests the teams returned to the pitch on Easter Monday, the Coldstream match seems likely to have been a one-off event. Around 45 miles further north, though, there is evidence that women were playing regularly. Not much is known about the game contested by the fisherwives of Fisherrow Harbour. Writing in his *Old Statistical Account of Scotland* in 1795, Dr Alexander Carlyle dedicates only 23 words to it: 'On

Shrove Tuesday there is a standing match at foot-ball, between the married and unmarried women, in which the former are always victors'. The last seven of those words, however, would suggest that this was an annual contest.

The fact that the married women are 'always victors' has been seen by some as evidence that the best player on the team of spinsters won themselves a husband and thus bolstered the opposition for the next year's contest. Such practices did exist, but what we know about the fisherwives suggests they did not readily conform to gender norms. 'They do the work of men, their manners are masculine, and their strength and activity is equal to their work. Their amusements are of the masculine kind', Carlyle writes, adding that they used their free time to play golf as well as football. Four days a week, it was the women's job to carry the catch from the harbour's fishing boats to market in Edinburgh. When those vessels came in late, it would not be 'unusual for them to perform their journey of five miles, by relays, three of them being employed in carrying one basket, and shifting it from one to another every hundred yards, by which means they have been known to arrive at the Fishmarket in less than 1/4 ths of an hour.' A gruelling endeavour, yes, but one that highlighted the women's physical prowess and would have honed the skills and teamwork needed for the annual football match.

*****

As the industrial revolution changed Britain, and people flocked from villages to the new cities in search of work, so the playing of folk football matches began to decline. The article carried by the *Berwickshire News and General Advertiser* in 1889 suggests that 'the ancient game of football, which seems to be neglected by the men of the present age, is likely to be handed down to posterity by the women'. Of course, there is a simple reason why this might have been true. The new forms of football developed in the English public schools provided men with a simpler and more regular outlet for their footballing passions. They didn't have to wait for Shrove Tuesday to tumble about with the rest of their village. Now they could head down to Rectory Field or Whalley Range on a Saturday, provided they had the right social connections, and take part in a contest which would last no longer than a couple of hours and not, unless something went wrong, impact on their ability to work.

However, these new football codes (whether Association, Rugby or indeed Australian rules) were designed explicitly for men; in rugby's case, a specific type of man. So, where did this leave women? As we have seen, evidence exists of the enthusiasm some women and girls had for football. A young servant and four female friends were found guilty by magistrates in the Lincolnshire town of Horncastle on Christmas Eve, 1813 of playing the game on the Sabbath. However, as the century progressed, Victorian views on what constituted 'lady-like' behaviour generally became more conservative. Popularised by predominantly male medical theorists, women began to be valued more and more for their ability to bear children. Any endeavours considered detrimental to their reproductive organs (whether mental or physical) were discouraged.

In 1894, the *British Medical Journal* released a paper on reports that 'female football clubs will shortly contest in public'. Noting that 'woman seems now to have a task before her in which we fear greatly she will fail', the article repeated many of the tropes which had come to dominate the debate on female participation in sport. 'If girls choose to kick a ball about a field between their lessons no one need object, but for young women to attempt to play at football as played is another matter. Many of the sudden jerks and twists involved in the game are exactly such as are known to cause serious internal displacements, and it is impossible to think what happens when the arms are thrown up to catch the ball, or when a kick is made with full force, and misses, without admitting the injury which may be thereby produced in the inner mechanism of the female frame. Nor can one overlook the chances of injury to the breast.'

Such attitudes were not uncommon in the *British Medical Journal* (BMJ) a publication which 16 years previously had featured an 'extensive correspondence' on whether it was safe for a menstruating woman to cure meat. The BMJ's objections appear to have been raised this time by the formation of the British Ladies Football Club, a female Association team set up with the help of Nettie Honeyball. However, the journal's outrage at women's football came at least 13 years too late.

Helen Matthews, a suffragette, was behind the first official football matches in Britain to feature teams of women. Between 9 May and 27 June 1881, Matthews, under the pseudonym Mrs Graham, organised a series of 'Scotland v England' contests which took place in various towns and cities in Scotland and northern England. Featuring two teams of 11 players, these matches are commonly thought to have been played under Association rules. However, the report of their penultimate encounter at the Cattle Inn Athletic Grounds in Liverpool suggests that the final two games at least were played under rugby laws. The report of that fixture in the *Manchester Guardian* relayed that Scotland had made 'several touchdowns and one goal' during a period of dominance over their English opponents. Under rugby laws of the time, scoring a try was not worth any points in and of itself. Instead, it gave the attacking team 'a try at goal' from which they could score.

Scotland went on to win 2–1 (presumably adding a drop goal to their one converted try) and returned to the ground two days later and won 2–0. In the context of football in 1881 and the various interpretations of the rules and laws which were applied depending on where a match was played, it is plausible that the two matches in Liverpool were played as an 11-a-side rugby match or to a hybrid set of laws. Rugby and Association football were a lot more similar in those nascent days than they are today.

What these matches undoubtedly expose are contemporary attitudes towards women playing sport. The fact that Matthews and her players performed under assumed names suggests they did not feel safe to reveal themselves as female footballers.[i] According to contemporary reports, a crowd of around 5,000 watched the teams in Glasgow while 4,000 turned up for their contest in Blackburn a few weeks later. These spectators had not necessarily come to show their support. Violence broke out at more than one of the matches, the players being forced to take refuge in their omnibus as a police baton charge kept hundreds of 'roughs' at bay at the Shawfield Grounds in Glasgow. On 20 June, the *Manchester Guardian* ran an article headlined 'Disorderly scene at a women's football match'. Reporting on the teams' second outing in a matter of days at Cheetham Football Club, it detailed how the players were again chased to their waiting transport 'amid the jeers of the multitude and much disorder'. It is understandable, therefore, that those women connected to the venture would do what they could to ensure their involvement did not impact on their day-to-day lives.

Later in the decade, Ogden's produced a series of cigarette cards depicting women's cricket and football teams. The cards featured at least four rugby players, the most famous of whom is pictured lining up a drop goal. These cards cannot be taken as an example of shifting attitudes towards women playing football and rugby, however. On Good Friday 1887, two teams of women attempted to contest a match in Hull. According to one spectator who attended the match on Holderness Road, though, the game 'had not proceeded more than two or three minutes

---

[i] It has been speculated that Matthews used two pseudonyms, one with which to organise the matches, Mrs Graham, and another to line up as one of the teams' goalkeepers.

before the spectators began to encroach upon the ground and immediately they "closed in" on all sides until the players and spectators were one inseparable, screaming mass of excited men and fainting women'.

According to the letter, which was published in the *Hull Daily Mail* on Easter Monday, if it had not been for the 'energetic efforts' of police, the players might not have made it to safety. The idea of women playing rugby football was enough to attract thousands of curious spectators to matches, but once there they were not prepared to sit idly by while women, in the words of the paper's correspondent 'Full Back', proceeded to 'bring the game into disrepute'. On reflection, it was probably not support for female emancipation that Ogden's sexualised drawings of buxom women in tight-fitting sports kit were designed to arouse.

*****

Victorian sensibilities might have been offended by the thought of women playing contact sport, but as we have seen that did not mean the 'fairer sex' was uninterested in them. On the contrary, as rugby became a pastime enjoyed by spectators as well as players, female fans were not an uncommon sight. Albeit to satisfy social norms of the time, women who wanted to get a closer look at the action would have been confined to ladies' enclosures. Indeed, Arthur Guillemard, an Old Rugbeian and president of the RFU between 1878 and 1882, praised the restraint of these supporters as he bemoaned the 'great nuisance' of crowds creeping onto the field of play at unenclosed grounds.[ii] It seems logical to suggest that some of these female rugby fans, and quite possibly more if the examples of Helen Matthews and the Hull match are

---

[ii] Later in the same chapter, Guillemard wrote that 'lady spectators used to say that hacking over "looked terrible"' as he lamented the disappearance of the practice. However, that could be read as a slight on the 'manliness' of those who questioned the tactic's legitimacy as much as evidence that female fans were flocking to rugby matches.

anything to go by, harboured aspirations to experience the game as players themselves.

That was certainly the case for young Emily Valentine, whose story provides conclusive proof that at least one Victorian girl seized an opportunity to live out her oval-ball fantasies. Around 1887, at the time Ogden's rugby-themed cigarette cards were being pressed into packaging, Emily was challenging late 19th-century gender expectations in more ways than one. The youngest daughter of William Valentine, who taught classics at Portora Royal School in Enniskillen, she had access to an education usually reserved for boys. Wandering round the school grounds, meanwhile, brought her into contact with the game her older brothers played on the large lush playing fields. The youngster quickly became besotted. 'I loved rugby football', Emily would later write in her memoirs. 'I used to stand on the touch line in the cold damp Enniskillen winter, watching every moment of play, furious when my side muffed a ball, or went offside, bitterly disappointed when a goal was missed.'

Portora had been, and would be again, one of the finest Royal Schools in Ulster.[iii] William Valentine himself would be described by one of his former pupils as a 'scholar of a calibre seldom found in Irish schools'. The problem for Valentine and his colleagues was they had very few boys to teach as enrolment bottomed out in the penultimate decade of the 19th century. In 1885, the school admitted no boarders, and three years later the number of day boys was down to just 18. Not exactly an ideal scenario for a fee-paying institution, but manna from heaven for an eager 10-year-old whose dream it was to play in a real rugby match.

Given the school's numerical challenges of the time, it stands to reason that finding enough willing boys to raise a rugby team would have been difficult. The Valentines were keen to revive

[iii] Oscar Wilde was educated at Portora Royal School between 1864 and 1871, as was Samuel Beckett around half a century later.

the sport, however, and events transpired to present Emily with her chance. According to her account, written years later, she had assumed her usual position on the sideline to watch a pick-up game between pupils of the school when it became clear that the teams were uneven. 'I plagued them to let me play,' she remembered, to which the boys eventually replied: 'Oh, all right. Come on then.'

Emily was more than ready. She hastily removed her overcoat and hat, knowing that her preference for boys' boots was finally about to pay dividends as she strode onto the pitch to take her place in history. 'I got the ball – I can still feel the damp leathery smell of it, and see the tag of lacing at the opening,' Emily wrote. 'I grasped it and ran dodging, darting, but I was so keen to score that try that I did not pass it, perhaps when I should; I still raced on. I could see the boy coming towards me; I dodged, yes I could and breathless, with my heart thumping, my knees shaking a bit, I ran. Yes, I had done it; one last spurt and I touched down, right on the line. I had scored my try. I lay flat on my face and for a moment everything was black. I scrambled up, gave a hasty rub down to my knees. A ragged cheer went up from the spectators. I grinned at my brothers.'

That her effort ultimately added nothing to her team's score did not erase the joy that moment gave Emily. 'I knew I couldn't kick a goal, but that didn't worry or disappoint me,' she added. It was a feeling of accomplishment which would stay with her into her autumn years. She had proven to her brothers that she could match them on the rugby pitch, but there was an acknowledgement, too, that her tale was not to be broadcast. When her mother congratulated her male siblings on winning, Emily was kicked to make sure she stayed quiet. 'My brother raised his cup, looked at me, and drank then winked. "Good luck, wasn't it mum?"' Her contribution to the game remained a secret.

It would have stayed that way, too, had Emily not chronicled her own life for her family while living in a London nursing home almost 80 years later. Those memoirs were passed on to John Birch, who brought the story to a wider audience through his work for the women's rugby website *Scrumqueens*. Birch suggests that Emily went on to play in competitive matches for the school (again, not beyond the realms of possibility given Portora barely had enough pupils to field a full team at the time), forming a fearsome three-quarter line alongside her two brothers William jnr and John. Although they both went on to study at Trinity College Dublin, Emily's academic and sporting endeavours ended when she left Enniskillen. She married Major John Galwey, going on to live in India for a time before settling in London, where she died in 1967.

'Although she wasn't what you'd conventionally call a feminist, she certainly believed that women could do anything that they wanted to do,' her granddaughter Catherine Galwey told CNN in 2016. 'I think she would be very pleased to support people who wanted to play rugby and were female.' Emily would certainly have enjoyed watching the players darting and dodging at the inaugural Women's Rugby World Cup in 1991.

*****

Had Emily Valentine lived in Auckland rather than Enniskillen, she would almost certainly have answered Nita Webbe's call for female rugby players in June 1891. The new codes of football had arrived in New Zealand in much the same way as they had in other outposts of the British Empire – through settlers and the armed forces. Australia and Aotearoa experienced a huge influx of immigrants from the UK in the mid-19th century, some escaping the Irish famine, others looking to start a new life or exploit recent gold strikes. One such colonialist was

David Monro, who in 1841 left Edinburgh for Nelson, via Melbourne, having purchased four allotments of land in the new settlement.

Monro would serve as the speaker of the New Zealand House of Representatives between 1861 and 1870, receiving a knighthood for his services, but it was his son Charles who left a more lasting legacy on the country's cultural identity. In 1867, aged 16, Charles was sent to school at Christ's College Finchley in North London. Intended to give him the platform from which to launch a successful career in the army, it instead introduced him to rugby football. On returning to New Zealand in 1870, he joined the Nelson Football Club and petitioned it to adopt Rugby rules.[iv] Fortuitously, at this time, the headmaster of Nelson College was an Old Rugbeian, Reverend Frank Simmons, who readily offered up his school as a potential opponent. And so, on 14 May 1870, the Football Club took on the College in the country's first recognised rugby match, the former winning the 18-a-side contest 2–0 in front of 200 spectators on the Botanic Reserve. The seeds of New Zealand's love affair with rugby had been sewn, and within 35 years the game had been recognised as the country's national sport.

Although the immigrants who arrived in New Zealand from the UK in the 19th century, and their descendants, very much still considered themselves British, the distance between them and the 'old country' dictated that society evolved at a different pace. Life was tough and thousands of miles away from home, Victorian gender roles were more susceptible to blurring. Rugby was certainly not immune to this, with Australia and New Zealand prepared to innovate to a degree that conservative committeemen in England, Scotland, Wales and Ireland felt bordered on bastardisation. Unfortunately, though, it seems

---

[iv] Prior to this, most teams in New Zealand had played a mixture of Association and Melbourne (Australian) rules.

attitudes towards women and sport did not differ too greatly in New Zealand.

W.W. Robinson remembered seeing 'a crowd of all sorts, sizes, ages and sexes punting a small black football' in Auckland as early as 1868. Twenty years later, meanwhile, Wellington Girls' High School played a rugby match, with modified laws, against the Salvation Army. The *New Zealand Mail*'s 'Round the Corners' column advocated schoolgirl participation in February 1888, highlighting potential benefits in the classroom and stating that 'there could be no better game for girls than modified football'. Although the *New Zealand Times* (NZT) reproduced and defended the article, the proposal elicited 'mild jokes' and 'derision' from other publications. The NZT was keen to qualify its support for the format that would later be played by the Wellington Girls' High School on the premise that it was 'free from all elements of roughness'. Nita Webbe would make a similar point three years later, but her appeal for 'lady footballers' to contest matches full of running, tackling and scrums would meet with a rather predictable response.

Webbe launched her endeavour by placing advertisements in several newspapers in New Zealand. Her goal was to compile a group of 30 women willing to learn to play rugby and contest matches in New Zealand, either side of a tour of Australia. Those interested were encouraged to apply, with parental consent, and Webbe would pay travel costs to Auckland for the successful candidates. Support would also be provided once they reached the city. If initial press reports can be taken at face value, it seems she had some early success. On 2 June, the *Poverty Bay Herald* carried a story which stated: 'Thirty girls are training here (in Auckland) in the game of football, and are shortly to travel the colonies and play against each other as separate teams of fifteen each.'

Two days later, though, an advert appeared in the *Otago Daily Times* which appealed for '20 Young Ladies (with parents' consent) to PRACTISE FOOTBALL, preparatory to playing Auckland Ladies.' It is unlikely that Webbe lost two-thirds of her playing squad in two days, but perhaps she had overstated the number of women already signed up when speaking to the *Herald* to boost support for the venture. Either way, it seems odd that there is no mention of the tour of Australia. However advanced Webbe's plans were by then, she received a public rebuke on 5 June when the *Auckland Star* ran an editorial critical of the female footballers. 'We subscribe most heartily to the doctrine that every sphere in which women are fitted to take their part should be as freely open to them as to men,' the author opened, 'but there are some things for which women are constitutionally unfitted, and which are essentially unwomanly. A travelling football team composed of girls appears to us to be of this character.'

The editorial, which was reproduced in several papers round the country, went on to suggest that it could not 'conceive of either men or women who have sisters of their own being attracted by such a spectacle'. It pondered whether the players would be left stranded in Australia were Webbe's scheme to flop. 'It would also be well for the parents of girls who think of engaging in this enterprise to consider what will be their position if the enterprise proves a financial failure, which we sincerely hope and believe it will be.'

Webbe was given the right of reply three days later, pointing out the hypocrisy of the *Star*'s stance when it supported tours by travelling female actors, cricketers and swimmers. 'And now a team of lady footballers is projected here, you charitably hope it will end in a financial disaster. The football team are being taught by a regular trainer to play a clever game without any of the roughness characteristic of men's play. Strict observance to the rules will be enforced, and when they play in public I am confident that the verdict will be not only that there has been not the slightest breach of propriety, but a cleverer game has seldom been seen here.' Webbe's arguments, though, fell on deaf ears. 'Nothing our correspondent has said modifies our opinion,' the *Star*'s editor retorted. 'The popular taste is still elevated enough to insist upon grace and beauty in such exhibitions by female athletes.'

Although not all publications were as damning in their assessment of the 'lady footballers' as the *Star*, some went further. The *New Zealand Methodist* deemed it a 'discredit to New Zealand' for women to resort to such an activity to make money. Ultimately, though, we will never know how close Webbe came to producing two teams of astute rule-abiding rugby players. Just over a week before the team was due to play its first match, on Cass Square in Hokitika on 22 July, the *Wellington Post* reported that the scheme had been abandoned. No reason was given for the cancellation; however, it seems Nita Webbe's husband Frederick was fighting a fraud case at the time, which would have been a drain on the couple and their finances. He won and later sued for damages, but the ship had sailed on Nita's rugby ambitions. She moved to New South Wales, petitioned for divorce in 1902 and does not appear to have had any further dealings with the oval-ball game.

*****

News of Nita Webbe and her lady footballers is unlikely to have reached the RFU in London, but had it done so it would have been met with dismay and disdain. Like Helen Matthews' matches in Scotland and northern England a decade previously, Webbe's enterprise was overtly commercial. It had to be as touring Australia and New Zealand (or Scotland and Lancashire for that matter) was not cheap, and neither Webbe nor Matthews had a line of creditors or benevolent backers ready to stump up the cash. However, the fact that players were remunerated for their travel to Auckland and subsistence while there would have marked them out as professional at a time when being paid to play was heretical to the amateur ethos of the game and those in charge of it.

While Webbe, Matthews, Valentine and other Victorian women were fighting for acceptance, those male custodians were involved in an ongoing battle to keep rugby under the control of the (British) middle class. Many of the arguments against professionalism extolled by Arthur Budd and his contemporaries centred on a fear of losing the supremacy they believed was inherently theirs. They had watched as the grip of the 'gentleman' had loosened in other sports, such as Association football and rowing, both on the field of play or in the boat and in the boardroom. They were determined that the working (bogey-) man would not usurp them, too, and so resisted concessions such as broken-time payments until the 'Big Split' became an inevitability.

By the dawn of the 20th century, the game in England had been irrevocably divided. While the northern clubs, free of RFU control, were able to innovate and refine the sport as they deemed necessary, the powers-that-be were more concerned with proving the provenance of the original, union code. That is where William Webb Ellis came in, as the handy tale of a daring schoolboy, however hazy, provided those who needed one with a genesis for the game that those in Lancashire and Yorkshire were now tinkering with.

Anyone who didn't fit with rugby's vision of itself at this point was left on the outside. This included those women who questioned Victorian gender expectations and attempted to plant a flag in a world that wasn't yet ready for them. As so much of their stories was not documented, Matthews, Valentine and Webbe faded from memory. It would take almost 100 years for a team of female rugby players to embark on an overseas tour from New Zealand. The Crusadettes headed to England, rather than Australia, at the end of 1988 on a trip which would prove to be a pivotal event on the road to the first Women's Rugby World Cup.

3

A PICTURE OF HEALTH?

THE DECISION MADE by Deborah Griffin and her
organising committee to hold the inaugural Women's Rugby
World Cup in the vicinity of Cardiff was a purely strategic one.
Although other locations were considered, the Welsh capital was
the common-sense choice for an organising committee operating
on a shoestring budget. It was a bona fide 'rugby city' which
possessed cheap university accommodation and an abundance of
clubs willing to host matches within easy reach. Some grounds
were more straightforward to reach than others, it must be said.

One thing that did not factor in the discussions, however,
was the historical significance of staging the first women's World
Cup final at the home of Cardiff RFC, Cardiff Arms Park. It was
undoubtedly a coup to secure the famous ground for both the
semi-finals and showpiece match of that inaugural tournament.
Rugby has been played on the site, which sits on land nestled
between Cardiff Castle and the River Taff, since 1868. It has
undergone much redevelopment in the intervening years. The
original pitch was enclosed and then expanded with the city

and its appetite for rugby, before splitting into two when the Welsh Rugby Union (WRU) assumed control of the National Stadium in the 1960s and built a smaller ground for Cardiff on the cricket pitch next door.

It would be onto the club pitch that England, France, New Zealand and the USA would run for the semi-finals in April 1991, and, unbeknown to the players, some very important women were looking down on them from one of the photographs in the clubhouse. When the portrait of the Cardiff Ladies Rugby Football Team 1917/18 was digitised and added to the Cardiff Rugby Museum in 2018, it was believed to be the oldest surviving photograph of a women's team.[i] Staring back at the camera, arms folded, wearing Cardiff's distinctive blue-and-black jerseys, is a squad of 17 women, the majority of whom worked for local brewers William Hancock & Co. and donned scrum caps for the occasion. Sat at the centre of the picture, clutching the match ball proudly, is captain E. Kirton, who would later lead her team onto the Arms Park pitch for a match against a team from Newport in aid of the ongoing war effort. The fixture, which was played on 15 December 1917, was Cardiff's first fundraising match for causes related to the First World War, but the latest in a series of such events contested by the Newport squad.

Britain's declaration of war on Germany on 4 August 1914 had an almost immediate impact on rugby. Since its earliest days, before Thomas Hughes had even set foot on the grounds of Rugby School, the game had been seen as ideal preparation for battle. It is no surprise, therefore, that within a month of the announcement, all matches in Wales had been cancelled as the WRU followed the lead of England's RFU and players rushed to enlist.[ii] Local sentiment among rugby men was summed up by

---

[i] Dr Lydia Furse has since uncovered a picture of the Newport Ladies Rugby Football Team, who inspired Cardiff to start a side, which is believed to have been taken earlier in that season.

[ii] The Arms Park quickly became both a recruitment office for local sportsmen keen to fight in the First World War and a hub for the athletes' volunteer force, a home defence battalion for those unable or ineligible to enlist.

A.W. Samuel at the start of September when he told a meeting of the Swansea and District Rugby League that 'this is no time for football. The youth of this country have the more serious game of war. They have to fight for honour and freedom and for the women and the children.'

The WRU was unique among the home unions in that it primarily drew its playing population and support from the working, not the middle, classes. Rugby was a part of the social fabric of South Wales, which meant two things during the war. First, for those unable, ineligible or opposed to fighting, there was a hole in their weekend which the oval-ball game (whether through playing, refereeing or supporting) had previously filled. Second, the popularity of rugby among the industrial working class meant those women filling the jobs vacated by enlisted men were familiar with the game. Those factors meant there were enough women in Newport and later Cardiff to form a team, and that helped ensure they received a much warmer welcome onto the pitch than their predecessors three decades previously.

A Newport Ladies Rugby Football team first played at the start of what would have been the 1917/18 season. The squad split into two sides, the 'Wasps' and the 'Whites', who competed against each other. Drawn from munitions workers in the city, the endeavour was overseen by Mr. J. Triggs and Mr. J. Hillman, who coached the women and reputedly ran the line in at least one of the matches.[iii] The team proved prolific fundraisers, helping to swell the coffers of the Royal Gwent Hospital, the Cwmbran Wounded Soldiers Fund and the Munitions Crèche. The teams also played at a carnival in Barry which raised enough money to buy a submarine.

Men had returned to the pitch intermittently by this time, primarily in 'internationals' between teams of servicemen or in

---

[iii] It has been reported in some places that the players worked at the National Cartridge and Box Repairing Factory and in others that they were employed at the Orb steelworks. It is entirely possible that the sides were recruited from more than one munitions factory.

charity matches, but that clearly had no impact on the pull of Newport Ladies. The Wasps and Whites played an exhibition match at the Arms Park on 6 October 1917 which drew 'thousands of spectators'.[iv] According to the following Monday's *Western Mail*, the women put on a 'wonderful display of scrimmaging, running, passing, and kicking', while referee R. Pollock 'stated that he had refereed many a worse game between male teams'. It was after that match that a fixture between Cardiff and Newport women's teams was first proposed, although it would take another two months to come to fruition. When it did, in aid of the City Battalion Comforts Fund, the Wasps and Whites put their rivalry to one side to form a united Newport side.

As the photograph which hung in the Hubert Johnson room of the Cardiff clubhouse shows, the exalted status of their opponents did not matter to Kirton and her teammates. The squad wore determined looks as they peered into the camera lens. It is thought the picture was taken shortly after the players had changed at the Grand Hotel for the match. The proprietor there at the time, Bessie 'Ma' Rosser, stands behind Kirton's left shoulder with a stern expression etched across her face. In another quirk of history, the USA would use the Grand as their base for the inaugural Women's Rugby World Cup in 1991. It means the Americans twice retraced the steps of those early pioneers as they made the short walk across Westgate Street and into the grounds of the Arms Park.

Newport's greater experience told on that December day in 1917 as the visitors won the match 6–0, but little else is known of the encounter. English journalist Edward Sewell wrote about it in his column in the *Illustrated Sporting and Dramatic News* a week later, but he gave the score erroneously as 22–0 (the result of the men's match held on the same day), so cannot be considered a reliable witness. He certainly did not share the positive opinion of women's rugby espoused by the *Western Mail*, Mr Pollock and

---

[iv] Some put the attendance for that match at 10,000.

the spectators who filled the Arms Park stands. 'There is little likelihood, happily, of Ladies Rugby Football ever becoming popular', he wrote. 'Indeed, it is a most unedifying spectacle, calculated only to lower the prestige of the game. In the 'eighties there was a "Ladies" Rugby team that used to go on tour, but it was a ghastly sight, and it is a pity anyone has thought of anything like a repetition. The fairer sex has come to stay in many spheres of life, but certainly not on the Rugby football field.'

Fortunately, the players did not take any notice of Sewell's criticism, if they were even aware of it, as both Cardiff and Newport continued to field teams for the remainder of the 1917/18 season. That is when their fun stopped, however. By the following September, the war effort was beginning to wind down and, as men returned home from battle, unofficial club matches became more frequent. 'We loved it,' Maria Eley (née Evans), who lined up as a 17-year-old full back for Cardiff against Newport, told the *Penarth Times* more than 80 years after the match. 'It was such fun with us all playing together on the pitch, but we had to stop when the men came back from the war, which was a shame. Such great fun we had.' It would be 74 years before another group of similarly determined young women returned to play at the Arms Park. It is heartening to think that the picture of Eley, Kirton and their teammates was hung in a room which still had a view of the pitch, albeit obstructed, at that time. Maybe even 'Ma' Rosser cracked a smile as New Zealand began their haka.

*****

The women of Cardiff and Newport who took to the pitch in 1917 did not do so in isolation. At the time when Miss E. Kirton was preparing, rugby ball tucked under her arm, to lead her team into the Arms Park, Britain was undergoing something of a sporting revolution. The First World War had been the unlikely catalyst for an increase in female participation.

Nine months after the declaration of war, the UK was gripped by what became known as the 'Shell Crisis' after a story in *The Times* laid bare the need for heavy artillery. Published on 14 May 1915, the report from the Battle of Aubers Ridge, an unmitigated disaster for the British, relayed that 'The want of an unlimited supply of high explosives was a fatal bar to our success.' The damning assessment was delivered by the newspaper's correspondent Lieutenant Colonel Charles à Court Repington, who had been permitted to watch the debacle unfold by his friend Commander-in-Chief Sir John French. 'To break this hard crust we need more high explosive, more heavy howitzers, and more men. This special form of warfare has no precedent in history.'

As Tim Tate observed in *Women's Football: The Secret History*, Repington's report had far-reaching consequences. The crisis toppled the incumbent Liberal Government, while a new Ministry of Munitions was set up under the control of David Lloyd George. By July 1915, Lloyd George and the new Coalition Government had assumed greater power over private arms companies in an attempt to streamline the production of munitions for the front. The government could now name their price for artillery produced by those firms and also had a say in the make-up of their workforce. This soon came in handy. On 2 March 1916, compulsory conscription was introduced for all men aged between 18 and 41 via the Military Service Act. Munitions factories had traditionally been staffed by skilled male labour, but as more of these men were called up to fight (and with private companies determined to cut overheads as the price of their products fell) so women were asked to fill the gap.

It was not only on the factory floor that women stepped into the void left by conscripted men. In October 1917, when the Newport Ladies were winning fans and raising funds in South Wales, Grace Sibbert, one of the new female employees at Dick, Kerr & Co., a munitions factory in Preston, received simultaneous requests. Around the same time that Sibbert was asked whether the company could hold a fundraising concert for Moor Park Hospital, some of her male colleagues, provoked by teasing of them about their footballing ability, challenged the women to play. Fusing those two appeals, Sibbert decided to help raise funds for the hospital by contesting a football match against a team of women from another local factory. In doing so, she set in motion a chain of events which would lead to the Football Association banning women's football entirely within four years.

Dick, Kerr's Ladies are undoubtedly the most famous of the women's football teams which sprang up during the war. At the height of their popularity, on Boxing Day 1920, they attracted a crowd of 53,000 (with 14,000 more locked outside) to watch them in action at Goodison Park in Liverpool. It was their popularity which prompted the FA to take action, but they were far from alone. Up and down the country, teams were formed by female factory workers who started playing in their lunchbreaks. Women's football proved so popular in the North East of England that a Munition Girls' Cup was held during the 1917/18 season, with the final played at Newcastle United's St James' Park and subsequent replay at Middlesbrough's Ayresome Park. Both matches attracted crowds in excess of 20,000. Unlike their rugby-playing counterparts, moreover, the footballers did not stop when the men came home from war. Instead, they set about strengthening the foundations laid while they were away.

On 5 December 1921, the FA moved to burst the women's football bubble. At a council meeting, the body said it felt 'impelled to express [its] strong opinion that the game of football is quite unsuitable for females and ought not to be encouraged'.

Under feigned concern that the majority of gate receipts from women's matches were not reaching the charities they were purporting to support, the FA requested that 'clubs belonging to the Association refuse the use of their grounds for such matches'.

Rugby's authorities in England, Ireland, Scotland and Wales had not been required to issue such a proclamation. In three of those countries, its player and supporter base was predominantly middle-class and therefore social norms dictated that women were not lining up either to work in munitions factories or to put on a pair of rugby boots, even if they were tempted to do so. Wales was the one home nation in which rugby had a truly mass appeal, and it is no surprise that it was in South Wales that women's rugby teams were formed. However, as the story of Maria Eley highlights, those female players were ushered back onto the sidelines and into the stands as soon as the war was over.

It is impossible to say what the WRU would have done had the employees of William Hancock & Co. decided to keep playing after normal service was resumed. In the wake of the ban, the Arms Park *did* host an international between England and France, the former drawn heavily from Dick, Kerr's. However, there is little evidence to suggest that rugby's authorities on the whole would have proved any more enlightened than the FA. On the contrary, the Yorkshire Rugby Football Union proved themselves to be just as narrow-minded. Unable to hold their matches at football grounds, the English Ladies Football Association hoped to play the final of their first and only cup competition in Bradford in 1922. The Yorkshire union, though, had previously made its opinion of female footballers abundantly clear as it rejected a request to use Bradford's Lidget Green Stadium, saying women who played football 'made a ridiculous exhibition of themselves'. The match was subsequently relocated to Cobridge, a small town north of Stoke, where the local team beat Doncaster to become the competition's sole winners.

Although things wound down for Maria Eley and her friends in 1918, there were at least two countries in which women continued to play rugby, or a game very close to it: New Zealand and France. Exhibition matches had been played in the former in aid of charities during the First World War, although the majority of these were either small-sided or shorter in length. One such example was a game organised by the Oriental Club and sanctioned by the Wellington Rugby Union, which took place at half-time during Oriental men's meeting with Wellington at Athletic Park on 29 May 1915. The 10-minute match featured 22 players and was overseen by a female referee, Mrs F. Roberts. According to newspaper reports the following Monday, it provided an 'entertaining interlude' on an otherwise dull day of rugby. 'Not all of the girls knew every rule in the game, and but for the colours it might have been difficult to judge always for what side the players meant to fight,' an article in the *Dominion* relayed. 'They did not fight strenuously at all, but they provided no end of amusement for the crowd and for themselves.'

Following the match, the whistle used by Mrs Roberts was sold at auction and raised £10 for the Wounded Soldiers' Fund. Although that can be counted as a success, the tone of the reporting suggests it was not taken seriously as a sporting contest. Up until this point, women's rugby had either been organised as speculative money-making ventures, as in the 1880s, or as fundraising exhibitions, as in New Zealand and South Wales during the First World War. It would be another six years before a group of women attempted to form a fully functioning rugby club. Unsurprisingly, given the examples of female participation in the city dating back to 1888, it was in Wellington that they chose to do it. Disappointingly, though, the endeavour came up against the same prejudice and pseudo-science, not parroted solely by men, which had hampered women in their attempts to play the game for the previous half a century.

When Phyllis Dawson stood up in a committee room in Wellington Town Hall on 5 July 1921 to address 'an enthusiastic band of young ladies', she did so with hope. 'The object of this club, which it is proposed to form … is to get together a party of girls to play the game of Rugby,' Dawson told those present, who included a reporter from the *New Zealand Herald*. 'I consider that if we form a club we can get the game going among the girls. To do this properly we will want a ground, a nice clubroom and some members.' An earlier speaker had warned 'the boys think we cannot do it. At present it is a big joke among them.' It was an observation which would be echoed and repeated on the decades-long road to the inaugural women's World Cup, and the implicit challenge those words carried was readily accepted. By the end of the meeting, the team had players, a kit (yellow and black jerseys with black shorts 'not more than four or five inches above the knee') and a name: Wellington Girls' Rugby Football Club.

Dawson chaired a second meeting for interested players six days later, where the Poneke club pledged the use of its gymnasium on Sunday mornings, but cracks in the plan began to surface. Three members resigned their places on the club's executive having advocated for the team to play Association rather than Rugby rules and lost the subsequent vote. The dissenters' concerns centred on the supposed physical dangers which playing the oval-ball code entailed. 'Who could imagine a girl being collared low? It might ruin her for life,' one was reported to have said. We cannot know what prompted those three women to get cold feet, but the reaction to their decision to sign up, at home or in work, might not have been positive. 'People [are] beginning to think the project ridiculous,' one of those who walked away, Miss Dingwell, told Dawson. Certainly, newspaper pages were filled with condemnation and condescension in the weeks following the second meeting.

Two of the most critical voices came from Reverend T.W. Vealie and a letter writer to *New Zealand Truth*, 'L.M.'. Both couched their opposition to the idea in terms of the perceived threat to the female reproductive organs, stating that a woman's primary, if not sole, objective in life was to bear children. Vealie, who described women as 'the mothers of the next generation', concluded a sermon in July 1921 by saying: 'God forbid that the young women of this generation should so far forget the true ideals of womanhood by seeking to indulge in masculine sport, as to become impotent in that which can make them true saviours of society.' If anything, L.M., a self-confessed 'old-fashioned woman', went further than the pastor. Her views, she admitted, were 'of a pretty strong variety'.

'I am coming to what some of your readers may squeal at,' L.M. wrote. 'All these rough, unwomanly pastimes are part of the cause of the sterility of the modern woman and a direct cause, for one thing, of the high percentage of maternity and infant mortality. The very parts of a woman's body which ought to be kept supple and non-rigid are toughened and ruined for the main purpose of a woman's wonderful vocation of motherhood.' She went on to characterise young women in New Zealand as 'fast bits of flappers' whose insatiable appetites in the bedroom were not only spreading venereal disease but producing 'rickety scrofulous children'. It was enough to make even a Victorian BMJ editor blush. As predicted, L.M.'s correspondence elicited a strong response from the *New Zealand Truth* readership, including a lengthy riposte from Dawson herself. However, support in the letters pages for the Wellington Girls' Rugby Football Club did not translate onto the pitch.

Dawson returned to Wellington Town Hall on 29 March 1922, but those inside the committee room were nowhere near as jubilant as they had been eight months earlier. Out of a membership which had hit 37 during the 1921/22 season, only 12 were present as the chair laid out the challenges facing the Wellington Girls. Dawson had not been able to realise her ambition to find a permanent home for the team, let alone one with a 'nice clubroom'. The lack of a ground had proven a large obstacle to the project. Although the squad played two 15-a-side matches during the season, presumably both inter-squad affairs, these had not been staged at a prominent rugby ground, such as Athletic Park. The city council was 'not very sympathetic' to the female players' cause, according to Dawson, fearful that it could be held responsible for any accidents which occurred during a match.

The apparent apathy of the Wellington public had sapped the club of momentum, hampering their ability to whip up interest in women's rugby and leaving them short of funds. Dawson remained upbeat, insisting: 'When we get going we shall draw the crowd.' Unfortunately for the chair and her players, though, the club doesn't appear to have made it back onto the pitch. It would take more than 60 years for women's rugby to truly get going in New Zealand.

Access to rugby stadiums was also initially an issue encountered by the women who picked up an oval ball in France in the 1920s. Femina-Sport, the first women's sports club in France, was founded in 1911, and in the second half of that decade, female interest and participation in sport increased exponentially as their role in society began to change. By 1917, enough clubs had sprung up that a national federation, the Fédération des Sociétés Féminines Sportives de France (FSFSF), was established. Four years later, an international governing body was launched. The influx of women into gyms and onto pitches and athletics tracks was met with hostility by the country's sporting establishment, however. Pierre de Coubertin, the godfather of the modern Olympics and a rugby enthusiast, was strongly opposed to women taking part in competitive sport. 'An Olympiad with females would be impractical, uninteresting, inaesthetic and improper,' he once said.

Given De Coubertin's relationship with rugby (he refereed the inaugural French championship final in 1892), it is understandable that women who sought to play the oval-ball game did so undercover. However, while Helen Matthews and her players in 1880s Britain used pseudonyms, their French successors gave the sport itself an assumed name. Officially, the teams which met at Stade Elisabeth in Paris on 2 April 1922 did so to contest a match of *barette*, a type of folk football which had been particularly popular in South West France during the 19th century. In reality, though, the women were playing rugby with some minor adjustments. Devised by Dr Marie Houdré and André Theuriet, teams were 12-a-side rather than 15-a-side, matches were shorter, pitch sizes smaller, and tackles could only be made round the waist.

In spite of the subterfuge, neither the authorities nor the media were fooled. Following some negative headlines, the newly founded Fédération Française de Rugby (FFR) banned the playing of barette on its clubs' grounds. Home to Paris Athletic Club as well as Femina-Sport, Stade Elisabeth was officially an Association football ground and offered Houdré and Theuriet a way round the ruling. Supported by the FSFSF and its influential general secretary Alice Milliat, barette proved popular with players, fans and even some media, and by 1926, nine clubs were competing in a national championship. The FFR was forced into a U-turn in 1928, when it relented and allowed barette to be played before matches at Stade Jean-Bouin.

As quickly as the sport had arrived, though, it vanished. Barette certainly appears to have slipped from public consciousness long before the Vichy Government decided to ban it, along with women's football and rugby league, in 1941. There are many reasons why its popularity might have waned in the 1930s; the economic impact of the Wall Street Crash on French women, the rise in popularity of league and the fact that Milliat's energies, and those of the organisations she represented, became more and more focused on athletics as she fought to secure greater female participation in the Olympics. Whatever forced it out of the spotlight, barette's fleeting success proved there was an appetite for women's rugby in France. The foundations laid by Houdré and Theuriet would eventually be built on by the French pioneers at the vanguard of the women's rugby revolution in the latter half of the 20th century.

*****

The inter-war years were a period in which a lot happened in the men's game, but not much changed. France had joined the home unions in the Five Nations Championship in 1910 and, following the resumption of competition after the First World War, made a request for membership of the IRFB in 1921. Their application was flatly rejected by the Board, though, which long into the 20th century saw itself as a law-making body working solely in the interests of England, Ireland, Scotland and Wales.

Francis Maule Campbell's worst fears were realised in 1927 when the French beat England 3–0 in Paris, five years after they had secured an 11–11 draw at Twickenham. France, though, had won only one Championship match (against Scotland in 1911) prior to the outbreak of war, and although they beat each of the home nations at least once in the 1920s, their results did not improve consistently. Les Bleus finished bottom of the standings six times between 1922 and 1929 and were expelled from the competition in 1931, although it was not on-pitch performance which led to their exclusion.

Rugby had been introduced as an aristocratic pastime in Paris at the end of the 19th century, but soon spread beyond the capital city and gained considerable popularity in the provincial villages and towns of the South and South West. As in Lancashire and Yorkshire before the Big Split, the game became a symbol of civic pride as teams battled for supremacy both at a local level and in the French national championship. One familiar outcome of this was the remuneration of players, either through jobs and inducements or more open forms of payment, but there was also a brutality to the way rugby was played in the South West of France. Violence was not an uncommon sight on the pitch or in the stands, and after its foundation in 1921, the FFR was unable to keep a lid on it. Control of the game was split between the establishment in Paris and the new order which had sprung up in Toulouse and the vast surrounding areas. The impotence of the governing body was highlighted when six of the country's biggest clubs, drawn from both the capital and the provinces, formed their own union in 1931, 'devoted to the ideals of fair play and friendship'. It was all too much for the home unions, who reacted to the allegations of foul play and professionalism by cutting ties with the French before the 1931 Five Nations had concluded. The result was an awkward 80 minutes for England in Paris as they lost 14–13 to France amid jeers and boos from the 25,000 fans in attendance.

In the immediate aftermath of their exclusion from the Five Nations, France threw in their lot with Germany, Italy and Romania while doing much, both directly and indirectly, to grow the game in mainland Europe.[v] Their absence from the Five Nations would only be temporary, as they were readmitted in July 1939, although they would have to wait until after the

---

[v] In 1934, the Fédération Internationale de Rugby Amateur (FIRA) was formed as a French-led organisation. As Rugby Europe, it continues to oversee the game (outside the Six Nations) on the Continent today.

Second World War to actually take the field. By that time, the FFR had also seen off the challenge of league in what was a rather shameful chapter in its history. At the end of the decade there had been almost as many 13-a-side clubs in France as 15-a-side ones as membership of the FFR fell by close to 40 per cent. Within days of the French defeat to Germany in 1940, however, the union began to exploit its connections to the far-right Vichy Government to help guarantee that league was added to its list of banned sports, alongside barette. The professional code was not so much prohibited as obliterated, with its assets turned over to union. League in France has never truly recovered.

Unlike France, New Zealand did not apply for outright membership of the IRFB at the beginning of the 1920s, most likely mindful of the answer it would receive. Instead, they asked for greater consultation over laws. The IRFB's response was less curt than its reply to the French but no less condescending. In 1924, it offered to host a conference on its laws every five years, a conference which the southern hemisphere's 'big three' could attend at their own considerable expense. The Board would be under no obligation to implement decisions or recommendations made at the conference. There was a commitment to set up a consultative body in 1929, following a visit from South African Paul Roos to London, but it never came to fruition. The home nations were preoccupied with issues relating to France at a pivotal time in those discussions, and there was also some resentment at the inducements already given to the big three.

In the early 20th century, the home unions had been happy to see the game flourish in the outposts of empire. Rugby offered the powers that be, particularly England's RFU, an opportunity to communicate with the 'Britishers' in the colonies and ensure the middle-class values they held so dear were being promoted in them. It did not matter that the game was developing at a faster pace, and in varying ways, in those countries. Or that rugby there had a much broader support base. Or even that Australia, while haemorrhaging players to Australian rules and league, could still raise a team to beat England, Ireland and Wales.

However, the fact that each of the big three had a certain amount of autonomy over the laws of the game in their own countries became more of a problem in the 1920s. Some of the variations would find their way into global use, such as not being able to kick directly into touch outside the 22, while New Zealand and South Africa were hotbeds of evolution in forward play. Other innovations proved less palatable, though, and the IRFB effectively banned the use of a two-man front row (as popularised by the All Blacks in the 1920s) by dictating that the ball had to pass through three legs when fed into a scrum before being hooked. Ultimately, it was the IRFB which won the day, and Australia, New Zealand and South Africa had all adopted its laws completely long before they were admitted to the body as full members in 1949.

France would have to wait another 29 years to take its place on the Board and become the first non-English-speaking member in 1978. In truth, having resumed playing in the Five Nations in 1947, it had only been a matter of time. Involvement in the Championship brought with it access to broadcast and sponsorship revenue as television companies began to pay handsomely for the right to show the tournament in the second half of the 20th century. Without a similar competition to monetise, the big three began to petition for a global tournament. It would take until 1985 for the IRFB to sanction a Rugby World Cup, to be held in Australia and New Zealand two years later, with the WRU representative Keith Rowlands crucially casting his vote in favour. By the end of the decade, another 34 nations, including Argentina, Canada, Fiji, Japan and the USA, were invited into the fold. Only ten years after Frenchman André Bosc had ingratiated himself to his new colleagues when he pleaded that 'the Board should not become a World Federation', it was taking steps to become exactly that. Was the IRFB ready for women, though?

NEW BEGINNINGS

ON 26 APRIL 1963, the *Herts and Essex Observer* ran an advertorial on central heating which asked its readers: 'Was your home warm during last winter's big freeze?' Had Harry Griffin picked up a copy of the newspaper on his commute to work in Stevenage, he would have answered *no*. Snow had arrived in Britain on Boxing Day 1962 and did not stop falling for the next ten weeks as temperatures dipped as low as –22 °C and a mile of sea froze off the Kent coast. 'Now is the time to think seriously of more warmth next winter,' the paper warned, and Griffin was one step ahead of them. His plan would cost considerably less than the £270 being quoted for a new radiator system but involve much more upheaval.

The big freeze of 1963 had convinced Harry and his wife Maureen that it was time to emigrate to Australia with their young daughters Deborah and Wendy. Later that year, the Griffins became '£10 Poms' as they boarded a boat and started their long journey, eventually landing on Queensland's East Coast. Life in Brisbane was certainly warm, and it was there that eldest daughter Deborah discovered the benefits of sport. A keen swimmer and runner (rugby did not yet feature on her radar), she loved the outdoor lifestyle made possible by the space and climate on offer in her new home.

Australia, though, was a long way from England, especially in the 1960s, and with airmail their only form of communication with friends and family back in Hertfordshire and East London, her parents began to get itchy feet. As Deborah approached her 13th birthday, Harry and Maureen became convinced that their daughters would receive a better education in England. 'It was absolute twaddle to be honest, but they didn't know that.' So, in 1971, the Griffins packed up and headed back to Stevenage.

When Deborah arrived at Stevenage Girls' School that September, she quickly realised she was an outsider, and not because of the accent she had picked up during eight years in Brisbane. To her frustration, her love of sport marked her out as different. 'It was quite formative, because it was a big change for me,' she recalls of her time at school in England. 'I was just absolutely shocked that the girls didn't do sport. Sport was there, but they used to line up with their excuses .... It was uncool, it was not the thing to do. I just couldn't understand that.' Deborah would spend her lunch breaks doing sprints with a friend who was a hurdler. 'The cool girls thought we were weird.'

Deborah found an outlet for her sporting energies at university through rugby. Much like for Grace Sibbert and her footballing colleagues at Dick, Kerr's in 1917, this was the result of a challenge. Having enrolled at University College London (UCL) in the autumn of 1977, she was introduced to the oval-ball game as a spectator by her first-year boyfriend. He played for the university team, and she would watch from the touchline with the other girlfriends. 'It sounds dreadful, doesn't it? Groupies!' she concedes. This was not a group of women who were content to sit on the sidelines, however, and when the opportunity for them to play arose, they grasped it with both hands.

UCL share a rivalry with King's College London which dates back almost 200 years, to the latter's foundation as an Anglican alternative to the institution which became UCL. The enmity between the two universities has arguably been most keenly felt on the rugby pitch, and it was given an added dimension in early 1978. Griffin and her friends discovered that, under the rules of competition existing between them at the time, a request for a match in any sport had to be met or the university unable to raise a team lost points in their annual head-to-head. Spotting a chance to get one over on their rivals down the road, the women had an idea. 'We challenged them to a game of women's rugby. We'd never seen women's rugby before, didn't even know whether there had ever been any,' Griffin recalled in 2019.

'We just thought it was a laugh. And that meant us going into the gym and training and throwing a ball around. They accepted, and we played, and the overwhelming feeling, which I've heard quite a few people say, was when we came off it was just like "Wow, that was fun." And they challenged us and then we started asking other universities if they would get a team up, and so it was done for the pure enjoyment of the game.'

The new enthusiasts in London might not have known it but, while women's rugby was in its infancy in the UK, it already existed elsewhere. Edinburgh University was the first to have a team, the Amazons, formed in 1962, and there are examples of women taking the pitch against men in fundraising matches around this time. Female participation spread to other institutions in the intervening 15 or so years, while in South Wales, the Magor Maidens became Britain's first women's club side.

In 1977, Keele University had even applied for membership of the RFU. Twickenham 'agreed that the legal implications of such a request in relation to RFU Byelaws and the Sex Discrimination

Act be examined'. Ultimately, following advice from its solicitors, the governing body rejected the application on the grounds that it failed to meet the criteria laid out in those byelaws. At the time, a successful club needed to have been in existence for at least a year, be a member of the 'appropriate Constituent Body' and be proposed and seconded by two member clubs. No matter how long the team at Keele had been playing, they would have struggled to satisfy the other two conditions without the support of the union. There is no evidence that they appealed the decision.

The RFU were clearly not ready for female rugby players, but that could not have mattered less to those women who wanted to lace up a pair of boots. And at the beginning of the 1980s, there were an increasing number who did. Enthusiasm for female participation had been stoked by touring teams from the USA, but it was domestic competition which sustained it. In those days before the internet and mobile phones, the pioneers of the women's game had to be resourceful as they attempted to fill their fixture lists. Griffin remembers asking her boyfriend to enquire whether the opposition had a women's team (or knew of any women who would be interested in raising one) when he travelled away with the UCL men's side. Others simply picked up the phone book and rang round student unions, often to the bemusement of the person at the other end.

However rudimentary their methods, though, they had a degree of success. In the years after Griffin and co. took on Kings, teams were formed at universities, colleges and polytechnics from London to Loughborough, York to Swansea, and many others in-between. Many of the players who filled the ranks of the new teams were drawn to do so by the camaraderie on offer and the opportunity to explore a different kind of femininity. The players could use their size, strength, speed and brains in ways they weren't allowed to in more 'traditional' women's sports.

The social side of the game was a bonus. 'I loved the physicality and I think that's something that people do, or they don't. I mean, being able to tackle someone or tap-tackle someone or get them down – there's a huge amount of satisfaction in that, isn't there?' Griffin says. 'It is one of those sports in which you need everybody on the park, you know. One person can't do it.'

By 1983, there were enough women's teams in England and Wales that it was decided a governing body, to organise matches and promote the game further, was needed. The RFU was again consulted, and its long-serving secretary Air Commodore Bob Weighill met those behind the plan at the beginning of 1984. Although the new body would not be affiliated to the union, it was recognised, given advice on its constitution, put in touch with insurance brokers and provided with a coaching weekend.

By the time that meeting took place, the Women's Rugby Football Union (WRFU) had already been formed with 12 member clubs, Magor being the only one that wasn't affiliated to a university or polytechnic. In its discussions with Weighill, the WRFU made clear its intention to add to that number, and it would not take long for that wish to come to fruition. At the start of the 1984/85 season, a group of graduates from UCL and York, Griffin among them, had grown tired of 'flooding the ranks of UCL with many a non-student member' and so convinced the committeemen at Finchley RFC in North London to let them form England's first female club on their back pitches. Soon, a second club sprang up in the capital, at Wasps, and a rivalry was born which would survive Finchley's move to Richmond two years later. The foundations had been laid, but there was work to be done if the game in England and Wales was to match that already being played in France and the USA.

*****

The revival of women's rugby in France was seeded by a series of charity matches in the mid-1960s in aid of the United Nations International Children's Emergency Fund (UNICEF) campaign against world hunger. These games, contested by students from Lyon and Toulouse, raised funds through ticket sales and bar takings. Capitalising on the social aspect of the game would also be a key feature of the rise in female participation in the USA, UK, New Zealand and elsewhere over the ensuing decades.

Fuelled by the success of the post-match socials, player numbers continued to grow, and on 1 May 1968, the first recognised women's club match was held at Toulouse Fémina Sports in front of a few thousand spectators. Within 18 months, a women's rugby association, the Association Française de Rugby Féminin (AFRF), had been set up to serve 12 member clubs, and by 1971 it represented 330 players and 70 administrators. A national championship was first contested in the following season, and around 5,000 people watched Lyon-Villeurbanne win the inaugural final in 1972.

However, the progress being made by the women's teams in France did not go unnoticed by those in power, and both the French government and the FFR came out in opposition to female participation. The union attempted to ban its referees from taking charge of women's matches; a pompous decision designed to check the advance of the AFRF which would backfire spectacularly. Henri Fléchon had first encountered the women's game in 1972, when he was asked to officiate a match. Angered by the FFR's attempts to undermine the burgeoning sport, he became a champion of it and served as AFRF president from 1975 until his death 11 years later. In that time, he helped to broker an agreement between the AFRF and the men's union which enabled FFR referees to officiate women's matches, and assisted the game as it took its first steps onto the international stage. When the inaugural European Cup was held in 1988, matches were played in Fléchon's hometown Bourg-en-Bresse, and the trophy competed for bore his name.

Women who wanted to play rugby in the USA did not, initially at least, come up against the same systemic discrimination encountered by those in France. Those keen to pick up an oval ball were able to ride the wave that was the boom in female sporting participation sweeping through the States in the 1970s and 1980s, a largely unintended consequence of educational reform. Title IX of the Educational Amendments of 1972 had been designed to ensure that women and girls were no longer denied opportunities available in the classroom to men and boys. However, the key tenet of the legislation (that 'No person in the United States shall, on the basis of sex, be excluded from participation in, be denied the benefits of, or be subject to discrimination under any educational program [sic] or activity receiving Federal financial assistance') would be most keenly felt on the playing field.

Although it took until 1979 for a full set of rules governing Title IX to be finalised, the preceding decade had already seen a dramatic rise in the number of opportunities offered to women and girls. Between 1971 and 1976, the number of female college-varsity athletes more than doubled to 63,000 while, in the same period, those at high school rose from less than 300,000 to 1.6m. 'When [Title IX] was proposed, we had no idea that the most visible impact would be in athletics,' admitted Representative Patsy Mink, who played a critical role in passing the legislation.

Women's rugby was an attractive option to universities and colleges looking to offset a large American football programme, and therefore teams were given access to funding which, while still small compared to that offered to men, had previously been unthinkable. It was in this land of increased sporting opportunity that two of the members of the organising committee of the inaugural Women's Rugby World Cup, Mary Forsyth and Sue Dorrington, were exposed to the game.

Forsyth had grown up in a sporty family, was an avid swimmer and basketball player and benefited directly from Title IX funding when a coach arrived at her high school to work with female athletes. A talented middle-distance runner, she blossomed into a high-school track-and-field prospect but could not devote the time required to become a varsity athlete on arriving at Penn State University in 1978. One of eight children, Forsyth needed to work to pay her way through college and therefore started a search for a more relaxed activity.

Introduced to rugby by her older sister, who had enrolled the previous year and told her about a woman who had played on the wing for the men's team, Forsyth was relieved to learn that a female team was in the process of being set up. She would represent the university for the next four years. Like Forsyth, a lot of her new teammates had been exposed to sport at high school but found themselves without an outlet as they either didn't want to, or couldn't, commit to the demands of elite varsity competition. 'You can't all float to the top,' Forsyth explains, 'so, they did other things, and we had a great sport. The women's coach was an English guy and there was a French coach as well who helped out.

'Penn State had an enormous [American] football team, therefore club sport got a lot of money. Not that we were awash in it, but it meant that they would give us a van to go [to matches] and a gasoline card, a credit card too.'

Dorrington didn't pick up an oval ball until the early 1980s, having been alerted to both the game and the formation of a women's team in Minnesota by her rugby-playing boyfriend. She had enjoyed an 'idyllic childhood', but life became difficult following the breakdown of her parents' marriage when she was 10. After leaving home in her early teens, Dorrington was cared for by friends and extended family, and it was through this loving network that she was convinced to attend college.

At the University of Minnesota, she learned the skills which would set her up for adulthood, securing a job in the office of the Mayor of St Paul, but she craved something more. Growing up, Dorrington had always been active, burning off energy by running, riding horses, water-skiing and cheerleading at high school. Rugby proved to be the missing piece in her jigsaw. 'It utterly changed my life,' she says. 'I found a place where I fit in and that was my community. That was the family I found.'

*****

It should not be a surprise that both Forsyth and Dorrington found themselves living and playing in England in the 1980s. Travelling was an important part of the game's social fabric in the USA and Canada as its popularity grew. The sheer size of the USA meant that teams were required to travel vast distances to fulfil fixtures or play in tournaments considered domestic. It is understandable that these women would take advantage of the falling cost of air travel to embark on international tours. These squads, usually drawn from players of several clubs, would prove integral to the development of the women's game in the UK, France and particularly New Zealand as they put on exhibition matches for interested locals in the towns and cities they visited. During a trip to Britain in 1979, one such adventurer, Pam Tittes, succinctly summed up the different challenges facing female players from the USA and countries where the men's game had more of a foothold. 'We would have been surprised to find a serious women's rugby team here, because it's difficult to overcome tradition, whereas in the States there was no tradition to overcome.'

Despite the best efforts of Nita Webbe and Phyllis Dawson, the women's game in New Zealand did not truly take off until two groups of US tourists showed up in 1980. Following the exploratory trips across the Atlantic, made predominantly by players from the East Coast and Midwest, two squads drawn from West Coast clubs decided to look south. In June 1980, the Rio Grande Surfers from San Diego completed an unbeaten four-match trip round the North Island, which included a victory against a Wellington XV. Dawson would have approved.

Two months later, the California Kiwis pitched up on their own excursion. They began what was also a four-match tour by playing an under-17 boys' side and ended it by taking women's rugby to the South Island, as they ran out at the iconic Lancaster Park. The Kiwis also headed back to the USA unbeaten, and the publicity generated by the matches ensured that the domestic women's game, having played its first inter-provincial match in the same year, was given a timely boost.

The tours also helped build the close relationship that existed between US and New Zealand women's rugby in the 1980s. Geography dictated that Aotearoa was isolated as the global playing numbers began to increase, something only exacerbated by the lack of a scene across the Tasman Sea in Australia. So, without a stream of competition on its doorstep, Kiwi women were grateful for the tourists who arrived from the USA. Rio Grande players would return to New Zealand as part of a San Diego Surfers selection in 1986 and helped raise the game's profile further by playing a Canterbury XV in a curtain-raiser to the All Blacks' test against France at Lancaster Park on 28 June. It was not until the end of 1988 that a team from New Zealand took on foreign opposition which wasn't drawn from the US West Coast.

When the country's first women's international team was put together the following year, it was to face another group of tourists from the States – the Pacific Coast Grizzlies. This familiarity would continue at the World Cup in South Wales, where the New Zealanders were destined to face the USA in the semi-finals. It would be an absorbing encounter from the moment the players walked onto the Arms Park pitch.

*****

Utrecht is not a place you would automatically associate with rugby. Its picturesque tree-lined streets and canals do not reverberate to the sound of people discussing the intricacies of a line-out drive or the fallacy of the 20-minute red-card replacement. Soccer is definitely king of the football codes, yet while that is the case, the fourth biggest city in the Netherlands holds an important place in the history of women's rugby. It was there, on the Sportpark Strijland de Meern to be precise, that the first ever women's international took place when the Netherlands hosted France on 13 June 1982.

The location was chosen because maintenance work was being carried out on the Nederlands Rugby Bond's pitch in nearby Hilversum, the match itself the result of discussions between the Dutch union and Henri Fléchon. Both parties left the meeting happy, the former full of tips on how to grow the domestic game and the latter impressed by the union's acceptance of female participation. A couple of months later, Fléchon received an invitation to send a France team to Utrecht to help celebrate the union's 50th anniversary. It was readily accepted.

Some of the players selected to represent the Netherlands had never played a full match of 15-a-side rugby; however, they acquitted themselves superbly, keeping the match scoreless until the second half. In the end, the teams were separated by a single unconverted try as winger Isabelle Decamp's score ensured a 4–0 win for the visitors. A curious report in the Dutch magazine *Panorama*, which focused as much on the 'third half' in the clubhouse as the two on the pitch, attributed the result to the gamesmanship as much as the skill of the 'sweet looking but dastardly Frenchwomen'. According to those who played that day, though, the occasion was more important than the scoreline. 'Representing France meant that women's rugby would be able to move forward,' France centre Monique Fraysse told World Rugby 38 years later. 'It was also a personal reward. We were there, we were not going to back down!' Teammate Viviane Berodier added: 'We were not immediately aware that we were living a historical moment, but we did hope that there would be other opportunities after that.'

France and the Netherlands would meet another six times before the end of the decade, but Berodier would have to be patient for further international opportunities. Italy would add their name to France's fixture list in 1985, and a year later, the squad travelled to Richmond to take on Great Britain. It would be an important match on the road to the World Cup. British eyes had been opened to the possibilities of international competition, and the standards being set overseas, by a team from a familiar location which toured England and France midway through the 1985/86 season.

The squad put together by Chicago-based coach Pat Foley was forbidden from using 'United States' or 'Eagles' (already the recognised nickname of the country's nascent men's side) in their name by the USA Rugby Football Union, but to all intents and purposes they were a national team. Under the banner of the 'Women's International Vagabonds, Emissaries and Rugby Nomads' (or Wiverns for short), the squad kicked off its two-week trip with a 44–0 victory against a Yorkshire Select XV and played a further seven full-length matches, winning them all. The dominance of the team was highlighted during a WRFU-organised festival in Shenley, in which the Wiverns entered two teams, both of which ended a day of 20-minute games unbeaten.

Emma Mitchell would represent England at the World Cup in 1991 and enjoy a long and distinguished test career. She was just starting out when the Wiverns arrived in Loughborough in November 1985 and missed out on selection for the Midlands XV. 'I remember just feeling such relief that I hadn't been picked because they were just being mowed over,' she admits.

'All we knew was playing against university sides,' remembers Liza Burgess, who played for the Midlands that day. 'When they arrived, we were like, "Oh my God!" because they looked so professional. The first thing that struck me was how athletic they all looked. It was that sense of how professional they were as a set-up. They had some phenomenal athletes there, you know, that played in that side. It was the sheer athleticism of them all.' It was not only on the pitch that the Americans made an impression on their hosts. '[They went] into the gym at Loughborough and the men's first XV were in training and lifting weights, and the women were putting more weights onto the bench press bar and the squat bar,' Mitchell adds. 'That was pretty impressive, they showed us what was [possible].'

Candi Orsini was one of the standout players in the Wiverns squad, scoring 36 points and being introduced to French hospitality when she suffered a broken nose, a fate she had avoided in her day job as a stuntwoman. The skilled centre would return to the UK six years later with the official national team for the World Cup, but there was no doubt in her mind about the quality of that touring team. 'We were like horses in a gate,' Orsini says. 'There was a lot of us on that tour, and so you were champing at the bit to get on the field. And once you got out on the field, it was like the start of the Kentucky Derby.' Deborah Griffin has described the tour as a 'wake-up call' for those running the women's game in the UK. 'It made people realise that the game could be played at a much higher level than we were playing.'

Many of the players who had been humbled by the Wiverns had an opportunity to put those harsh lessons into practice the following April, when France travelled to Richmond to provide the opposition for Great Britain's international debut. There was an early hiccup when Fiona Barnet, sent by the WRFU with a French-speaking friend to welcome the squad to London, realised she had gone to the wrong airport. Following a frantic dash from Heathrow to Gatwick, Barnet then had to bluff her way out of another hole when it transpired the visitors had expected a coach to ferry them into the capital. The misunderstanding only served to inspire the French, who ran out 14–8 winners at the Athletic Ground.

The match was not merely a springboard for the international game in the UK, and therefore the World Cup, but a useful and timely advert to the club acting as host. One of the oldest rugby clubs in England, Richmond was willing to welcome the women as full members and let them use their first-team pitch. Neither of those 'perks' was on offer in North London, while the Finchley players involved against France were impressed by the quality of facilities available on the banks of the Thames.

'My husband was the secretary of the [Finchley] men's club and I understand that the women were not wholly approved of there. They had only let women in the clubhouse a couple of years before,' Mary Forsyth recalls. 'We had to pay our subs, still buy our own kit, go in on a Sunday, sweep the mud out of the changing rooms to make it palatable for anybody else to be in there, go clean and wash up all the glasses from the bar from the night before and cook our own meals. And just then, Richmond was like: here's your shirts, here's the clean changing rooms, here's where you can have your teas, we have nicely groomed pitches, you have floodlit pitches. You know, it was a no-brainer.'

*****

The USA would make its belated entrance into international rugby on 14 November 1987, when the first Women's Eagles squad travelled north to take on Canada in Victoria. It is not a coincidence that it was the Americans who were required to hit the road, again, to take the step they craved. The Canadian Rugby Union had been more receptive to female participation than their counterparts south of the border, and it was only due to a request sent directly to the women that the game was organised, as a double-header with the annual men's test.

In the eight years since Pam Tittes spoke to a reporter while on tour in England, it seems sections of the male rugby community in the USA had become more vocal in their opposition to women playing the game. This was evidenced in the USA RFU's refusal to sanction the Wiverns tour, but none of the players who lined up to represent their country for the first time at Royal Athletic Park were prepared for the incident which would mar that occasion.

The team's inspirational late captain Kathy Flores, who would play a prominent role in South Wales three-and-a-half years later, was in high spirits as she led the players into a function room on Vancouver Island on that November evening. The visitors had enjoyed a comfortable triumph on the pitch, beating Canada 22–3, and were ready to celebrate. Flores had scored one of her side's five tries and was looking forward to an enjoyable night alongside her country's men, who had lost 20–12 to the hosts. Flores and her teammates, however, would not make it to dessert. Comments made by USA men's captain Fred Paoli about female participation prompted a walk-out of both women's teams and several male attendees. 'It's unfortunate that it was some of the men that actually had some power that were being so sexist. A lot of the men that were actually players didn't have that,' Flores said in 2020. 'I think a few of us that were there probably still carry a bit of a grudge.'

Reminiscing about those events more than three decades later, several players feel that the representatives of the USA RFU who were present at the dinner were at least aware of the content of Paoli's speech before he got up to address the guests. At worst, some accuse them of giving his message their approval. It would have been crushingly disheartening to sit and be denigrated by such an influential figure for nothing more than having the temerity to play a game enjoyed by millions round the world. Like their counterparts in the UK and France, the Americans had come face to face with 'tradition' and men who wanted rugby to remain a closed shop.

It is testament to the players involved that they didn't hang up their boots en masse. Instead, they redoubled their efforts to grow the women's game, putting all their energies and money into becoming the best players they could be. They played and beat Canada again in 1988 and 1989, neither match tied to a men's contest, and travelled to New Zealand as a national team for the first time in 1990. By the time the USA arrived in South Wales for the World Cup, they were the favourites to win it.

5

GOING GLOBAL

ALICE COOPER STILL has a copy of the letter which won her both a bottle of whisky and her first paid writing gig. Like many of her contemporaries, Cooper has kept a meticulous record of the clippings, programmes, faxes, invitations and awards which document her involvement in the women's game. Maintained in a pristine plastic wallet is the correspondence she sent into *Rugby World & Post* during the off-season of 1988. A relative newcomer to rugby, she had stumbled into the sport completely by chance less than two years previously. Cooper had walked into the Sun Inn in Richmond in October 1986 looking for some midweek fun, but left with more than she'd bargained for. Having got chatting to a couple of Richmond players, she was introduced to Jane Addey and Sue Butler, members of the club's recently acquired women's team. 'We could do with tall people like you,' they told her. 'Why don't you come to training?'

Cooper was not a complete novice when it came to rugby. Her uncle Philip had captained Middlesex and played on the same Rosslyn Park team as Alexander Obolensky, while she spent much of the mid-1980s freezing on the touchline watching an ex-boyfriend. 'I liked the whole vibe of rugby clubs,' she says. Cooper had excelled at lacrosse at boarding school in Salisbury, but had played no team sport since leaving more than a decade previously. Unperturbed, she dusted off an old pair of lacrosse boots ten days later and headed to the Athletic Ground to finally experience rugby as a player. 'I never looked back. Once I started playing and I also got into the whole [scene], there was just such a fun group of people and we used to have all these mad pranks and sing-songs and whatnot,' she remembers. That enthusiasm for the game came through loud and clear in her correspondence with *Rugby World*.

The letter she submitted echoes much of what had been said by advocates of women's rugby for more than a century. The insistence that women 'play a clean, running game' could have been written by Phyllis Dawson or Nita Webbe. However, there is also a sense of the empowerment which women felt at the end of the 20th century, in the UK at least, and the self-assuredness which had enabled the WRFU to take up space and grow the game even as many male players and administrators treated them with disdain. As Cooper points out, her teammates and opponents in 1988 were drawn from the professional classes. They were graduates who worked in various fields. These women were used to succeeding, even if they had to experience some discrimination and adversity to do so. Why would they listen to people who told them they shouldn't play the sport they loved? 'It's going to take something akin to a nuclear explosion to stop us playing!' Cooper wrote. 'Because after all we're not trivialising the sport – quite the reverse in fact: we're expanding it and fostering a wider interest in it. Why should you guys have all the fun?'

The magazine's editor, former England scrum half Nigel Starmer-Smith, was so impressed with the correspondence that he made it that month's 'Litre Letter', earning Cooper a litre and a half bottle of Whyte & Mackay special reserve Scotch. She subsequently received paid work too, becoming *Rugby World*'s third women's rugby columnist, following on from Tricia Moore and Deborah Griffin. It was reward for the hard work she had put in since leaving school with 'absolutely no qualifications'. Cooper had enrolled on a secretarial course in Oxford and followed that up with a writing one which enabled her to begin a career in advertising as a copywriter. Her new relationship with *Rugby World* did not require Starmer-Smith to publish everything she wrote, however. Cooper got used to seeing her work get spiked, and WRFU meeting minutes include instances in which she apologised to the committee for articles failing to make it into print.

'The editor had a habit of, if he got an ad in, he would just dump the women's section and you would never know until the following month,' Cooper recalls. 'So, you're trying to build this ongoing thing; "You remember last month, we talked about this and la, la, la ...." And then you'd find that by the time you'd done the next article, the last month's one didn't come out, so then this one didn't make sense. That was endlessly frustrating ... and then, of course, you didn't get paid, either. I might have gone to Scotland and back to cover a match or to get some information or have done something [but if it wasn't published] – I never got paid for that. I mean, I got 60 quid or something for 400 words.'

An irregular column in the UK's most popular rugby magazine was better than nothing, though, and it at least gave the women an opportunity, in modern parlance, to control their own narrative. In the days before designated sports supplements and wall-to-wall coverage, space in the broadsheets, which primarily covered rugby in the UK, was tight. Other sports reporters were also battling for acreage, and oval-ball reporters needed to get their elbows out to secure vital column inches from those covering football, horse racing, league, golf and snooker to name but a few. 'Women's team sport in Britain had to fight desperately hard for space,' remembers retired *Times* journalist David Hands, who alongside Stephen Jones was an important ally for the women's game on the road to South Wales. 'There was a limited amount of space for sport. It hadn't quite become the significant part of the paper that it occupies now. So, you know, you were fighting your corner for men's sport never mind women's sport, which might have been regarded as a curiosity.'

In this context, tabloids and local papers offered a potentially easier route into print, but it was one that came with a pay-off. Articles in these publications would often focus on the more titillating aspects of female participation. Back in 1979, a *Daily Mirror* preview of the tour of the UK by Pam Tittes and her teammates from the US Midwest was headlined 'Happy Hookers'. In the copy, readers were warned that the 'hallowed he-man traditions of the British rugby club' were 'about to be violated. By AMERICAN women rugby players to boot. And to cap it all by PRETTY American rugby players.'

Almost a decade on, it was debatable how far things had progressed. Players were often described solely in terms of their appearance and femininity and grew tired both of questions about why they played a 'manly' game and requests to pose for suggestive shots. Even supportive articles, such as a report on the Wivern tour which appeared in the *Guardian* on 24 November 1985 and warned chauvinists 'if you go there to patronise the little women you might find the smile wiped off your face', could not escape hints of sexism. The headline of that particular piece referred to the players as 'Rugger dolls'.

'You would have people like Stephen Jones and Chris Jones, for the *Evening Standard* who were doing, you know, sensible articles – and David Hands was always incredibly supportive. And then you get the red tops all doing twatty stuff ... But that's what sells their newspapers,' Cooper says. 'My view was, you know, any publicity is not necessarily good publicity.' That was a stance that would be put to the test in April 1991.

*****

There was a grudging acceptance from some that the winks, nudges and double entendres of the popular press were something which had to be endured to ensure women's rugby progressed. And, as the 1980s drew to a close, the game was certainly developing. England and Wales met for the first time as individual nations at Pontypool Park on 5 April 1987. The visitors, essentially the Great Britain squad minus Liza Burgess and Amanda Bennett, ran out 22–4 winners with Karen Almond and Carol Isherwood, not for the last time, the stars of the show. Burgess would be back on the same side as Almond and Isherwood four weeks later as Great Britain travelled to Châlon-sur-Saone to renew their rivalry with France. The French won again, this time by a bigger margin (28–6), but the British would secure their first international victory before the end of the year as the Netherlands were beaten 16–0 in Richmond in November.

France were undoubtedly the most experienced team and the best of the period, going unbeaten in the 11 matches they played during the first five years of international women's rugby. The side put its reputation on the line as it hosted the inaugural European Cup over a long weekend in May 1988, but the tournament almost didn't happen. The brainchild of Henri Fléchon, the referee who had done so much to aid the women's game both at home and on the Continent, it came close to being torpedoed by a dispute between the women's unions in France and the UK. In April, the French had pulled out of their scheduled match against Great Britain in Newport, citing a lack of funds. In reality, there was also disquiet on both sides of the Channel due to the expectation in France that the European Cup would become an annual enterprise. The WRFU was against that proposal, as it would reduce the number of home fixtures for Great Britain, England and Wales (vital vehicles to raise both funds and profile), and therefore withdrew. It was only following a meeting between the parties to discuss the future of the competition that the Brits relented and confirmed they would send a team.

Fléchon did not live long enough to witness his vision of a European Cup become reality, but he would have admired the diplomacy which got it over the line. An honorary member of the Dutch Women's Federation due to his role in organising the first women's international in Utrecht, he later helped to broker an agreement with the committeemen at the FFR which enabled men's clubs in the country to have women's sections and allowed the union's referees to officiate women's matches. Those in charge of the 1988 tournament ensured his presence was still felt. That first European Cup was held in Fléchon's home town, Bourg-en-Bresse, and featured four nations (hosts France, Great Britain, Italy and the Netherlands) competing for the Henri Fléchon Trophy. 'The European Cup was therefore born in Bourg-en-Bresse', the town's mayor Jean Moreteau wrote in the tournament programme. 'It remains for me to wish it a long life, for the good of women's rugby.'

The inaugural European Cup got underway 365 days after the first men's Rugby World Cup had kicked off in Auckland, but the late May start date was as far as the similarities went. The World Cup had consisted of 32 matches played over four weeks in the Australian and New Zealand autumn. If that seems a tight schedule by modern player-welfare standards, then spare a thought for the women who arrived in Bourg-en-Bresse the following year. The realities of the women's game at the time, still very much amateur with a playing population unable to take huge amounts of time off from their studies or work, dictated that all six matches were scheduled to take place across three days. A condensed format also made financial sense for the organisers, who paid for the participants' accommodation, and so each team was required to play on Saturday, Sunday and Monday. This feat was made even more exhausting by the late spring heat which scorched the turf and sapped the players' legs. Great Britain found this out to their cost before a ball had even been kicked. Having driven through the night to reach their accommodation, they arrived too early to check in. The team's coach, future World Rugby Hall of Fame inductee Jim Greenwood, had banned sunbathing in a bid to conserve energy, and so the players instead had to invent games to keep themselves occupied as they waited and wilted in the heat.

France and Great Britain were scheduled to close the tournament on Monday 23 May in what organisers hoped would be a de facto final. So it proved as both teams beat the Netherlands and Italy without conceding a try. British captain Carol Isherwood remembers being introduced to the idea of a warm-down following her side's opening 32–9 defeat of the Italians, something which clearly helped soothe aching muscles as they followed that up with a 26–0 win against the Dutch. France had not been quite so prolific in their victories, beating the Netherlands 13–3 before a 16–3 win against Italy, and had never lost against their final opponents.

It was Greenwood's team who started brightest, however, and took the lead when Cheryl Stennet finished off a move involving Almond and Claire Willets to score a converted try. That would be as good as it got for Great Britain, though, as France hit back with two unconverted scores to secure an 8–6 victory and take the trophy. Perceived refereeing injustices still rankle with several of the British players. 'It was tremendously disappointing because we genuinely believed we had a team to beat them. We should have beat them,' Bennett recalls. 'We were pretty exhausted by the end of it,' Emma Mitchell admits. 'It was a very close game and they won and deservedly so. But we were just so disappointed. We felt that we didn't play our best and that we had the ability to win that game.'

The British squad did not have long to lick their wounds. Less than an hour after France had been presented with the cup at Stade Marcel-Verchère, the 30-strong party was required at the town hall for a wine reception and formal dinner. The gap between drink and food was stretched dangerously long by a succession of speeches from local dignitaries. 'We were in joyous mood. We were singing, getting all the other teams to sing "We Sing, You Sing",' Bennett recalls. 'It was that very, almost local club-type atmosphere. We had a brilliant time. But I do recall that by the next morning, my lovely white skirt was covered in red wine.' It was in that exhausted, disappointed yet upbeat mood that the Great Britain players and coaching staff clambered onto their bus and began the overnight trek back to normality. It would take more than six hours to even reach Calais, but as they boarded the ferry to Dover, there was a sense of accomplishment despite the defeat. 'Things were happening so fast in those times,' Mitchell explains. 'To go and play in more of a stadium environment (even though it was really just a big stand) and have a crowd and to be singing an anthem, and the nerves and the adrenaline, and again, that whole team spirit of being together and trying to achieve something as a group, that was inspirational.'

It was a no-brainer that there would be another tournament, and the WRFU, forgetting its earlier scepticism, offered almost immediately to host the next European Cup in the UK in 1991. Planning for it would not begin until the start of 1990, by which time interest from Canada, the USA and New Zealand would ensure that the scope of the competition became bigger. Women's rugby was going global.

*****

Bourg-en-Bresse is located at the foot of the Jura Mountains, roughly equidistant from Lyon and Geneva. It is a typically quaint French town famous for the quality of its chickens, *poulets-de-bresse*, which are bred to exacting standards and sold for often extortionate prices. It is not necessarily where you would have expected to find a future Hall of Fame coach at the end of May 1988. Jim Greenwood did not need to spend three days stood on the touchline of Stade Marcel-Verchère. At 59 and approaching retirement, he certainly could have done without the long bus journey to eastern France, his 6 ft number eight's frame crammed into his seat as the coach sped through the night to reach its destination. However, at that precise moment, there was nowhere else in the world he would have rather been.

Greenwood had captained Scotland and represented the British and Irish Lions, playing all four tests on the 1955 tour to South Africa. It is as a coach, or more accurately a tutor of the game, that he had his biggest impact, however. A qualified teacher, Greenwood moved to Loughborough in 1968 to work in the university's English department and coach its rugby team. Over the next two decades, he shaped the careers of a series of internationals, including Sir Clive Woodward, Fran Cotton and Andy Robinson, many of whom took with them the lessons he taught when they launched their own coaching careers.

It was not only in the East Midlands that his philosophies took root. An advocate of an expansive 15-player game, the Scot shared his vision through courses, both at home in Loughborough and across the world. Greenwood travelled extensively, spreading his gospel through clinics in Canada, Japan, the USA and New

Zealand, where he was known simply as 'Mr Rugby'. Somehow, he also found time to write three books on the subject, two of which (*Total Rugby* and *Think Rugby*) became hugely influential. 'I was extremely fortunate as a player as I came under the influence of three great coaches – Earl Kirton, Chalky White but most importantly Jim Greenwood,' his former pupil and men's Rugby World Cup-winning coach Woodward wrote in 2003. 'I was a student at Loughborough when I first read *Total Rugby*. Twenty-five years later, its [sic] still the only rugby coaching book I regularly refer to.' Famed former Scotland and Lions coach Sir Ian McGeechan is also a disciple: 'I didn't feel I'd started coaching properly until I'd read Jim Greenwood.'

It was at the start of the 1986/87 academic year that Greenwood first noticed a couple of unfamiliar faces at the back of his coaching lectures. In truth, it would not have been difficult to spot the two women in a room full of men, and the Scot was intrigued by the newcomers. He spoke to one of them, Chris Gurney, to understand what had brought them to his class. Gurney had taken up the game the previous year alongside Claire Williets and the Mitchell twins Emma and Jane. All four would go on to play international rugby. Gurney explained to Greenwood that, in the wake of the Wiverns tour and the introduction of international rugby, the women's team were keen to improve. Would he be interested in attending one of the squad's training sessions? After some cajoling, Greenwood agreed.

When Greenwood set off to watch the women train for the first time, he expected only to 'observe and maybe help out a little'. His plans quickly changed, though. His wife Margot would tell Emma Mitchell, one of his early protégées at Loughborough, that 'he came home with a skip in his step …. He explained it was [because] he had a group of people who were just so eager to learn.' Greenwood's infectious love for rugby and his clear ideas about how it should be played had a huge impact on the university's players. Amanda Bennett, Liza Burgess and Mitchell are just three who have gone on to have successful careers in coaching and sports administration, and he was soon convinced to take on both England and Great Britain as well.

He took on those roles at the beginning of 1987 and would continue until he and Margot returned home to Scotland at the end of the 1988/89 academic year, following his retirement from teaching. 'His detail was intricate. He used to give us all little letters (I've got all my letters from him) before we played about what he wanted us to think about, what we should [take] into the game, what our preparation should be,' Burgess recalls. 'He was meticulous in his preparation, and he treated us as rugby players, you know. So, we weren't just women, we were rugby players. His preparation was phenomenal, and that's something I've always held close to my heart.'

'He absolutely loved it, you could tell that,' former England and Great Britain winger Cheryl Stennett says. 'I think because we were at the developmental stage, he could see the potential. So, that was really exciting for him. And he became our friend as well as our coach because he was just so passionate about how much potential we had as a squad. It was a real shame when he had to step down. I remember going round his house to have a meal. There were quite a few of us who got invited round there, and it was just lovely to see him in his home environment.'

In ten matches in charge of England and Great Britain, his only defeats were the two inflicted by France. He signed off from international women's rugby with a 13–0 victory against the French in Roehampton, as Mitchell fittingly scored the hosts' opening try. Greenwood's contribution to the women's game in the UK cannot be measured solely by results, though. At a crucial time in its development, he gave it credibility. At a time when several high-profile male players and coaches unashamedly played to the chauvinist gallery, the great Scot gave women's rugby the respect it deserved.

'A group who have attained unexpected importance are women players. Undeterred by the criticism of prejudiced men and women, more and more women are taking up rugby as players,' Greenwood wrote in the later editions of *Total Rugby*. 'I've thoroughly enjoyed coaching Loughborough, England, and GB women's teams. A nicer bunch of people and a greater degree of dedication to the game or pleasure in playing, I've never encountered.

'But as a coach, what stands out is the talent the best women players show for the game. In terms of reading the game, intelligent decision-making, improvising answers to unexpected problems, range of skills, the women give nothing away to the men. They are equally committed to attack and defence, and equally whole-hearted in contact. When you consider that none of the players has any experience predating higher education, their feeling for the game is remarkable.' In his resignation letter, Greenwood recommended Rex Hazeldine and Herbert 'Chalky' White be considered to succeed him as Great Britain coach. Wales boss Jeff Williams was initially given the job but quit before his first match in charge due to a disagreement over selection. In the end, Steve Dowling agreed to step into the void and coach both Great Britain and England. A former student of Greenwood's at Loughborough, it seemed a fitting appointment.

*****

Great Britain's experience in Bourg-en-Bresse lit a fuse inside the players involved. They wanted to compete at another international tournament and they wanted to beat France. They really wanted to beat France. However, as Isherwood, Almond and co. focused their attention on the French, Jim Greenwood was using his rolodex of global contacts to help the game take another step towards a Women's Rugby World Cup. It is not known exactly how the Scot came into contact with Laurie O'Reilly, but given the latter was a dedicated student of the game then it most likely occurred during one of Greenwood's many trips to New Zealand. Both men were a huge influence on the early coaching career of Wayne Smith, and it would not be a stretch to imagine the three of them sat in O'Reilly's downstairs lounge discussing the game late into the night. Greenwood and O'Reilly certainly had a lot to discuss, and their shared passion for rugby and determination to provide female players with the opportunities they deserved led to a mammoth tour which would have far-reaching consequences.[i]

O'Reilly liked to help people, whether in court as a respected family lawyer, at the rugby club or at home. Sport was a big part of O'Reilly family life. Laurie coached the University of Canterbury men's team, which is where he met Smith, and wife Kay was an elite netball coach and New Zealand selector. The couple's children got used to spending time with their parents' players, who would drop in at all hours for a chat or to grab some food. 'Growing up, there were always sporty people [around],' daughter Lauren remembers. 'Our house was a bit of a drop-in centre.' One day, a couple of former charges walked through the front door and made straight for the kitchen. While looking round the fridge, one lifted their head to ask the unfamiliar figure standing behind them where Laurie and Kay were. 'They haven't lived here for a year,' came the stern reply.

Whether the players eventually managed to track down the O'Reillys or not, the number of young people hanging out round the house, many of whom were living away from their own home for the first time, only increased after Laurie took an interest in

---

[i] Their friendship was so strong that Greenwood would dedicate later editions of *Total Rugby* to O'Reilly, following the latter's death from cancer at the beginning of 1998.

the women's game. It was Lauren who introduced him to the idea of women playing rugby, and initially he wasn't entirely sold on it. Not quite able to force her way into her mum's netball team, Lauren first picked up an oval ball in 1984 after beginning a teacher training course at the university where her dad taught and coached. 'I was playing in the front row and dad was concerned,' Lauren remembers. 'He said: "If you're going to play, you're going to play properly and I'm going to make sure you're taught the correct technique." And, then he really got involved.'

Once he had committed to doing something, O'Reilly was unable to give anything less than 100 per cent, especially when it came to rugby. His passion for the oval-ball game was such that, even on family holidays, if he saw a training session under way, he would stroll over to offer his services. On one occasion, near his home in Canterbury, he proffered some advice to a young father coaching his son only to realise it was the current provincial half back.

O'Reilly also had a knack for convincing people to do what he needed them to, and that came in handy in two particular ways once he got involved with the women's game. First, he was able to spot and coax a stream of players from other sports, including several of Kay's netball squad. 'He was very good at picking girls who would actually be good players,' says Anna Richards, one of the players to swap a round ball for an oval one. 'He was a bit of a horse breeder, I suppose. He was a good picker of those players.' Second, he used his contacts within the New Zealand Rugby Union and further afield to help the game develop. One of those connections was Greenwood, and it was the Scot who helped him plan the Crusadettes. The latter enabled women's players from New Zealand to measure themselves against those in Europe for the first time.

At the end of 1988, a squad from Canterbury, drawn primarily from O'Reilly's university side and featuring Richards, left New

Zealand on a two-month odyssey. The whirlwind schedule for the tour included stops in the USA, England, France, Italy, Spain and the Netherlands and would open the eyes of those involved to the possibilities of international competition, just as the Wiverns had for those in the UK three years previously. By November 1988, Lauren was living in London's Shepherd's Bush where she worked as a teacher, and so missed the US leg of the trip. It was in Europe that the tour really kicked into overdrive, though. Following ten days in England and Wales, in which they played at a tournament in Keele and against three regional select sides, the party drove to Paris to take on an Île-de-France XV on 13 December. Four days later, they were in Madrid, and from there stopped off in Catalonia, Nice and Amsterdam on their way to Treviso for a match against the Benetton Red Panthers on 29 December. In total, the Crusadettes played 21 matches, winning 17 while scoring 520 points and conceding just 67.

For a few of the matches, the women had been billed on promotional flyers as a New Zealand national team, something which gave several members of the squad an idea as they criss-crossed the Continent. 'That's kind of how talk of a women's World Cup came about,' Natasha Wong recalls. 'As we were travelling around, we made connections with the key people in different countries, and it all started from there. When we came back from that tour in '89, a few of us, with Laurie obviously, pulled together the first Women's World Rugby Festival.' In August 1990, Canterbury's Lincoln College staged a three-tiered women's rugby tournament which consisted of club, provincial and international competition. No clubs from the UK could afford to make the trip, but RugbyFest, as it was known, attracted sides from Japan and a four-team international tournament pitted hosts New Zealand against the USA, the Netherlands and the USSR.

Each of the visiting nations also played matches against regional sides while in Canterbury, making it a full-on experience for everyone involved. New Zealand won all three of their international matches and then repeated the trick against a 'World XV' on 1 September to bring the curtain down on RugbyFest in style. 'For some of us who were in all three teams, we played 15 games in 14 days. I can remember one day we played a club game and then in the afternoon we played a provincial game. I mean, they wouldn't do that in this day and age! After the tournament it was like, "Wow, did we just do that?"' Wong adds. 'To actually play an international team was a big deal. In those early days, even from a provincial [point of view] we were stuck on the South Island because it was all about cost …. It opened our eyes up to the possibilities and the fact that, Oh, my God, it's actually a community. There's a whole group of women.'

RugbyFest was not billed as a World Cup, but the event did not go unnoticed by a group of women on the other side of the globe, whose plans for a World Cup accelerated once they heard about it.

6

'WE SHOULD HAVE A WORLD CUP'

AS THE 1988/89 season drew to a close, Richmond's women were riding the crest of a wave. Despite a run of injuries, the club ended its third campaign in South West London as cup and sevens champions.

The league had eluded them, won by their perennial rivals from across the city Wasps. Nevertheless, excitement swirled round the Athletic Ground, and not merely as a consequence of results on the pitch. Richmond was a club forged by the pioneering spirit of women who had found a home in what wasn't just a male-dominated space, but a men-only one.

Thanks to the work of Deborah Griffin, Tricia Moore, Carol Isherwood and many others, that perception was beginning slowly to change. Women's rugby in the UK had grown from an informal university pursuit into a thriving club game. Teams from across England and Wales competed domestically, while there was a burgeoning international scene. Since Griffin and co. had moved south from Finchley, in pursuit of better facilities and more equal rights, Richmond had been a club at the forefront of this movement.

So, it should come as little surprise that it was Richmond who were to become the first British women's club to embark on a tour of rugby's spiritual home, New Zealand. 'This tour is the icing on the cake of a series of achievements in Women's Cup and League Rugby and is a reflection of Richmond's own strength and commitment to the long-term structure of the game,' tour organiser Pru Watkins wrote in the programme produced to commemorate the trip. 'Thanks to everybody who has given time, money or support towards this tour – we still can't quite believe we're going!'

Richmond's tour of New Zealand would prove an important staging post on the road to the first Women's Rugby World Cup, but as the players excitedly packed their bags and prepared to travel halfway round the world, storm clouds were gathering over the sport. A rather more clandestine expedition would soon expose the lengths to which those in charge of the game, particularly in the UK, were prepared to go in order to maintain the status quo. Many of those blazered committeemen were not interested in promoting female participation, far less a global tournament. In their minds, rugby was a man's game that promoted the ideals of amateurism, and they were determined to keep it that way.

Griffin and her Richmond teammates had not fallen in love with rugby because of the politics or values of its custodians. Some had become addicted to the feeling of freedom which came with running down the pitch with the ball tucked under their arm. Others delighted in the physical nature of the game and discovered an outlet for (and celebration of) attributes they might otherwise have been required to curb while playing hockey or netball. However, as female playing numbers continued to increase and the nascent women's international game took shape, cooperation with men's clubs and the traditional unions became more important.

Although they had several high-profile male allies, including legendary coach Jim Greenwood, women playing rugby were still seen as a novelty by the majority of club members. Promoting female participation was a progressive act in a distinctly conservative world. Just how conservative became clear in April 1989, when it was finally confirmed that the IRFB, rugby's global governing body, had agreed to allow South Africa to host a World XV on a five-match jaunt which included two tests against the Springboks. The tour, a centenary celebration for the country's union, would take place in August and September.

Rugby had always maintained an uncomfortable relationship with the apartheid state. South Africa had been admitted to the IRFB in 1949, a year after the National Party swept to victory in the country's general election and began to impose the racist policies which segregated the population and disenfranchised and dehumanised its non-white citizens.

Nelson Mandela would later use rugby as a vehicle for social change, but while the National Party remained in power, and Madiba (the clan name by which he was known among admirers) languished in various prisons, the sport's power brokers failed to grasp the potential at their fingertips. The British and Irish Lions toured South Africa as late as 1980, Ireland did so 12 months after that and England did likewise in 1984, while New Zealand hosted the Springboks in 1981. Protests and demonstrations greeted each trip, and a few players suffered from their decisions to visit the ethnostate. Some even lost jobs back home and opted to stay.

South Africa retained their place on the IRFB with full voting rights, a fact which proved pivotal in 1985 as the decision to host a first men's World Cup was passed by ten votes to six.[i] The Springboks would be banned from the first two editions of

---

[i] The eight members of the IRFB shared the body's 16 votes equally. Australia, France, New Zealand and South Africa used both of theirs in favour of the World Cup. Ireland and Scotland voted against, while England and Wales were split.

that tournament, but in 1986, the global governing body invited a host of South African players to the UK for its centenary celebrations. Two rebel tours to the Republic followed, but although the country's union was threatened with expulsion it managed to emerge instead with an official visit.

There are many reasons why the powers that be might have been keen to consent. Putting aside the well-worn and wrong-headed argument that sport and politics should not mix, South Africa was simply too big for the IRFB to jettison completely. Some 16 nations competed in the inaugural men's Rugby World Cup in Australia and New Zealand in 1987, but less than half of those began the tournament with any real chance of winning it. Co-hosts New Zealand were the only country involved where rugby union was the undisputed national sport, and their All Blacks won the Webb Ellis Cup at a relative canter, scoring 298 points and conceding only 52 in their six matches.

South Africa remains the only country that can rival New Zealand for the depth of passion for rugby found within it. That fact does not make the decision to allow the 'World XV' to tour the country in 1989 any more palatable, but there were real concerns at the top end of the game that refusing to do so could cause a catastrophic split. South Africa, it was feared, could be pushed to adopt professionalism more openly or lose its considerable playing population to rugby league. Either scenario, they felt, would throw the long-term future of union into considerable doubt, so the game's administrators instead chose to mollify.

'The Board will do everything in its power to ensure the tour becomes reality,' IRFB secretary Keith Rowlands told the *Johannesburg Citizen* newspaper in June. The governing body had agreed to sanction the tour at an interim meeting in London on 4 November 1988, although it favoured a Five Nations rather than World XV – as did each of the home unions, bar

England and France. Publicly, the responsibility was shunted onto individual players to decide whether they wanted to accept invitations sent their way. Several high-profile players, led by Finlay Calder who had recently captained the Lions in Australia, declined,[ii] but a squad of 23 managed by Willie John McBride (described in the *Irish Independent* as a 'long-time advocate of sporting links with South Africa') did make the journey. The Springboks won both test matches.

Rowlands would later become the point of contact at the IRFB for the Women's Rugby World Cup Organising Committee. Although not required to, or apparently interested in, supplying the tournament with official consent, he did hold two meetings with Griffin (one of which left her in tears) and was intrigued enough to accept an offer of hospitality for the final.

'If you want to raise a snigger about women's liberation, the [rugby] clubhouse remains the best place to do it,' journalist Eamon Dunphy wrote in a column scathing of Irish involvement in the centenary tour of South Africa. Richmond's women had fought such prejudice themselves over the previous decade and had no interest in waiting for male approval as they plotted their next step, whether that be a trip to New Zealand or hosting a World Cup.

*****

The identity of the 23 players selected for the World XV tour of South Africa remained a closely guarded secret until they congregated in Johannesburg, but with up to £50,000 'expenses' on offer to those involved there was never much doubt a squad would be raised. Rugby was still ostensibly an amateur sport, and for a five-match trip that sum, equivalent to £132,549 in 2022,

---

[ii] David Campese, Nick Farr-Jones, Michael Lynagh, Simon Poidevin and Brian Moore were among those who declined the opportunity to tour South Africa in 1989.

would have been difficult to resist. If only the women of Richmond could have benefited from such a bountiful influx of cash.

Griffin and co. had moved south to Richmond in 1986 in search of more privileges and better facilities. The players had been allowed to become full members, something denied them at Finchley, but while they were affiliated to one of the country's most prestigious clubs, and had access to manicured pitches, they were required to scrimp, save and fundraise to keep the club moving forward.

One case in point was the club's own trip to the southern hemisphere. That Richmond were the first female team from Britain to visit New Zealand is not surprising given the prohibitive costs involved. Tour organiser Pru Watkins was grateful for a donation of £5,000 from Chelsfield PLC,[iii] but it was a concession stand at Wembley Stadium which proved to be the biggest source of funds.

Sue Dorrington had moved to London from her native Minnesota in 1983 in search of competitive rugby and, despite initially struggling to find a team, she became a fixture for Finchley and was part of the mass exodus to South West London. Short in stature but possessing a steely determination, Dorrington had become a Great Britain and England international, and her skills as a fundraiser made her as integral off the pitch as on it.

Ahead of the trip to New Zealand, Dorrington was alerted to the fundraising potential of the Wembley stalls, which at the time were run by charities and volunteers. 'It was very funny because one of our teammates, my best friend Pat, worked at Wembley part time and she was on the team that ran all the bars,' Dorrington says. 'And the old Wembley had these little red huts and they had volunteers, so they had the scouts, they had charities in to run their bars. That's what they did! They didn't

---

[iii] Club secretary Mary Forsyth worked for Chelsfield PLC, and the company's London offices would later provide the venue for early-morning meetings of the Women's Rugby World Cup Organising Committee.

hire people, they hired charities. Such a scam! But the brilliant thing is that you took ten per cent of the takings on your bar as your charitable donation, as your payment.

'So, Pat said, "Well, why don't you see if we can't get you in, Sue?" You know, I was looking for fundraising opportunities and she said, let's do this. And I went along, and they said, yes, and then what I did was get [access to work at] all the Wembley events and then whoever was going on the tour had to sign up for an event and then we allocated a points system in terms of how many events you worked and how much money we took and how much money you made personally.

'So, every player that went on that New Zealand tour had the opportunity of working at Wembley over two summers and generating personal funds for their personal tour payment. And we made probably £26,000 that was split between those 30 people and we went on tour.'

Dorrington paid for her whole trip through her work in the red hut, but she admits it was 'absolutely terrifying as women' at certain events. Drunken fans would sometimes clamber onto the top of the structures and walk along them, and the unsophisticated way in which Wembley staff collected the takings presented its own problems. In a sign, perhaps, of a more innocent time, a security officer would knock on the door of the hut and simply ask for the money. On one occasion, tour organiser Pru Watkins handed over the cash without question, only to soon realise that she had been scammed.

'She handed him everything,' Dorrington says. 'Then ten minutes later it was like, "Can I have your money please?" "I just gave it to someone." "Well, what do you mean you just gave it to someone?" So, we were robbed and so we had some really quite funny stories about it.

'When we were promoted into the major bar, a guy broke into our bar and was trying to steal a case [of beer]. Now, you have to understand we had to be accountable for every bottle in that bar, so I tackled him and laid him flat and got the case back and called security. And the brilliant thing is it was during a concert, and I had to go back of house and they walked me past Paul McCartney, Eric Clapton, all those really big names, in a photoshoot.

'So, I get to walk 5 ft from all those ... you know, arresting this chap and then I had to go to court and testify, which was very, very scary – and he got done. But it's ridiculous really, he was drunk and broke in and tried to steal a case, but it was so important to us to try to balance our books because we had been promoted and given the privilege of running this bar because of our reputation, and I wasn't going to let that drop.' Dorrington had made her citizen's arrest at a tribute concert to celebrate Nelson Mandela's 70th birthday. The event at Wembley Stadium was watched by hundreds of millions of people worldwide, although it was not broadcast in South Africa or, one may deduce, the IRFB's offices.

Dorrington's fundraising abilities would be put to the test on the road to the inaugural Women's Rugby World Cup, but for now they had helped to ensure Richmond was on its way to the Land of the Long White Cloud. 'Throughout our visit to New Zealand we hope to play rugby to the best of our ability and provide worthy opposition to the formidable sporting inhabitants of this famous rugby nation,' Watkins wrote in the tour programme. 'We hope to make lots of friends and act as a good advertisement for our sport – one of the fastest growing in the country.'

Richmond would enjoy a fruitful tour on the pitch, but it was in the friendships which were made and strengthened during the post-match functions that the seeds for the first women's World Cup began to take root.

*****

By the time that Richmond's women touched down in Auckland in May 1989, the furore over the morality of the IRFB-sanctioned World XV tour of South Africa was at its height, but it is safe to assume that those on board Richmond's plane cared little about that. A tour party of 28 players (four of whom would start the Women's Rugby World Cup final for England two years later), two coaches, two husbands and a sexagenarian Second World War veteran were intent on enjoying their trip of a lifetime.

Touring had played an integral part in the growth of women's rugby over the previous decade-and-a-half, primarily thanks to the US teams which ventured to Europe and New Zealand intent on spreading their gospel. As detailed previously, British teams had been a little less adventurous, sticking largely to the more cost-effective environs of Europe. Now it was time for something rather different.

'We were quite adventurous,' Griffin remembers. 'We'd already toured France and Italy, probably other places as well, and it was just a case of, "Well, that's it, that's the home [of rugby], let's go there."'

'It was incredible for us because we had worked two years running bars at Wembley to fund the tour,' Dorrington says. 'We had worked really hard and then went over there and played for two weeks, and just had the most incredible time.

'How couldn't you, touring north and south? I'm sure everybody else who went on that tour would wax lyrical about it. We loved it. It was a lifetime experience.'

Following some 'time to recover from the perils of jet lag', the squad began a whirlwind tour which featured stops in Auckland, Dargaville (home of Richmond player Denise Grantham), Hamilton, Rotorua, Kawerau, Queenstown, Mount Cook National Park, Ashburton and Christchurch. In total, Richmond played nine matches in just two weeks and, unlike the World XV, they won them all.

The trip came to an end in Christchurch, on New Zealand's South Island, where the tourists were reacquainted with Laurie O'Reilly and his University of Canterbury side, the bulk of whom had toured Europe less than six months previously as the Crusadettes. It was while O'Reilly and the Crusadettes had been in Europe at the end of 1988 that the coach had first discussed the idea of hosting a global international tournament with some of his players.

Although women's international rugby had been building in Europe since the start of the decade, and the USA and Canada had first played a test match in 1987, New Zealand were cut off. The lure of hosting an international tournament was obvious for O'Reilly and his players. Some time after they returned home to Christchurch, most likely over the Kiwi winter according to organiser Natasha Wong, plans for what would become the Women's World Rugby Festival (or RugbyFest 1990) began to take shape.

It was as those plans were being formulated that Richmond arrived in Christchurch, and it seems likely that the tournament would have been discussed, however informally, as the teams shared post-match beers and food. Shortly after Griffin returned home, an official invitation for RugbyFest arrived, which she still retains, but the players would not have been able to raise the funds required to send a team back to New Zealand so soon, and therefore it was declined.

In August 1990, the Netherlands, USA and USSR national sides, as well as two club teams from Japan, arrived on New Zealand's South Island to take part in RugbyFest 1990. The event comprised club and provincial competitions alongside the showpiece test tournament, with organisers determined to use it to encourage new players to pick up an oval ball. 'The whole idea was to showcase women's rugby,' Wong says. 'What we wanted to do was to ensure that women at all levels were able to participate.'

RugbyFest was never billed as a World Cup, but the notion that a global women's tournament could become reality had flicked a switch in at least one mind in London. 'I think that's what sort of prompted us to do it,' Griffin told me when I visited her at home in Cambridge in January 2020. 'What happened was when we were out there we found out that probably Christchurch or Canterbury were having a sort of tournament, a club tournament, and inviting countries, clubs and everything,' she added.

'I think we were a bit miffed that they thought they should have the first [World Cup]. They weren't billing it as a World Cup – I think it was sort of a world club competition. So, we thought in our wisdom, "Well, we should have a World Cup and have it here."' It is telling that the competitive spirit that had helped build Richmond into a force on the pitch was evident off it, too, as some of the club's leading lights strove to put on the first, global women's tournament.

*****

Those who were planning to guide the women's game on its next step forward might have been based in the UK, but that journey had begun in the universities of North America in the 1970s. Almost simultaneously, there had been an awakening across a number of nations in Europe (influenced, at least in part, by touring teams from the USA) and, later, New Zealand. Female participation had spread to non-traditional rugby nations in Europe largely thanks to the Continent's geography and the increasingly affordable cost of travel between countries such as France, Spain, Sweden, the Netherlands and the UK.

It was in Europe that women's international rugby first took root, and, since the first match between the Netherlands and France in June, 1982, it had grown to such an extent that a European Cup was held only six years later. It was not a surprise, therefore, that teams such as Canada, New Zealand and the USA, without a plentiful supply of opposition on their doorsteps, would want to join the party.

Although the USA had played such an integral role in seeding the growth of female participation across the world, the country remained a novice on the international stage. It was not until 1987 that the blazers in charge of the USA Rugby Football Union consented to a women's team being raised in its name, and even then it was only in response to a request from their counterparts in Canada. The post-match events which followed that first international in North America, moreover, only served to underline the attitudes those American players were required to fight.

Eight months after the USA's 22–3 defeat of Canada in Victoria, as Kathy Flores and her teammates prepared to welcome their neighbours to upstate New York for a rematch, a fax found its way to Deborah Griffin. It had been sent by Anne Stephen, as a representative of the National Women's Rugby Committee of the Canadian Rugby Union, and dispatched to unions round the world who oversaw the female game in their respective countries. The correspondence sought, among other requests, information on the 'existence and history' of women's rugby in each country as well as international matches and tournaments which were in the pipeline.

'Last November, the Canadian Rugby Union hosted the inaugural Senior Women's Can-Am match in Victoria, British Columbia,' Stephen wrote. 'It is our intention to maintain this annual fixture with the United States.

'We are now seeking information regarding women's rugby in other countries. Specifically our interests are in national teams and international competitions, both past and matches planned for the future.

'Initially, it is the Canadian Rugby Union's intention to establish an information exchange with the national union's [sic] with respect to women's rugby. The importance of opening communications in this regard is obvious. Ultimately, of course, we anticipate taking a Canadian women's side off the North American continent.'

Although Griffin retains a copy of the memo in her many files, there is no record of how she or anyone else at the Women's Rugby Football Union responded. Having arrived only two months after the inaugural European Cup had been held in Bourg-en-Bresse, it is safe to assume that Stephen was informed of the recent tournament and that the WRFU had agreed to host the second edition in 1991. It is important to remember that this was a time before information was available at the click of a button on the internet, and the correspondence is evidence of an impressive network which was being built using little more than fax machines and airmail. It is a sign, too, that Griffin had been alerted to the appetite for international competitions in North America.

Those women working to promote rugby in Canada and the USA would have loved to have access to an international tournament such as the European Cup. Given that some North American players were happy to plough their spare cash, savings and Air Miles into plane tickets in order to play in weekend tournaments on the opposite side of the country, it is unsurprising that both would declare an interest in joining the next running of that competition in 1991.

The USA's thirst for international competition meant that they found a squad of players willing and able to pay their way to New Zealand for RugbyFest 1990. That tournament had unearthed two newcomers to the women's game in the Soviet

Union and Japan, while through Laurie O'Reilly the host nation would make clear their own ambition to make the European Cup a more global affair.

Following the first iteration of the European Cup in 1988, it had been decided that Great Britain would host the next edition in 1991. It was becoming increasingly clear that the tournament's remit would have to be broadened, but the WRFU still faced an important question: Who would head the organising committee?

*****

Midway through the 1989/90 season in England and Wales, the stars began to align for the inaugural Women's Rugby World Cup. Although the WRFU had not yet started organising the tournament, the interest it had received from nations outside Europe meant it was inevitable the event would take place. On 9 January 1990, WRFU treasurer Kim Rowlands met the governing body's insurance broker and sought advice on hosting a tournament featuring teams from Italy, the Netherlands, France, the USA, Canada and Sweden. Four days later, at a committee meeting in Loughborough, Deborah Griffin shared a rough proposal for 'European/World Cup 1991' as 'a starter for discussion'.

Griffin's plan envisaged only eight to ten nations competing in two pools of four or five in a provincial location. The top two in each group would qualify for the semi-finals, followed by the final, both of which she argued should be held in London. 'The final obviously needs to be prestigious. We are unlikely (though we will try) to get Twickenham just for our games,' she wrote. Griffin suggested the competition would take eight days to complete and estimated it would cost at least £35,000. Even in this rough sketch, Griffin extolled the virtues of hosting teams in affordable university accommodation and warned about the dangers of holding it too close to the men's Rugby World Cup.

'The above are purely my own thoughts to start the ball rolling,' Griffin concluded as she requested opinions from across the WRFU membership be sent in by the middle of March. Her proposal was so persuasive, however, that she was asked to chair the organising at the next committee meeting. Although already the WRFU press and publicity officer, and responsible for the union's *In Touch* magazine, Griffin accepted. According to minutes from the meeting, both Sue Dorrington and Mary Forsyth had already indicated their willingness to help their clubmate, but Griffin hesitated about confirming their appointments, wary of the 'possible perception of Richmond bias'. Ultimately, though, she accepted the role on the proviso that she could put together her own team.

Griffin turned to three women she had come to lean on during Richmond's rise. Dorrington, whose fundraising drive at Wembley Stadium had done so much to help the club on its way to New Zealand, was a no-brainer as commercial manager. In her day job at Help the Aged she worked on nationwide campaigns, turning bright ideas into real-life events. Dorrington had also served as a spokeswoman for the charity and was therefore used to working with journalists and getting publicity that could, in theory, be turned into commercial opportunity.

The committee's sponsorship target of £100,000 (around £250,000 today) might only have been equivalent to the 'expenses' incurred by two male amateurs on the recently concluded World XV tour of South Africa, but it would not be easy to meet, not least as the UK slipped towards a recession. But the presence of two accountants on the team (Griffin and Forsyth) would ensure that the budget for the tournament was watertight. Like Dorrington, Forsyth hailed from the USA and had found a community thousands of miles from home in the changing rooms of first Finchley and then Richmond. She had been a high-school athletics prospect in her youth, but turned to rugby while at Penn State University. Her height proved a useful tool in her new pursuit, and she would become a good enough player to earn a solitary cap for her adopted country, England.

The Pennsylvanian retained a link to Finchley. Her husband Piers, whom she had married in 1987, played for the club, like her in the second row. She proved to be a force at Richmond both on and off the pitch. Forsyth had been named Player of the Year in the team's final season at Finchley and had an even greater impact on the new club as she helped to pull the men's section 'into a sensible shape with their accounting'. Her acumen as a bookkeeper also helped to smash through more than 125 years of misogynistic tradition when she became the first woman to attend the club's annual dinner.

It was left to Griffin and Forsyth to draw up the budget for the tournament and to make sure the organising committee did not commit to spending money it did not have. The pervading attitude within British women's rugby was that extending the scope of the European Cup, and thus making it a World Cup, was the next logical stage of the game's evolution. However, the cost of hosting teams from around the world would inevitably be significant, hence the desire to land a big sponsor.

The fourth and final member of the organising committee was Alice Cooper. The least experienced of the quartet, Cooper had taken up the game just three years previously, having been cajoled into picking up an oval ball while out trying to 'pick up boys' at a Richmond pub. She had long harboured a desire to play, however, and the previous season had been her best to date. Cooper had shared the award for the club's Player of the Season and was also named Richmond's Most Improved Player. In terms of the organising committee, she provided publishing knowledge and had a presence in the wider rugby landscape, having taken over *Rugby World & Post*'s women's rugby column. She was all too aware of the sexism which still pervaded the scant column inches dedicated to women who played rugby.

At the end of the 1980s in the UK, such articles were incredibly rare, especially in the national press. When they did appear, they were often full of faux outrage, condescension and thinly veiled sexual references. It is impossible not to think of Eamon Dunphy's assertion that the contemporary rugby club remained a bastion of male chauvinism when reading Frank Gilfeather's column from April 1989. Commenting on a match which was due to be staged between Scottish Universities and a team representing the North of England in Edinburgh, the author was apoplectic. In *The Press and Journal* under a headline reading 'Better stick to netball, girls', Gilfeather opined:

> Women playing rugby sounds about as fascinating as watching paint dry. I wonder what makes women want to take part in such a sport. They're built the wrong way for a start. And they yelp and scream a lot when it comes to things physical.
>
> These are not sexist remarks, I hasten to add, although I know some women will accuse me of being chauvinistic.
>
> It's just that I do feel that girls should not be cavorting round a rugby field trying to inflict the kind of torture and injuries we see in that rough and tumble sport. Can you imagine people like Roy Laidlaw and Gavin Hastings wearing short skirts and turning out on a netball pitch?
>
> So girls, leave rugby to the big brawny brutes who like that sort of thing, and stick to your own sports.

Thankfully for millions who now play the game round the world, women such as Griffin, Cooper, Dorrington and Forsyth refused to take such bigoted advice.

Gilfeather did not speak for every journalist or club member, of course. The first women's World Cup would receive the backing of several influential rugby writers, including David Hands and Stephen Jones. Both penned articles for the official tournament programme, but could not guarantee getting their stories on the women's game into *The Times* and the *Sunday Times*, for whom they wrote.

Griffin and co. were certainly not prepared to 'stick to netball', and coverage would be essential if they were to hit their ambitious sponsorship target. It is understandable that the organising committee would have been confident of doing just that. They were successful people who had achieved pretty much every goal they had set themselves since picking up an oval ball, taking on misogyny and breaking through sizeable barriers as they did so.

However, the search for a title sponsor would be the biggest challenge the four women had faced and left the prospect of a World Cup truly in the balance. In July 1989, journalist Fiona Murray wrote in an interview with England and Great Britain player Liz Whalley that 'despite the increasing credibility of the female game, most companies have performed a quick side-step when it comes to sponsorship'. British corporations would prove just as difficult to tackle over the next 18 months.

As the 1980s drew to a close and a new decade appeared to offer hope, the inaugural Women's Rugby World Cup was beginning to take shape. Events in New Zealand and North America had proven there was an appetite for a global tournament, and Griffin had enlisted the help of three trusted friends to make that dream become a reality. Operating in a male-dominated and sometimes hostile environment caused no one involved any anxiety, but one question remained: How do you organise a World Cup in your spare time?

HOW TO ORGANISE A WORLD CUP BEFORE WORK

IT WAS THE low hum of the engine which woke Alice Cooper as Mary Forsyth swung her Saab into Ernest Gardens. Cooper's alarm clock had failed miserably at its one important function, but as she reached out to turn it off, she caught sight of the time. It confirmed what she already knew: she had overslept. It was just before 7.00 am as Cooper raised herself from bed, threw some clothes on, brushed her teeth and hurried downstairs and out of the door. Forsyth was waiting on the quiet West London street, as she would at least once a month while the first Women's Rugby World Cup was being planned. Apologies proffered and accepted, the pair set off for Mayfair, the journey taking them past the construction site of The Ark, the mammoth, ship-shaped office building which was rising from its mooring alongside the Hammersmith flyover. As time ticked down to the World Cup, it would have been tempting for the pair to wonder which was the more ambitious project.

Deborah Griffin and Sue Dorrington were waiting for them by the time Forsyth reversed into her space in the underground car park at 67 Brook Street. Home to Chelsfield PLC, the property company which Forsyth worked for, it was the regular early morning meeting point for the Women's Rugby World Cup Organising Committee. The first time the four women had convened formally to discuss their plans for the tournament, on 24 April 1990, they had done so in the evening. However, each had busy work and home lives, as well as their commitments to Richmond and the WRFU, so it was decided that mornings would be best.

Chelsfield had been incredibly supportive of Forsyth's rugby career, providing a donation to Richmond's 1989 tour of New Zealand and stepping in at late notice to sponsor the England–Sweden match the previous year, in which the Pittsburgh-born forward had already been selected to make her international debut. The company's central location was perfect. Nestled in one of the city's most exclusive neighbourhoods, surrounded by embassies and upmarket hotels, its proximity to Bond Street tube station ensured the organising committee could meet for an hour in its boardroom from 7.30 am, and Griffin, Cooper and Dorrington would have time to travel to their own offices and be in place when the working day started at 9.00 am. That was how Brook Street became the unofficial planning hub of the inaugural women's World Cup.

The meetings themselves were led by Griffin but were more informal affairs than WRFU committee meetings, which at the time were stipulated to last for at least three hours and include lunch. Although she headed the group's efforts, especially in those early days when the search was on for a host venue, each of the organising committee's members had their own defined speciality. Forsyth was an accountant, like Griffin, and therefore kept an eye on the budget as financial controller. Dorrington, a charity fundraiser by profession, was responsible for finding sponsorship. Cooper, working hard to build her profile as a rugby writer, was in charge of press and publicity.

'I'm an organiser, I'm an administrator, and it was a case of saying "Right, what are the things we have to do?" and divvying up the tasks to go away and do them,' Griffin remembers. 'Then the four of us used to meet at about 7.00 in the morning at Mary's office. And it was a matter of "What are the things we need to do?" … It's not really rocket science is it? You need places to play, accommodation, you need transport, you need referees, you need hospitality, you know. That's it really, isn't it?'

Locating a place to play with suitable and affordable accommodation would be Griffin's first task, but the biggest challenge facing the organising committee would prove to be finding companies willing to sponsor the tournament. Competing nations at the 1988 European Cup had been provided with food and board in Bourg-en-Bresse, and it was a favour Griffin and co. were determined to extend in 1991. The organisers of the tournament in France had found it a stretch to do that for four teams, though, leading to a breakdown in relations with their counterparts at the WRFU. The World Cup was set to be a more ambitious undertaking, meaning the strain on its finances would be even greater.

Griffin had estimated the cost of an eight- or ten-team tournament would be around £35,000, a sum which would only increase if more teams committed to taking part. The organising committee's desire to leave money in the pot for the next hosts, moreover, meant they needed to find a business, or businesses, willing to part with considerable cash to be able to cover their overheads. The target eventually agreed upon was £100,000, and although all four women pitched in, it was Dorrington, as commercial manager, who would take the lead in that search. It would prove harder than anyone expected, leading them to bring in an outside agency to help with a quest which almost derailed the World Cup entirely.

*****

More than three decades on, Griffin cannot remember what prompted her to put together a proposal for the structure of the inaugural Women's Rugby World Cup. But, at the beginning of 1990, she did exactly that. Given the amount of correspondence which was pushed through the letterbox at 224A Camden Road or came flying out of her fax machine at Panell Kerr Forster, though, it makes sense that she would have felt the pressure more than most at the WRFU. It was Griffin and incumbent secretary Rosie Golby who received the bulk of enquiries from teams inside and outside Europe that were keen on taking part. It is understandable, therefore, that she would see the sands of time slipping away and opt to act. She had done so much previously to help the women's game move forward in the UK, why wouldn't she kick off the discussion about the World Cup?

It is also impressive how closely the two A4 pages of typed-up notes resemble the actual tournament. Yes, Griffin initially only envisaged a tournament of eight–ten teams, floated the idea of a two-centre event and was in favour of a much bigger organising committee, but the skeleton of the World Cup is already there. Griffin's initial plan was to hold the tournament across a week, with the first group matches on a Saturday and the final on the following Sunday, using a 'provincial' location for the pool stage and a bigger city (i.e., London) for the showpiece match. On the possibility of staging the final at Twickenham, Griffin wrote: 'In April they may allow it as a "curtain raiser". In September it would be more difficult.'

Griffin suggested three months to hold the tournament (April, July or September) and favoured the first as it would be possible to secure university accommodation, was not out of season and, arguably most important, would not clash with the men's Rugby World Cup. In terms of the location, the proposal stated that the host city, or cities, needed to possess appropriate accommodation, a supportive rugby community and, ideally, a local women's team. Cardiff and South Wales ticked all those boxes, but it would take more than six months for Griffin to be able to confirm that was where they were going. Letters were sent to clubs, universities and polytechnics in Bath, Birmingham, Bristol, London and Nottingham requesting help. Waterloo put itself forward, and at one stage it looked as though the World Cup would be played in Leicester.

By the time the organising committee met formally for the first time at the end of April, it had been decided to hold the tournament in one location during the Easter holidays. To cut down on costs while maximising advertising and broadcasting revenue it was a no-brainer. It may seem strange that a tournament organised by a governing body based in England would be held in South Wales, but in 1990 the WRFU was not an English union. The body had responsibility for the women's game across the UK, albeit the majority of clubs and players were based in England and it was there that most of its energies were focused. Wales, whose regional and international matches were organised by a committee of the WRFU, and Scotland were beginning to push for a bigger voice, but it would take another four years for those countries to break away.

It is important to remember that the pinnacle of representative women's rugby in the UK remained Great Britain until at least the end of the 1989/90 season. England and Wales had each played only five tests by April 1990, four of which were against each other. The inexperience of the nations as individual teams was such that the respective captains, Karen Almond and Liza Burgess, both told Golby that they should join forces and compete as Great Britain at the World Cup. In the row that ensued, Almond was summoned to a WRFU committee meeting in Warwickshire on 7 April to explain herself, and while she and her opposite number both insisted they had changed their minds by then, Golby felt it necessary to apologise to her colleagues for reopening the debate. Although feeling was clearly strong on both sides, it made sense that an ostensibly British union would host its tournament in South Wales, especially given its suitability.

The case for taking the tournament to Cardiff and the surrounding areas was made by the Sports Council for Wales, rather than the WRU. As the 1989/90 season drew to a close, Welsh rugby, as it often does, found itself in turmoil, the game still reeling from financial decisions made by a number of its most high-profile players in the preceding 18 months. This was a time when the flow of talent from the country to rugby league was as strong as ever, but it was the mercenary actions of the internationals who took part in the centenary tour of South Africa that left the biggest scar. Wales coach John Ryan had expected two or three of his players to go on the tour, not least because three senior WRU officials (Clive Rowlands, Terry Vaux and Gwilym Treharne) were in favour of it. However, he could only watch on in astonishment as ten were airlifted out of Aberystwyth by helicopter, two of whom had played no part in that weekend's national-team training camp because of injury.

A subsequent inquiry into the affair found that at least one of the Welsh tourists was paid £30,000 for his services, while the behaviour of the players and officials involved provided 'the gravest cause for concern for both the present and future for rugby football in Wales'. The report was written by Vernon Pugh QC and, although suppressed at the time, put him on course for a successful career in rugby administration. He would come to the aid of the Women's Rugby World Cup organising committee on the eve of the tournament, when they found themselves in sudden need of a venue.

Given everything which was going on in Welsh men's rugby in 1990 (there were also fervent debates about the merits of playing on Sundays and the use of kicking tees), it seems the WRU's attention was not fully on the women's World Cup. There were also concerns within the WRFU about the state of relations with the union, due primarily to the latter's refusal to allow the most recent Wales v England match to be played at the National Stadium in Cardiff. The WRU, though, *did* offer to help with referees and sold tickets for the semi-finals and final through its box office, while its administrative officer Peter Owens sat on a hospitality committee for the tournament. Otherwise, though, Griffin and co. were left to get on with things themselves. Fortunately, the Sports Council for Wales was keen to be more hands-on.

Griffin first met a representative of the Sports Council for Wales, John Evans, on 16 June 1990, at which stage Leicester had been earmarked for hosting duties. Following a much more positive and supportive discussion than she had experienced elsewhere, though, her head was turned. Evans was confident elite clubs could be convinced to make their pitches available for pool matches, while Griffin, keen to keep her options open, had already sounded out the Cardiff Athletic Club about the use of the Arms Park for the semi-finals and final. Evans offered his organisation's help with finding local university accommodation as well as pledging access to its facilities at the National Sports Centre in Sophia Gardens.

Built in 1971 at a cost of £545,000, the Sports Centre was perhaps in need of modernisation two decades on. However, it provided the organising committee with a central location, two training pitches (one grass and one Astroturf), and a main hall which Evans suggested could be used for a formal dinner following the final. It also meant participating players would have a cheap way to amuse themselves on non-match days. Evans pledged full access to the centre's facilities for the duration of the tournament, meaning that when not playing or training, the teams could use the gym, swimming pool or squash courts in Sophia Gardens free of charge. The site also comprised enough rooms to accommodate the organising committee, key volunteers and the Wales squad.

As for the accommodation of the other teams, Evans favoured the use of the University of Wales College, Cardiff due to its proximity to the National Sports Centre. A prior booking meant that most of the remaining participants would instead be housed at the Cyncoed campus of the Cardiff Institute of Higher Education, as it became in 1990. Despite its out-of-town location, around four miles from the city centre, Griffin was attracted to the Institute as it possessed three rugby pitches of its own. Those playing fields provided the squads staying there with somewhere to train, and it was ultimately there that the World Cup's Plate competition, for teams which did not make the semi-finals, was held.

Griffin was clearly impressed by what she had found in Wales' capital. Nine days after her meeting with Evans, she wrote to National Sports Centre for Wales principal Gwynne Griffiths to confirm Cardiff as the World Cup host venue. In July, Griffin reported to the WRFU committee that while there were 'one or two matters to finalise' before the Welsh capital could be confirmed, 'everything is in hand although going a little too slowly for my liking'. It would not be until much later in the year, when the paperwork was completed and deposits had been paid, that she felt comfortable going public. Yet, the case for Cardiff was as obvious as it was compelling. It was the beating heart of a rugby nation, was close to several thriving women's clubs, while the tournament had the support of Cardiff's City Hall and South Glamorgan County Council (both of which had offered to lay on civic receptions) as well as the WRU and the Sports Council of Wales.

The latter was key as it opened up a potential avenue of funding. The WRFU had previously applied for a grant from the UK Sports Council, which appeared to have been kicked into the long grass of bureaucracy when Griffin was scouting for venues. Working so closely with its subsidiary in Wales could only help their cause on that front, surely? It was certainly no coincidence that when tournament rules and regulations for the women's World Cup were drawn up, they closely resembled those stipulated by the Sports Council.

'I think they were keen, the others,' Griffin remembers of the process, 'but these guys just said, "Oh, we'll do this for you, we'll do this for you." They were very keen to have it and were prepared, whereas the others would have just hosted it, I think. These guys were really wanting to help.'

Money would be a pivotal issue on the road to Cardiff and beyond. Now that the organising committee had found a host, they just needed to convince teams to take part, clubs to offer up their grounds and sponsors to provide the cash to pay for it all. There would be issues associated with each of those requirements, but one would prove much more difficult than the other two.

*****

The organising committee set about their task of finding sponsorship for the Women's Rugby World Cup with their eyes wide open. In her rough proposal for the tournament, Griffin had priced the cost of the tournament at £35,000, but there was agreement early in the formal process that they would need to find considerably more money than that. The target Dorrington was initially given as commercial manager was £75,000 although that soon became £100,000, a fraction of what the men's World Cup hoped to attract but still a considerable sum and much more than the women's game had attracted up to that point.

Due to the size of the task, it was not left to Dorrington alone, although she led the efforts, and each member of the organising committee dug into their contacts books to try and find a company willing to pay part or all of that money. As they did so they would have known exactly how tough extracting money from the corporate world would be. England's match against Sweden in 1988 had not been an anomaly in the sense that the WRFU struggled to cover its costs. The WRFU draft accounts for 1989/90 indicate that the body raised £2,530 through subscriptions and a further £1,000 from TV rights, but nothing from sponsorship. The lack of funding meant that those called up for international duty were often required to pay for the privilege, being reimbursed only if the match made a profit. Great Britain players selected for the clash with Italy in Moseley on 18 March 1990, for example, were asked to contribute £20.

An initial shortlist of 24 companies, ten of which were breweries or distillers, was drawn up while each member of the organising committee was provided with a crib sheet detailing the benefits of partnering with the women's World Cup and a list of numbers to cold call. On offer to a business willing to part with cash for the tournament were a host of branding opportunities, including on souvenir publications, merchandise and the England team's playing and training kit, match tickets and hospitality for the semi-final and final. Meanwhile, a dedicated press and PR manager to 'ensure that maximum media coverage is obtained' was also touted, as were perimeter advertising boards at the Arms Park, something they would soon learn was not possible.

By June, Dorrington had received a series of 'thanks but no thanks' letters from companies, Courage and Toshiba included. There was a hint of interest from an agency that represented ADT Security Services, the sponsors of that season's County Championship, but it looked as though the women would need some help. They had known that might be the case from the off and compiled a list of potential sponsorship and PR consultancies at the same time they identified companies. One name on it was Allan Callan, the commercial head for the men's Rugby World Cup who was having his own problems finding outside investment. Another, which quickly emerged as the favoured candidate, was John Taylor International (JTI).

Like Griffin, Dorrington, Cooper and Forsyth, JTI's eponymous chairman was a member of Richmond Football Club. However, it was not at the Athletic Ground that they became acquainted. Taylor had caught the organising committee's attention through an article he wrote for *Sponsorship News* which posed the question: 'Are certain companies blind to the benefits of women's sport?' The piece highlighted how British society was changing at the dawn of the 1990s and presented evidence that not only were women avid watchers of sport on TV, but they also had money to spend on products being advertised to them while they did so.

Taylor paraphrased an old Guinness advert when he concluded why companies were reticent about sponsoring women's sport, even though it was a much cheaper alternative to sport played by men. 'They haven't tried it because they don't like it.' Unperturbed by that pay-off, the organising committee met with JTI director Tom Purvis on 25 June with a view to contracting the agency as consultants on sponsorship and TV. It took until 22 October for agreement to be reached on the terms of a contract, but those negotiations had not prevented the parties working together in the intervening months.

When Purvis eventually sent the final agreement to Griffin to sign in October, he stated that 'JTI feel very confident that the first ever Women's Rugby World Cup will be a great success, and providing BBC Wales come up trumps with their coverage, between us should be able to find four sponsors each to pay £25,000.' That would prove a considerable 'if'. While the ink dried on the contract with JTI, the UK was heading deeper into recession as the boom of the late 1980s gave way to rising inflation. The impact of this was felt in every sphere of life as budgets were tightened in homes and boardrooms across the country – even the Sports Council was impacted. The women were going to have to think outside the box if they were to secure the funding they needed.

*****

The organising committee felt, quite understandably, that the key to finding sponsorship for the inaugural Women's Rugby World Cup lay with television. The broadcast landscape in 1990 in the UK was very different to what it is today. Satellite TV was in its infancy, meaning the viewing needs of the vast majority of homes were served by just four channels. This cut down the number of options available to the organising committee but increased the benefits of a deal if one could be struck. Were the World Cup to be shown on terrestrial TV, regardless of whether the matches were broadcast live, on delay or as a highlights package, the tournament would potentially be beamed into millions of homes. That, in turn, would make it an attractive proposition for sponsors.

It is only recently that women's rugby has been deemed worthy of free-to-air attention by television executives. The Women's Rugby World Cup 2017 final, between England and New Zealand in Belfast, was the first to be shown on prime-time terrestrial TV when it ousted *Catchphrase* from ITV's Saturday night line-up. It would take another five years for the BBC to move their Women's Six Nations coverage from behind the red button and the iPlayer streaming service to a more visible slot on BBC 2; even then, not every match made the jump. It might surprise some to discover, therefore, that Griffin and co. had reason to believe the very first Women's Rugby World Cup would secure broadcast exposure.

Television coverage of women's rugby in the 1980s had amounted to one documentary. Aired on 24 April 1985, it was part of the BBC 2 *Open Space* series which enabled members of the public to explore subjects important to them. Titled *Ungentlemanly Conduct?* it focused on Magor Maidens and shone a light on the challenges the team faced and the enjoyment they took in playing the game. 'Their menfolk may not understand what it is they are trying to prove, but the women know all right,' a write-up of the programme in *The Times* stated. 'They are challenging the male monopoly in pushing, shoving and tumbling about in the mud.'

At the beginning of the 1990s, though, it looked as though TV might be starting to treat the women's game as more than just a curiosity. Channel 4 commissioned Rugby Vision Ltd, a Welsh production company, to make a one-hour documentary on the scene in the UK. In doing so, they agreed to pay the WRFU £1,000 for broadcast rights of both the annual Wales v England match and Great Britain's encounter with Italy. At 5.30 pm on Sunday 6 May, almost three months after Dorrington helped her adopted nation to an 18–12 defeat of Wales in Neath, Channel 4 broadcast *Rugby Women*. Featuring highlights of both internationals, the programme was hosted by England men's captain Will Carling, to the chagrin of many WRFU members.

In its annual report for 1990, Channel 4 credited the documentary with helping to extend 'its unique coverage of neglected sports', and there was early hope that the broadcaster might agree to commission three one-hour programmes dedicated to the women's World Cup. Although 700,000 viewers tuned into the programme, despite it clashing with *Rugby Special*, it seems that women's rugby was perhaps too obscure even for Channel 4. By the time that Rugby Vision began working on behalf of the organising committee to find a broadcast partner, the production company's head, Martyn Williams, identified four other main targets; the BBC, BBC Wales, Welsh-language channel S4C and British Satellite Broadcasting. Channel 4 had disappeared from view.

Given his role in producing *Rugby Women*, it makes sense that the organising committee would ask Williams to take care of broadcast negotiations. However, it seems as though they kept a close eye on developments. Griffin wrote to BBC Wales head of sport, Gareth Davies, in November and outlined exactly what she hoped to get out of any deal. 'It is of vital importance for us to obtain television coverage of our competition in order to obtain sponsorship. We have several sponsors who are interested in the event but all are dependant on television coverage,' she wrote. 'Ideally, we would like some two hours of coverage, with perhaps the first programme showing some of the preliminary rounds. This might also involve some "documentary" coverage of the participating teams. A further programme might cover the semi-finals and finals. It would also be of advantage to a sponsor if we could guarantee some coverage nationwide as well as Wales.'

It is unclear whether Griffin fell out with Williams or others at Rugby Vision, but as time ticked down to the World Cup and 1990 became 1991, JTI began to take the lead on these negotiations. Again, that is not surprising given the importance of a TV deal to attracting sponsorship, and the fact that JTI had commission riding on landing commercial investment. It is also true that a lack of movement on this was not only having an impact on the organising committee. Japan and New Zealand were among the teams that needed television coverage of a certain standard to be able to get a sponsorship deal of their own over the line. Time ultimately ran out on their hopes of commercial funding.

The inaugural Women's Rugby World Cup would be shown on UK terrestrial TV, but the coverage was not quite what Griffin had hoped for. Both BBC and BBC Wales were interested in showing highlights of the tournament on their *Rugby Special* and *Rugby Special Wales* programmes but dragged their feet on finalising the details of their offering as their attentions were focused on the showpiece tournament of the men's season, the Five Nations Championship. Match coverage of the pool stage had already been ruled out as it would cost the organising committee £4,000, but it was not until 19 March, just two-and-a-half weeks before the first match was due to kick-off in South Wales, that a plan was communicated by the BBC to Tom Purvis at JTI. Johnnie Wetherston, *Rugby Special*'s executive producer, agreed to air two packages: a feature on the event and coverage of the final, 'the duration depending on the quality of the match'. Davies committed to similar for the BBC Wales edition, albeit with separate coverage of the semi-finals and final as part of around 20 minutes of total coverage. 'In order to edit the women's final for a 1700 transmission, we would request a kick off time of 1415,' *Rugby Special Wales* producer Gareth Mainwaring wrote.

Confirmation of the coverage came too late, and was too little, to have any impact on the organising committee's search for a sponsor. However, Griffin and co. had not put all their eggs in the broadcast basket. If television companies were not prepared to anoint the women's World Cup as a tournament to be taken seriously, then its organisers would have to find the credibility they craved from another source. Surely, no sponsor could ignore an event that had been given Royal approval.

WRFU secretary Rosie Golby had written to Princess Anne in June 1990, offering her the presidency of the union. The Princess Royal had been a regular visitor to Murrayfield to watch men's internationals since the early 1980s and became patron of the Scottish Rugby Union in 1986, so as a female supporter of the game she was an obvious target. 'Your interest in rugby is becoming increasingly well known,' Golby stated. 'I am writing to ask if you would honour us by becoming our president.'

Unfortunately for the union, Anne felt 'unable to accept'. Her response, communicated through her private secretary

Peter Gibbs, did raise hopes concerning the inaugural Women's Rugby World Cup, however. Golby had informed the Princess of 'our most important event' in her original letter, and it seems it got Anne's attention. 'With regard to the Women's World Cup,' Gibbs wrote to Golby, 'Her Royal Highness has said that if the event was taking place in Britain in 1991 she might be able to attend.' That was by no means confirmation that she would attend, but the organising committee were happy to cling to the hope it conveyed.

A brief produced for the tournament in September stated, under the heading 'World Cup Presentation', 'Princess Anne has expressed interest in the event and we have asked her to make the presentation.' According to letters sent to Griffin by both Gibbs and Joanna Hockley, secretary to the office of the Princess Royal, Anne (or at least those responsible for her diary) did consider attending the final at the Arms Park at a meeting in November. However, she ultimately came to the decision that it would not be possible to make the trip to South Wales or present the trophy.

This would have been a considerable blow to the organising committee at a time when they needed everything to go their way in order to woo potential sponsors. A subsequent request to present the World Cup was sent to Sarah, Duchess of York in December, but this approach was met with a much speedier rejection. 'Her Royal Highness has asked me to convey her best wishes,' private secretary Neil Blair wrote to Griffin on 17 January 1991. It was becoming increasingly apparent, however, that the women's World Cup would not run on best wishes alone.

8

INTERNATIONAL RELATIONS

THE SEARCH FOR sponsorship was clearly complicated, but the struggles in finding outside investment could not distract from the task at hand. The organising committee never once contemplated not pressing forward with the Women's Rugby World Cup, regardless of the personal cost to those involved. 'Every meeting was another reason why it couldn't happen,' Alice Cooper remembers. 'It was the IRFB or the RFU or the clubs or something, there was just constant "No it can't be done, no it can't be done, no it can't be done" and us fools going "Ah, yes it can." So yes, crazy. We had the foolishness of youth.'

Mary Forsyth has a similar recollection of those early-morning conferences at Chelsfield. 'It was like, "No, we will [do it]," and that is the way we operated. It was the nature of the women. We needed to do this. Oh, you come up [against] a wall here, you go around the wall, you knock the wall down. Whatever it was you just found a way, it was the workaround. "OK, that's not going to happen, what about this?" It was the nature of everybody who was working on it.'

What Cooper, Forsyth and co. needed more than anything else, arguably even money, were teams to make the trip to South Wales to take part. The decision to enter England and Wales individually rather than Great Britain ensured they were starting from a base of two teams. Add to that the early interest from Italy and the Netherlands, who had competed at the 1988 European Cup, and Sweden, as well as the enquiries received from Canada, the USA and New Zealand and it quickly became clear that the World Cup would be the biggest international women's tournament yet staged. Assuming, of course, that each of those nations was able to get to the UK.

Griffin had based her initial proposal for the tournament around eight or ten teams, but the organising committee quickly recognised that the ideal number of nations was 12. Having a dozen teams would be beneficial for the structure of the tournament as it would allow for four pools of three, with the winner of each qualifying directly to the semi-finals. It would mean one more matchday than an eight-team World Cup, but that meant extra work for the organisers, not the players. Because there would only be three teams in each group, they would still only play two matches in the pool stage, providing a much-appreciated rest day.

However, despite the promising early indications from potential participating nations, finding a dozen teams to commit to play in South Wales in April 1991 came with its own challenges. Early outlines of the World Cup had included Belgium and West Germany (Germany from late 1990) in the list of prospective competitors. Both European nations had nascent women's rugby teams at the time, the Belgians having made their international bow against Sweden in 1986 and the Germans three years later, against the same opponents. The matches represented the Swedes' only test victories heading into the World Cup, by 32–0 and 8–0 respectively. Belgium also lost

66–0 to France in Brussels in November 1988, and, perhaps unsurprisingly neither nation felt ready to take on the world.

Women's rugby had only been played in West Germany since 1988, and the national championship consisted of just eight teams. 'For this reason neither our ability nor our financial situation allow our participation in the Women's Rugby World Cup 91', Christiane Huck from the German Rugby Union wrote to Griffin in September 1990. 'But we would be very glad if we could stay in contact and participate later on in Women's Rugby World Cup.' It was not until 1998, the first women's World Cup run by the IRB, that Germany would send a team to the tournament.

When it came to other nations, the organising committee wasn't entirely sure who they should contact. It should be remembered that this was a time before the internet, which made the search for information about the state of women's rugby in other nations incredibly difficult. That is why publications such as *In Touch*, the WRFU magazine, were so important. Not only did they provide stories on what was happening in national, regional and international competitions, and provide room for debate on the state and direction of female participation, they also gave their readers information on union meetings and other events, and printed contact details for those driving them. Copies of the magazine would sometimes find their way into the luggage of tourists, who once home could use those names and phone numbers to ask for advice and arrange international fixtures or future tours. The same was true in many other countries, and that is how a global database of women's administrators began to take shape.

But what to do when you had sourced the information that you needed? You couldn't simply fire off an email because they did not exist. You might have had a phone number for a union volunteer in Canada or Sweden, but the cost of dialling an international number was prohibitive. Letters were obviously one low-cost option, but the time it took for airmail to be delivered and the ensuing wait for a reply meant that, while frequently used, it was not an ideal form of communication. The time-saving option for the organising committee was the humble fax machine. For younger readers today: a fax machine was a phone-cum-printer which enabled its user to scan documents and send them via a phone line to another such lumbering piece of tech anywhere in the world.

As Forsyth would discover on the road to the inaugural women's World Cup, faxes were very loud; however, they were a staple of British offices in the early 1990s and so each member of the organising committee had access to one, even if they had to employ varying clandestine methods to use them. These machines enabled the organising committee to communicate quickly with contacts across the globe and were pivotal to its success in staging the tournament. Fortunately, when Forsyth later went on maternity leave, Chelsfield even paid to have one installed at her home.

*****

Fax machines would have been scant use to the organising committee had Forsyth, Griffin, Dorrington and Cooper not had numbers to dial in, and as they sat down to draw up the list of potential participants, they did not have access to all of them. Beyond the seven or eight 'established' nations that were expected to take part from the get-go, other countries were included as much in hope as in confidence. Echoing the days Griffin spent as a student ringing round universities or sending requests for matches via her college boyfriend, they were alerted to possible rugby-playing women by hearsay.

Wales had toured Catalonia, so maybe Spain would send a team? Word would also undoubtedly have reached the UK from New Zealand following RugbyFest 90 that a national team from the Soviet Union had taken part. However, it seems Griffin attempted to establish dialogue with female administrators in Japan long before it became apparent that they would send clubs to the tournament in Christchurch. The catalyst for her to do so, before she had even agreed to chair the organising committee, was cash. An unnamed Japanese company indicated that it might be interested in sponsoring the event were a team from Japan to compete.

It is unclear how the offer was communicated to Griffin given this was before Dorrington had been brought on board and a formal list of companies to canvas had been drawn up. While the exact make-up of the World Cup was still being debated by those at the WRFU at this time, it could be that it was proffered informally during a conversation at work or the rugby club. Either way, it was considered serious enough that on 1 February 1990 Griffin sent off a fax from her office at Pannell Kerr Forster to the Japan Rugby Football Union (JRFU). 'The Women's Rugby Football Union would be interested to know if there are any women's rugby teams playing in Japan,' she typed. 'If there are we would like to know how many teams there are. If you have any contact names and addresses we would be most appreciative.'

A reply from JRFU chairman Shiggy Konno was received within a matter of hours: 'I understand there are a few women's rugby teams in Japan but as they do not have any connections with us I am afraid I do not have any information regarding the teams or their organization.'

Unperturbed, Griffin used the WRFU's contacts in the travel industry, namely Bob Rees at Rugby Travel, to get a fax number for a rugby-playing agent in Japan. 'In April 1991, we will be hosting the first Women's Rugby World Cup. There will be at least eight teams including the USA, Canada, France, Holland

and Italy,' she wrote to Toshi Hori of Pacific Tours Co. Ltd on 13 February. 'We have interest in sponsorship of the event from a Japanese company but they would like to have a team from Japan competing. The Japan Rugby Football Union informs me that there are women's teams in Japan but does not have a contact.

'Would it be possible for you to find a contact name for us? Perhaps you will be able to provide the travel arrangements if the team travels to England.'

Again, Hori's reply was swift, and he committed to making contact with women's teams while also looking for sponsorship for a Japanese national team. By 6 March, Hori confirmed he had 'started to have a negotiation with some Women's Rugby Clubs'. However, whether the original interested party had cooled its intent in the intervening month or merely the magnitude of organising a World Cup had begun to sink in, Griffin was now less sure of securing outside investment. 'We will have to charge teams for this (accommodation) unless we can sign up a major sponsor for the event. The participation of a Japanese National side is therefore important to us in also extending the range of sponsors which we can approach,' she responded. Reading between the dot-matrix lines, it certainly seems that the original offer of sponsorship had been withdrawn.

Although it is debatable how helpful Hori was, Griffin had important confirmation from him that women's rugby was played in Japan. Later in the year, another letter fell onto the doormat at 224A Camden Road. Addressed simply to the WRFU, the hand-written correspondence came from Noriko Kishida and had been sent 'in order to establish a contact and to obtain any available information about future fixtures, either in England or elsewhere' as well as to invite England to the third Friendship Tournament, which was due to be held on 4 November. The lack of a direct reference to the women's World

Cup could be interpreted as proof that Hori had not succeeded in his mission to find those responsible for running the women's game in Tokyo. Certainly, this was a time when female players in Japan were beginning to look outwards, as highlighted by their participation in RugbyFest, and it could be that plans were already afoot to reach out to the WRFU before Griffin contacted the travel agent.

Either way, Japan were soon added to the list of World Cup definites, and Kishida would act as the point of contact as they finalised the details of their trip to South Wales. In the end, Griffin's suggestion that Hori could cash in on Japan's involvement in the tournament proved ill-founded as Ohshu Express took care of the team's travel arrangements for the tournament rather than Pacific Tours.

When it came to Spain, the problem for the women's World Cup organisers was not locating a contact but working out who they were talking to and how many teams intended to compete. José Moreno, the secretary general of the Federacion Española de Rugby (FER), the body which oversaw both the men's and women's game in Spain, wrote to Rosie Golby at the beginning of May to express interest in participating in what he believed at the time was going to be another European Cup. However, in the time it took Golby to pass that correspondence on to Griffin, she had already sent an invitation for the World Cup to a contact at the Catalan federation provided by the WRFU Welsh Committee secretary Maddy Austin.

Subsequently, Begoña Montmany began liaising with the women's World Cup organising committee over plans to send a team to Cardiff, but there was more than a little confusion. Her faxes were all sent with the Catalan federation's insignia embossed on them, and the historic information requested for the official tournament brochure included only the region's match results. Was Montmany acting on behalf of the FER or did she intend to enter a Catalan team? Would two teams from the Iberian peninsula arrive in Cardiff in April? Nationalist feeling in Spain's autonomous regions was probably on Griffin and Forsyth's minds as they contemplated making room for an extra entrant. On a fax sent to the Catalan federation on 4 February 1991 which has survived in tournament records, is scrawled in frantic handwriting, 'Please ring Ann McMahon she speaks Spanish … URGENT.'

Ultimately, Moreno sent a fax to McMahon, who had answered the organising committee's SOS, in Spanish assuring the women that Spain would indeed be sending only one team to the tournament. Montmany was organising the trip, but the side would play under the flag of Spain and the FER. In the end, a squad of 25 players, made up of women from the Basque Country, Catalonia, Madrid, Galicia and Valencia, travelled north to South Wales to take on the best female teams in the world.

*****

In the decade or so since André Bosc had pleaded with the IRFB not to become a 'World Federation', the role of the body had changed significantly. The Frenchman's comment had been made at the IRFB's annual meeting in London in 1979 in response to a paper presented by New Zealand Rugby Football Union chairman Ces Blazey on the role of the Board. In the document, New Zealand urged the body to seize the initiative of the game's burgeoning popularity by opening up lines of communication with non-member unions. Despite the strength of response, it did not advocate drastic reform, warning that allowing associate membership 'could create a dangerous precedent. Associate membership could (and probably would) lead to full membership with full voting rights.'

As both New Zealand's discussion paper and Bosc's input (recorded in the official minutes as a 'very useful contribution') highlight, there was little appetite to expand further.[i] The Board's role at the end of the 1970s remained much the same as it had been for the previous 90 years: to oversee the laws of the game, schedule international tours and uphold the ideal of amateurism. It did not run or own tournaments, did not make money and did not serve any union other than the eight deemed worthy of membership. The IRFB did not even have a permanent office until Keith Rowlands moved it to Bristol in 1990, hosting meetings primarily in gentlemen's clubs and hotels round London and using Twickenham as its postal address.

One momentous event would change all that, and, although it was led by Blazey and New Zealand, it was not the discussion paper on the role of the IRFB. Two days before he presented that document at Hobart House, he also raised the idea of a men's Rugby World Cup to the body's tours sub-committee. The meeting minutes record that 'while the idea found no support in the Sub-Committee it was considered important enough to be referred to the Board'.

Blazey was by no means an idealistic reformer. Approaching his 70th birthday and with more than 40 years of sports administration behind him, he had a chequered past. His naive insistence that politics should be kept separate from sport ensured that he found himself on the wrong side of history on several occasions when it came to the question of South Africa. He was resolutely pro-tour without ever disclosing his personal opinion on the matter, always couching his answers to interrogation in terms of the New Zealand RFU's interests and statutes. Whatever his politics, and however distasteful his actions look now more than 40 years removed, he did more than most (along with like-minded peers on the IRFB such as John Kendall-Carpenter and Keith Rowlands) to modernise the IRFB.

---

[i] Only two years previously, the JRFU had applied to become an associate member of the RFU, not of the IRFB.

It would take another six years, and the threat of a breakaway rugby circus in the image of Kerry Packer's World Series Cricket, to force the IRFB into seriously considering a World Cup. Australia and New Zealand were asked to produce a feasibility study on the potential tournament, and at the annual meeting in Paris in March 1985 those in favour won the day by ten votes to six. Australia, France and New Zealand all voted in favour, having lobbied repeatedly for it, while South Africa followed suit despite its isolation. Kendall-Carpenter and Rowlands ensured that the England and Wales votes were split.

The inaugural men's Rugby World Cup, hosted jointly by Australia and New Zealand, kicked off at Auckland's iconic Eden Park on 22 May 1987 and highlighted the damage done by running the game as a closed shop for a century as the All Blacks dispatched Italy 70–6. With the Springboks banned, New Zealand won the tournament at a relative canter, racking up eight tries in a 49–6 defeat of Wales in the semi-finals in Brisbane and then beating the French 29–9 back at Eden Park to lift the Webb Ellis Cup. Coming only a year after ten members of the victorious squad displayed a fine disregard for the wishes of their union, and much of the Kiwi public, by embarking on a rebel tour of South Africa, it was not necessarily an ideal outcome for those concerned with the game's image.

If anything, though, New Zealand's victory and the manner in which it was achieved helped to heal the wounds of the previous six years and bring the country closer together. Certainly, the first men's World Cup was a qualified commercial success. The tournament made a profit of NZ$2.3m (the equivalent of around $5.7m today), of which $1.4m was split between the competing nations and $522,760 was kept by the IRFB. Suddenly, the Board had money, which it used not only to fund a salary and office for its first paid secretary, Rowlands, but to grow in size and importance. Steadily, the IRFB became exactly what Bosc had warned against: a world federation.

The nine non-traditional nations which competed in the first men's World Cup (Argentina, Canada, Fiji, Italy, Japan, Romania, Tonga, the USA and Zimbabwe) were invited to become members in 1987. Over the next three years, another 28 unions were brought into the fold, initially as associate members, each of which would pay an annual subscription. Keen to build on the foundations laid in Australia and New Zealand, the IRFB needed to be commercially savvy to ensure that it had funds to arrange subsequent tournaments. This was one way of doing that. Opening the Board up to new nations did not alter its dynamic, the same eight unions (arguably with the addition of Argentina and Italy) still effectively run the show today, even if their interests and those of the IRFB diverged a quarter of a century ago.

Whatever its underlying motives, the IRFB had begun to take on a more fatherly approach to 'emerging' unions, and nowhere was this more obvious than in its plans for the revenue generated by the 1991 men's Rugby World Cup. Instead of sharing the profits from the tournament with the participating nations, the Board kept the money and set up a fund for developing nations. Cynics may suggest this was a power grab, but it was also an early attempt to curb the power of the established unions. Clearly, there was a benefit to helping those emerging countries develop as it would strengthen the World Cup and help make the competition a more valuable asset.

If the women's game could be used as a tool to communicate with nations like the Soviet Union, which had been admitted in 1990, then so be it. Replying to a query about female participation sent by USSR Rugby Federation president Viktor Sviridov on Boxing Day of that year, Rowlands relayed that although 'Rugby Union has been historically a male sport ... the Board has expressed its support for Women's Rugby and encouraged Member Unions to develop this aspect of the game as they see it appropriate by encouragement or by including the women's section within their national organisation'.

Although he did not mention the women's World Cup in his fax, Rowlands did send a copy to Griffin 'as I believe she is the best person to give you an accurate and up to date account of the world-wide development within Women's Rugby'. Those introductions were not necessary, Griffin having first received an enquiry about the women's World Cup from the USSR Rugby Federation in October. According to a letter sent by Griffin to Moscow in January 1991, the organising committee 'were all anxious' for the Soviets to attend. Their excitement at that possibility blinded them to several red flags that had been raised in the weeks and months before the tournament got underway in South Wales. It would be a time-consuming and costly oversight as the Soviet squad landed the organisers on the wrong side of both UK customs officials and their hosts at the Cardiff Institute of Higher Education.

*****

The IRFB only formally discussed the Women's Rugby World Cup once, at a meeting of its policy committee in Edinburgh on 8 October 1990. Minutes record that Rowlands was 'requested to write expressing the Board's best wishes for a successful Tournament'. Given the Welshman was present at the meeting, it seems strange he did not inform his colleagues on the committee that he had already done so, but the following month he went further than advised by meeting Griffin and Dorrington to hear more about their plans.

It is unclear why Rowlands sought an in-person audience, considering neither he nor the IRFB had given any indication that formal assistance would be forthcoming. However, as his original correspondence with Griffin suggests, he would most likely have been keen to gauge how much of a threat to the commercial viability of the men's Rugby World Cup the women's tournament would be. It is important to remember that Rowlands and his colleagues on the IRFB's organising committee were struggling to find sponsors ready to stump up the cash they wanted. Heinz had come on board since Rowlands first wrote to Griffin in August, but the condiment company were only willing to pay £1m for one of the eight packages on offer, half the amount which had been hoped for.

As Rowlands' reply to the USSR Rugby Federation shows, the IRFB secretary did not see himself as a roadblock to the Women's Rugby World Cup. Following the meeting with Griffin and Dorrington in Bristol on 20 November 1990, he sent a letter to the latter to express the global governing body's 'best wishes' for their tournament. 'I have noted the involvement of and support given by Unions in Membership of the Board and would commend them for their actions', Rowlands wrote. '[It is] our sincere hope that the Tournament is a resounding success enjoyed by all participants and supporters alike and that it will make a significant contribution to the development of Women's Rugby throughout the World.'

Successful tournaments are not funded by hope alone, however sincere, and there is evidence to suggest that not all Rowlands' colleagues at the IRFB (particularly those on the men's RWC 1991 organising committee) shared his goodwill. Indeed, when Griffin, her newborn baby daughter and Dorringnon travelled down the M4 motorway towards Bristol, a legal challenge, focused on the Women's Rugby World Cup logo, was rumbling, which threatened to destabilise the tournament and would cause its organising committee considerable stress in the months ahead.

Four months earlier in July, Alice Cooper's cousin James Young had submitted his design for the women's World Cup logo. It consisted of an angled rugby ball, which had 10 stripes running halfway across it from left to right, inside a black rectangle with a green border. Underneath the box was written WOMEN'S RUGBY WORLD CUP 91. Griffin thanked Young for his hard work in 'producing an excellent logo to represent us … [and] help us to maintain a professional image for the event'. However, there was one large problem. It bore more than a passing resemblance to the emblem of the men's event, which featured a rugby ball made up of angled lines within a box.

Griffin was first made aware of potential problems by John Taylor of JTI in September. Given that the IRFB was attempting to establish the men's World Cup, and itself, as a commercial entity, it is no surprise it would seek to safeguard its logo. Unbeknown to Griffin and co., the IRFB had gone to great lengths to secure ownership of the emblem it commissioned for the first tournament in 1987 and to then register it as a trademark. It was therefore understandably a contentious issue for them. 'In the interests of maintaining good relations,' as Griffin told the men's World Cup's solicitors Townleys in December, Young modified his design, removing the stripes and instead layering the ball with a map of the world. Coincidentally, this was not dissimilar to the IRFB's letterhead of the time, but at the 20 November meeting in Bristol, Rowlands 'raised no objection whatsoever to the new logo'.

If the women's organising committee thought Rowlands' ambivalence constituted approval, they were to be disappointed. Dorrington subsequently received notification from Townleys that they believed the new logo was still in breach on two grounds: 'firstly that it consists of a slanted ball inside a box and secondly that the typeface is too similar to the RWC logo'. This was a considerable problem for Griffin. By the time Dorrington received the official objection, they had spent significant money printing letterheads, labels, press packs and other promotional material which featured the revised logo. With little to no money coming in, they could ill afford the associated costs, both in terms of cash and time, another redesign would entail. In a bid to head off a protracted dispute, Griffin offered to produce a third logo so long as the men's RWC committee covered the costs involved, something she put at £3,889.20.

Townleys do not appear to have agreed with Griffin's approach, and this was an issue which hung over the women's organising committee well into 1991 as the IRFB dithered and Griffin sweated. However, at the end of 1990, there was still reason to believe things were coming together. The organising committee had secured a host city and iconic venue for the showpiece matches. A good number of teams had confirmed their entry, while others had intimated that they would attend, and at that point things even seemed positive on the broadcast and sponsorship front. It was time to make things official. It was time to launch the inaugural Women's Rugby World Cup.

*****

As the clock approached 11.00 am on Tuesday 27 November 1990, two rooms around 150 miles apart continued to fill with journalists and dignitaries. To ensure maximum exposure for the inaugural Women's Rugby World Cup, its organising committee had made the decision to host its official launch simultaneously in both Cardiff and London. The Tudor Room at the Arms Park and the Members Bar of Richmond's Athletic Ground had opened at 10.30 am and both reverberated to the sound of clinking coffee cups and chatter as the attendees waited for proceedings to get under way.

Alice Cooper had spent the previous Thursday morning at the offices of JTI in Chiswick, West London. Alongside Deborah James and Moira Swinbank, she had rung round members of the press who had not yet RSVP'd. Their hard work had certainly paid off. In London alone, writers from *The Times, Sunday Times, Daily Telegraph, Independent, Evening Standard, Rugby News* and *Rugby World & Post* were among those munching on peanuts and crisps at the bar. Meanwhile, a press pack had been mailed out the previous evening to regional and overseas journalists as well as others who could not make either event in person.

The concurrent launch events would take place in Cardiff's Bute Room and the Conference Rooms in Richmond. Both had been set up so that a large display board plastered with the new tournament logo sat behind a top table from which Sue Dorrington, in Cardiff, and Deborah Griffin in South West London, less than four weeks after she had given birth, would walk those who had congregated through a half-hour presentation. There was, though, one significant addition at the Athletic Ground. On a small side table, a Gilbert rugby ball and flowers served to frame the prize which the participating nations would compete for in South Wales: the Women's Rugby World Cup trophy.

Although insured on Griffin's home policy, the original women's Rugby World Cup had been selected by Dorrington during a trip to London's Hatton Garden. She would not be able to unveil the trophy to the world in person, the organising committee in consultation with JTI reasoning that there was more chance of broadcast coverage of the event in Richmond than Cardiff. Described in the official launch press release as an 'antique solid silver' cup which 'we believe presents a strong but feminine image to portray our game', Dorrington had been attracted to it by the unique lace-like detail on its rim.

'I didn't want some tinny fake trophy,' she told me more than three decades later. 'I wanted something proper, like a silver cup, and that's where I headed. I went into Hatton Garden and found this cup and have since learned through Phill [McGowan] at the World Rugby Museum that it was commissioned in 1924.'

Dorrington added: 'It just looked different; it was more feminine. I know that one shouldn't choose one's trophies on that basis, but it stood out for me, and it was the biggest one I could afford because then they got bigger and got more and more expensive. So, it was the biggest and the most attractive one I could afford.' The price tag on the ornate trophy landed the World Cup's commercial manager in hot water with her chair, however, as JB Jewellery and Antiques invoiced the organising committee £1,007.50 for it. At a time when the women were struggling to attract sponsorship, that was a not inconsiderable sum.

'I think we had a bit of a barney about how much she spent on it,' Griffin recalls. 'There we were with no money, and she goes and spends £1,000 or whatever on a bloody cup!' The organising committee would not pay the invoice for the antique trophy until the following March, when some much-needed funding came in, but no one present at the Athletic Ground on 27 November knew that, as England players Karen Almond, Debbie Francis, Carol Isherwood and Sam Robson posed for photos with it. Having such a striking piece of silverware on display gave the tournament a veneer of credibility in the eyes of the assembled press pack.

The Women's Rugby World Cup was not the only thing which had been launched on 27 November. Confirmation that John Major had won the race to replace Margaret Thatcher as leader of the Conservative Party, and therefore of the UK, was splashed across the front page of every national newspaper on Wednesday morning. Head of press Cooper would have been pleased with the coverage events in Richmond and Cardiff received, however. the *Daily Telegraph* and *Independent* carried small reports on the tournament, both of which focused on the fact that the Arms Park would host the semi-finals and final while highlighting that the organisers' hopes of finding the commercial backing they craved rested on the outcome of the ongoing broadcast negotiations.

'They may lack sponsors at the moment, but there is no shortage of enthusiasm for, and commitment to, the inaugural women's rugby World Cup,' Robert Cole wrote in the latter.

As Cole and others reported, nine nations (England, Wales, the USA, Canada, Spain, Italy, Sweden, the Netherlands and Japan) had confirmed their entry, while Glamorgan Wanderers had offered to host the second and third rounds of pool-stage matches. Contact had been made with several top-level clubs in South Wales concerning the opening fixtures on Saturday, 6 April, but with the Schweppes Cup semi-finals scheduled for that weekend, none was able to confirm whether their pitches would be available.

Challenges awaited the organising committee. Despite earlier interest, France, New Zealand and the USSR had yet to confirm their attendance, a fact which left serious question marks over the scheduling of the tournament. As the newspaper reports suggested, meanwhile, they were no closer to landing a sponsor. There was no turning back now, though. The inaugural Women's Rugby World Cup was no longer a hypothetical concept being discussed within committee meetings and changing rooms. It was a very real event with an antique trophy, and by hook or by crook, Griffin, Dorrington, Cooper and Forsyth would do everything in their power to make it a success.

The pioneering Cardiff Ladies team pose for the camera ahead of their match against Newport in 1917, captain E. Kirton proudly clutching the match ball. The triumphant USA would retrace their steps 74 years later. *Cardiff Rugby Museum*

Sue Dorrington (far left) and Mary Forsyth (second from right) pictured ahead of England's match against Sweden in October 1988. Forsyth won her sole international cap in the 40-0 win.

Forsyth receives her original England
cap from WRFU secretary, Rosie Golby.

Sue Dorrington prepares to throw into a
lineout for England. Brian Moore helped
Dorrington with aspects of her game,
including throwing, leading into the
World Cup.

Mary Forsyth poses for a photo with newborn baby Kathryn, under the watchful gaze of her mother, Clementine.

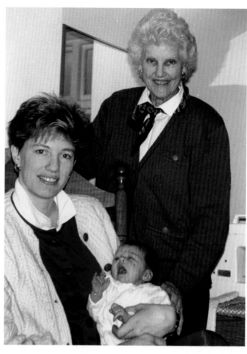

A flag bearing the Women's Rugby World Cup logo flutters in the wind during the opening ceremony. The logo had been approved by the IRFB only weeks before the tournament. *Getty*

Liza Burgess holds the Welsh flag as she leads her team-mates into the courtyard at County Hall. She would later take to the stage alongside Amanda Bennet (second left). *Getty*

The Italian squad line up behind captain Mafalda Palla at the World Cup opening ceremony at Cardiff's County Hall.

The Italians, in their eye-catching turquoise tracksuits, take part in the parade
around the National Stadium pitch at half-time of the Schweppes Cup semi-finals.

The World Cup's commercial manager Sue Dorrington pictured in action for England against Italy. She was determined to win the tournament she had helped organise.

England captain Karen Almond makes a break through the Italian defence. The fly-half was widely considered to be one of the best players in the world at the time. *Getty*

Italy turned heads for their style on and off the pitch in South Wales.
Here players pose for a photo at the Cardiff Institute of Higher Education.

Another late night for Alice Cooper as she types up teamsheets in the bunker.

Having eventually found Llanharan's Dairy Field, Alice Cooper conducts media interviews on the touchline. *Copyright, 1991, Dawn Cooper, All Rights Reserved*

A USSR player runs with the ball against the USA. It was a mismatch on the pitch but the American players happily bought Soviet trinkets to help their opponents with their off-field problems. *Getty*

Wales take on the mighty New Zealand. Despite acquitting themselves
well, they had no answer to the Women's All Blacks' attacking prowess. *Getty*

Head of press Alice Cooper talks to
media at the Arms Park.

Alice Cooper stands on the Arms Park pitch as she gives another television interview.

Debbie Chase leads the Haka ahead of the semi-final against the USA. The American players did not face the ritual, remaining in their huddle chanting 'Harder, Stronger, Faster'. *Getty*

New Zealand's Anna Richards attempts to evade a tackle during her side's bruising semi-final defeat to the USA. *Getty*

Ahead of their historic victory against France in the semi-finals, England gathered for a team shot under the floodlights.

Alice Cooper in action for a side made up of the organisers/volunteers, who played against the USSR on the eve of the final. In the background is Laurie O'Reilly, who refereed the match. *Getty*

Sue Dorrington was attracted to the tournament's antique silver trophy by its ornate lace detailing, something that made drinking from it difficult. *Getty*

England pose for a squad photo ahead of the inaugural Women's Rugby World Cup final at the Arms Park. They would run into a physical and fit USA once the whistle blew.

England centre Sam Robson leads the charge in the final against the USA, who would ultimately prove too streetwise. *Getty*

England number eight Gill Burns can only watch on as opposite number Kathy Flores gains possession at a lineout. *Getty*

WRFU secretary Rosie Golby presents USA captain Mary Sullivan with the Women's Rugby World Cup trophy. *Getty*

Sullivan, right, hoists the trophy high into the Cardiff sky with squad captain Barb Bond, who had been dropped to the replacements' bench for the final despite scoring the winning try against New Zealand in the last four. *Getty*

The winning USA squad celebrate with the trophy at the VIP dinner that brought the tournament to a close. *Getty*

Mary Forsyth (left) and Deborah Griffin pose for a selfie during the
VIP dinner at the National Sports Centre for Wales on 14 April, 1991.

Alice Cooper (left) hits the dance floor at the VIP dinner.

John Taylor and Deborah James, who worked on the World Cup
for John Taylor International, pictured during the VIP dinner.

Official tournament photographer
Eileen Langsley finds herself on the
other end of the lens.

9

LEAVING NOTHING TO CHANCE

IT WAS NOT only from an organisational perspective that Sue Dorrington was determined to make the Women's Rugby World Cup a success. Although born and raised in Minnesota, her time in London qualified her to play for England and Great Britain on residency grounds, and in the previous three seasons she had won a cap for each. Dorrington was named as a replacement in nine further test matches and had been a member of the European Cup squad in 1988, but as substitutions were only permitted in the event of injury, she had to bide her time. Having sat tight on the sidelines for three years, her international debut eventually arrived in February 1990 when she lined up at hooker as England beat Wales in Neath. As the World Cup approached, she was intent on winning both her place in the side and the tournament itself.

When Dorrington travelled to Cardiff for the tournament launch at the end of November, she was locked in a committed contest for the England number two jersey with Waterloo hooker Nicky Ponsford. Nine years Dorrington's junior, Ponsford was an all-round sportswoman. A talented sailor, she had represented Great Britain on the water as well as in rugby and worked as a development officer for the Welsh Yachting Association. Ponsford had spent a year away from rugby as she chased a place on an Olympic boat but, following her return, she was the woman in possession of the jersey, while Fiona Hackett was also in contention. Dorrington, though, was driven to become England's undisputed number-one number two by the time the World Cup kicked off in April.

A converted centre, Dorrington knew she had work to do if she was going to oust Ponsford from the England front row. The press coverage of the tournament launch shone a light on the lengths to which its commercial manager was prepared to go to make her ambition a reality. The following day's *Daily Mail* carried an interview with her which was headlined, 'Ruling the world is the goal for Susan and her rugby converts'. Under a picture of Dorrington sat on a rugby ball on the hallowed turf of the National Stadium in Cardiff, the article revealed that Dorrington and her international teammates had trained with male England and British and Irish Lions hooker Brian Moore in a bid to improve their game. 'He has committed himself to another session,' she told Peter Jackson. 'Brian's been brilliant. When he talked to us he said, "This is how I do it." Thanks to him, I've changed my technique in the way I go down into the scrum. I've learned a lot from him.'

Moore cannot remember exactly how he was recruited to help the women, but according to Dorrington it took a great deal of persistence on her part. Solicitor Moore had moved south from Nottingham midway through 1990, accepting a job offer at a City of London law firm and taking his considerable talents to Harlequins. That the Twickenham-based club had excellent contacts within the City was a mere coincidence, the England hooker insisted. 'Moore, 28, said he was making the move purely for job purposes,' the *Nottingham Evening Post* reported on 21 April, barely concealing its cynicism.

Dorrington was not about to let an opportunity to learn from one of the best players in the world in her position slip through her fingers. She was a member of the Metropolitan Club, as it was known, which was a gym next door to Harlequins' home ground the Stoop, and so she would attend midweek training sessions in the hope of convincing Moore to work with her. 'He was right up his own backside back then and he never responded. I'd rock up at the Stoop, at the training sessions, and would kind of hang around and just when he was finished, I'd say, "Can you help me with my line-out?" He just ignored me for two or three consecutive weeks, and then one day he said, "OK, right. What is it that you want?" And I said, "I need your help, technically. Tell me how best to throw the ball."'

Moore had developed a reputation for being abrasive both on and off the pitch, equally happy to go toe-to-toe with a blazered RFU committeeman as a grizzled front-row forward in a test match. In Dorrington, though, it seems he met his match. 'She's quite insistent. She's one of the few characters in rugby who's ever intimidated me because she's so intense,' Moore says. 'It wasn't that I thought, "Oh, this is the right thing to do." I just thought, "Well, someone wants my help with rugby. If they want to play, that's absolutely fine by me …" It was a case of, "Oh, yeah, I can do that. I can help."'

The Harlequins star, who had the men's Rugby World Cup to prepare for as he settled into a new job and city, laid on several training sessions for Dorrington and her colleagues in the England forward pack. They took place at the Athletic Ground and Old Deer Park in Richmond, both only a few miles down the A316 from the Stoop. As Jim Greenwood had been half a decade previously, Moore was particularly impressed by the players' ability to listen and their willingness to learn.

'I remember in particular I took them through a back-row move that we'd tried with England and failed to do right in two years,' he adds. 'They got it right first time … in the game.''' Moore would have beamed with pride when the story of that try was relayed to him, but there were boundaries. On one occasion, Dorrington dialled his work number in search of more tips on her line-out throwing, a key tool in the hooker's armoury. 'She said, "Brian, I'm having a bit of trouble with my strike",' Moore recalls. 'I said, "I'm in a conference with a client, Sue, as a lawyer. I can't speak to you now!"' Dorrington's laser focus on winning her place in the England team for the women's World Cup meant it was not only Harlequins' latest international acquisition she had on speed dial.

*****

Dorrington's quest to play at the World Cup began almost as soon as it became clear that the tournament would take place. Having experienced life as a non-playing replacement during Great Britain's long weekend in Bourg-en-Bresse in 1988, she was determined not to be left watching on as Ponsford had all the fun once again in South Wales. Dorrington, moreover, was not someone who needed outside inspiration to get up in the morning and give her all. Her inner drive had been apparent since her early teenage years and was evident at every important juncture of her life.

It had required an innate enterprise to uproot her life in the US Midwest in 1983, leave the community she had discovered and travel more than 4,000 miles on a one-way ticket for nothing more than the hope of a better playing experience. 'I wanted to get better, and I wanted to get better fast. I'd never travelled abroad before, but I knew that being in Minnesota wasn't really where I wanted to be, and I just thought, "Right, I'm going to the UK",' Dorrington says. 'None of this was scary to me. I just did it. I'm not risk-averse, so I jumped on that plane and never went back.'

The reality of Dorrington's decision quickly became apparent as she struggled to find both a paying job and a women's rugby club. The terms of her initial six-month visa meant she could only work as a volunteer, while the dearth of publicly available information about female teams meant her first taste of a British rugby club came with the men at London Cornish, not all of whom were happy to be training alongside a woman. 'Some of them liked it, some of them couldn't stand that idea,' she recalls. '[When] we'd be in the gym training in the winter, I'd get a knock just that much harder from those guys who didn't want me around. But I stuck at it.'

Dorrington's breakthrough came during a jog round Hyde Park when she stumbled across a group of women throwing a ball about. 'I ran over to them and said, "Who are you? What are you doing?"' Dorrington explains. 'They said, "We're the Imperial College rugby team" and I said, "Oh my word, I've been looking for you – can I play?" And they said, "Absolutely!"' Following a few months playing for the student side, a York graduate she met on a rugby tour of the Netherlands pointed her in the direction of Finchley, where she would hook up with Griffin and later Forsyth and Cooper.

The trip to the Netherlands also aided Dorrington's hopes of making a success of her new life in the UK. On returning to London, her passport was stamped with a fresh six-month visa, and in that time she met her future husband, policeman Mark. The couple were quickly engaged, which benefited Sue as it gave her the right to remain in the country. 'At our wedding he said, "Some people think this is a marriage of convenience, but marrying Sue is the most inconvenient thing I've ever done",' she recalls. 'Thank you, Mark. He was kidding, of course.'

It was that drive and determination that would stand Dorrington in such good stead, from both a playing and administrative point of view, on the road to South Wales. It was also what prompted her to enlist personal trainer David Crottie in her bid for the England number-two jersey. Crottie had earned his break as a fitness coach with the Melbourne Demons Australian rules football club in his native Victoria, and although he had no previous rugby experience, he was taken on by London Welsh after he relocated to the UK in October 1987. He built a business as a personal trainer, while his work at Old Deer Park, in an area of the sport which was still primitive in the late amateur era, helped attract other high-profile clients from the oval-ball game.

Crottie also wrote articles about fitness and rehabilitation for *Rugby World & Post*, which is how Dorrington was alerted to his talents. At around the same time that she agreed to work with Griffin, Forsyth and Cooper on the women's World Cup organising committee, Dorrington began working with Crottie, paying him £25 an hour for between two and three training sessions a week in the year or so leading up to the tournament. Those sessions would take place either in the gym or on the track at Battersea Park, where Dorrington worked on her speed. 'She was very intense about what she wanted,' Crottie remembers. 'It wasn't like she was coming for a jolly. She was clear on what she wanted, and she thought by the way I wrote that I could produce some stuff she was after.'

What Dorrington wanted was to get fitter and faster round the pitch. 'She was always looking to get anything extra I could give her. Her main problem at the time was stamina and just basic off-line speed. She's only small of stature – that's why she obviously suited the position of hooker very well. But it didn't help her round the ground, so she wanted to get more involved in ball-carrying and in getting to the breakdown, the maul, things like that,' Crottie adds. 'Part of that was sports nutrition, which obviously was chopping body fat. She was very intense on not carrying around an extra pound of fat. We were doing a lot of testing on the guys; even Jason Leonard, who looked big, was only 14 per cent body fat at the time. So she goes, "I want that. That's what I'm after." So, we worked on the dietary aspect, checking her body fat literally every six weeks.'

Dorrington was doing everything she could physically to stake her claim for a place in the England World Cup squad, but on Crottie's suggestion she also began working with a sports psychologist to help her with the mental strain she was under. Alma Thomas had worked with Saracens' men the previous season, helping the first team to a fourth-place finish in their maiden season in the English top division. 'I worked with her on things like staying in the moment because if I did something wrong on the pitch, I would just drag it around,' Dorrington says. 'It would drag my game down.

'I had to start living in the moment and to make sure that I was playing throughout the game. Then in terms of visual imagery on my line-out, [I needed to] work with the mental aspect, not just the physical of being strong with a good core through David and the technical with Brian Moore. I needed the mental aspect. God help me, I surrounded myself with all these people and paid for all of it myself. I had to work on visual imagery. Literally, Alma worked with me on "Where's that ball going? Visualise that ball going and throwing it there." So, I had Alma with me, who was amazing, and she'd come and watch my games and then we'd sit down, and we'd have an analysis of it and comment on it.'

Interestingly, throwing into the line-out was something that Ponsford also felt she needed to work on ahead of the inaugural women's World Cup. Although she had more on-pitch international experience than Dorrington, she knew she needed to up her own game when she returned to rugby. She might not have hired outside help, but her determination to retain her England jersey was every bit as intense as Dorrington's. 'For a long time, it was definitely a rivalry,' Ponsford says. 'We didn't get on and we just had to fight. We just fought it out and we each had our own battles, you know.

'Sue was incredibly, incredibly fit, had worked really hard. I definitely wasn't as fit as she was. Probably, some of my skills were different to hers and therefore different coaches look at them slightly differently. I tried to make sure that I had a point of difference. She had a point of difference with her fitness. I had to try and make sure I had a point of difference and I worked really hard on my throwing to try and make sure that was better. And, you know, that's how rivalries work. It's just always trying to battle against the person that's in possession; or, if you're in possession, you've got to just be focusing on how you can get yourself better.'

Three decades on, the former foes are now great friends, and neither has any doubt that their shared experience at the beginning of the 1990s made each a better player. 'Her fitness levels in particular were probably what she was renowned for,' Ponsford adds. 'I knew that if I didn't really work hard on that, I was never going to get to where I wanted to get to. So, it definitely made me focus in on my skills and focus in on my fitness because I needed to do that. I needed to be better. You can't just be as good as; you've got to be better in order to jump over somebody.'

'I had to be the best player I possibly could be to get rid of Nicky,' Dorrington says. 'She decided to take a bit of time out and I moved into that space, and she didn't get it back for a number of years.' Dorrington's focus on fitness was also due in part to her belief that England would have to be able to match the USA in that department to have any hope of winning the

World Cup. However, as she and Ponsford trained relentlessly in pursuit of their goal, that determination was not shared by every member of the women's rugby community. As the tournament began to take shape, concerns about players' on- and off-field behaviour became a potential issue for the organising committee.

*****

Although women who wanted to play rugby met with resistance from many male traditionalists, the majority of those coming into the game did not want to reinvent the wheel. They merely wanted access to the clubhouse. As we have seen, the social side of the game was a key ingredient of its appeal to women in the UK, France, New Zealand, the USA and beyond. Rugby gave these women an opportunity to explore a different side of their personality on the pitch, and that also extended to the bar after matches and training. When female players began to approach clubs about setting up women's teams in the mid-1980s, the WRFU produced a crib sheet for its members on the benefits such a move would entail. Top of that list was increased bar takings on Sundays, when they would be at the club, which was usually a slow day in terms of revenue with only mini and junior teams in action.

'The camaraderie of women's rugby is quite different from other friendships,' Cooper explains. 'You have friendships with these women that are uncomplicated by emotion. These are people who are saving your neck. If the scrum goes down, you're a tetraplegic, so these are people who are coming in to save your neck … I don't think we ever went shopping together. You'd go drinking together, go singing together, but you wouldn't go and do girly, girly things together, which now we're all older we do. I don't know what the girls are like now, but it's a very uncomplicated friendship, and I found it very insightful because I never understood the camaraderie of men, but now I understand that much better.'

In October 1990, the RFU used its column in that month's *Rugby World & Post* to warn that 'there is concern about the changing atmosphere in some clubhouses', and that disquiet about behaviour, both on- and off-field, was mirrored in the women's game. Two years previously, the WRFU banned Leicester Polytechnic for a year following 'allegations of rough play and drunkenness' during and after a match against Pontypool. 'Members of the team were drunk, impersonated monkeys and pretended to be 'dying flies' by lying on their backs and waving their legs in the air', the *Daily Telegraph* reported.

The punishment handed down to Leicester Poly did not seem to act as much of a deterrent. Less than a month into the 1990/91 season, the WRFU sent a letter to all member clubs reminding them of their responsibility for holding their players to account following three incidents in the previous six months. It was also recommended that the union's disciplinary code should be updated, but at the next WRFU meeting on 24 November, two players were temporarily suspended due to their on-field conduct. Anne McMahon was instructed to draft a second letter to clubs which would 'emphasize the need for good discipline in the run-up to the World Cup and in light of increased publicity'.

However, this was not an issue confined to the club game. Later in the meeting it was agreed that a disciplinary hearing should be convened to consider the misbehaviour of three Wales players on the eve of their international in Catalonia. Coming days before the official launch, concerns about player behaviour had consequences for the women's World Cup organising committee as well. Griffin and co. needed to present a credible image if they were to attract funding. Understandably, they were anxious that negative headlines arising from disciplinary issues could harm their chances of convincing sponsors, broadcasters, the UK Sports Council and, of course, the IRFB to part with support, time and, most importantly, cash.

'I love this word, "narrative". We never used to have that word,' Griffin says. 'But what was the narrative which the press was going to pick up on? Drinking and behaviour ... all of those things would have been things that we would have been very conscious that in the wrong hands they could put things out there that weren't complimentary, let's say. What was great is that actually it was largely covered by the rugby writers. They were the people that were concerned. They wrote about it from a rugby perspective, and that was brilliant.'

Participating nations were warned about the 'risk of adverse publicity during the World Cup' in January, but by then other concerns had superseded the behavioural issue in the minds of the organising committee. Christmas 1990 was Griffin's first as a mother, while Forsyth was pregnant, and both were kept very busy as they searched for a sponsor, waited on the IRFB to make a decision on their redesigned logo and attempted to convince the final few nations to commit to travelling to South Wales for the inaugural women's World Cup. Things were definitely taking shape as 1991 began, but (much like Dorrington in her training sessions with Crottie) there was a great deal of pain to go through before the gains became clear.

10

CHILDBIRTH WAITS FOR NO MUM

DEBORAH GRIFFIN'S SCHEDULE in November had been packed by any standard as she criss-crossed the country to attend meetings with the IRFB, JTI and ultimately launch the inaugural Women's Rugby World Cup. What made her stamina more impressive, though, was the fact that she had her newborn daughter in tow every step of the way. Victoria had been born on 1 November 1990 at University College Hospital, London – a mere stone's throw from where Griffin had plotted her oval-ball delivery a dozen years previously. She could ill afford to take too much time away from her responsibilities as chair of the tournament's organising committee. On the contrary, she approached maternity leave from her day job at Pannell Kerr Forster as an opportunity to devote even more of her time to the World Cup. It would prove more difficult than she envisaged, but Griffin was determined to use her time off wisely.

'I don't recall thinking it was going to be an issue,' she remembers about finding out she was going to become a mother. 'I don't know at what point, but it was bloody useful having maternity leave. You don't know how exhausted you're going to be, you don't know any of that. You think, "Oh, I'm just going to pop out this baby and carry on as normal." I'm sure I felt that way, so certainly I remember thinking, "This is great having some maternity leave because I've actually got time to do stuff.'"

Griffin had met her husband Chris when the pair were students at University College London. Chris was in the year below, and it was not until she had graduated that the friends started dating. The couple shared a love of rugby, and though Chris did not play after leaving UCL, he was a big supporter of his partner's endeavours at Richmond and with the WRFU. She and Chris were married in 1987, the same year Griffin lost her place as starting scrum half at the Athletic Ground due to a couple of work trips to Asia which took her away from Richmond for weeks at a time. By the time that she became pregnant with Victoria, she had reinvented herself as a centre, following a serious injury to Jane Addey, and was back in the first-team picture long before the squad departed for New Zealand in 1989.

The couple had also moved from Griffin's third-floor flat in Tufnell Park into the much more spacious property on Camden Road. Featuring three bedrooms and a garden, it was a flat fit for a family. Deborah and Chris did not attend antenatal classes ahead of Victoria's arrival; what with work and a World Cup to organise, they simply didn't have time. They *did* go to hospital for check-ups, but the scans available to expectant parents in 1990 were not as detailed as they are today. Technology has improved to such an extent that ultrasound scans can now detect a range of serious health conditions. However, that was not the case three decades ago.

It was not until Victoria made her entrance into the world on that Thursday in November that her parents discovered all was not entirely well. Their daughter had been born without an arm or hand below her right elbow. This did not dim the loving glow Chris and Deborah felt in that moment, but would have made the first few months of their lives as a family more fraught than they already would have been. 'It was a shock. It was a big shock,' Griffin remembers. 'But, you know, I just had to deal with that as well. I couldn't not do the World Cup. There wasn't a choice really.'

Within 24 hours of giving birth, Griffin was wheeled to another part of the hospital alongside Chris to be given the verdict on Victoria's long-term prognosis. In a consulting room, a paediatric orthopaedic doctor, accompanied by what seemed like a rugby team's worth of medical students, told the couple that there was nothing further they could do. 'I was quite relieved because [when you've] got a child, having to make decisions about them is one of the hardest things,' Griffin says. 'I remember being, even at that stage, really pleased, if pleased is the right word, that I didn't have to think. I didn't have to make a decision. That was it. She is what she is.'

When Victoria was three months old, she was referred to the Royal National Orthopaedic Hospital in North London, where her right arm was put in a cast, and she was fitted for her first prosthetic limb. Chris and Deborah, meanwhile, were offered genetic counselling, but with a happy baby to introduce to the world, they declined. And by all accounts, Victoria was a very happy baby. 'Oh, she was delightful, delightful from the word go,' Griffin says. 'She's still one of the happiest people you could find.' That even temperament would come in handy as she accompanied her mum to meetings relating to the inaugural Women's Rugby World Cup from only a few weeks old. It was only on rare occasions that Griffin would hand Vicky to her husband and implore him to 'Take her out for a few hours to let me get on with some stuff!'

*****

'It was tough, and had I not had the World Cup, perhaps I'd have talked about it a bit more, I don't know,' Griffin admits 32 years later. At the time, though, both she and Chris were keen to get on with things. They accepted that no one was to blame for what happened to Victoria during pregnancy and were determined to ensure that the disability did not impact on her or her image of herself and what she could achieve. 'I hadn't really thought about motherhood, but having Vicky, and having her disability, really made me think about it,' Griffin says. 'I really wanted her to be confident, so I was full of praise for things that she did.' Later in life she would take her water-skiing and horse riding, but for now Victoria had to settle for trips up and down the M4 motorway as her mother frantically tried to tie up the women's World Cup's many loose ends.

Depending on your point of view, Griffin could not have picked a better or worse time to be on maternity leave. So much had been achieved to turn the idea of a global tournament into something that was becoming reality, but question marks remained. Griffin and co. did not yet have 12 teams confirmed for the World Cup, they did not have a venue for every pool-stage match, nor had they secured funding to pay for it all. On 25 October 1990, a week before she gave birth, Griffin wrote to the eight nations which had accepted invitations asking them to provide an update on how preparations were going and various details to be included in press materials for the launch and the official tournament brochure which Alice Cooper was compiling. In the letter, the Chair laid out that 'sponsorship is still a problem'.

The four teams which were reluctant to commit at the end of September were France, New Zealand, the USSR and Spain, although Begoña Montmany would soon contact Griffin. Women's rugby in each of those nations was overseen by the men's union, although that is likely to have been a coincidence rather than anything sinister, given Canada, the Netherlands, Sweden and the USA were all in a similar boat and had accepted. That said, there was certainly feeling in New Zealand that the nation's union were not making it easy for their women to sign up to play at the World Cup. Laurie O'Reilly had written to Griffin and Forsyth on 3 October to assure them that 'most of the current squad are available and are enthusiastic about participation'. However, he warned that the New Zealand Rugby Football Union (NZRFU) 'have made it clear there will be little or no funds available'. Considering O'Reilly believed it would cost around NZ$150,000 to send a team to South Wales, that was a significant hurdle to be overcome.

The women's game in New Zealand was overseen by a two-person committee which consisted of John Dowling and Margo Cory-Wright. In O'Reilly's own words, though, 'During the last few months the New Zealand Rugby Football Union seems to have been content to allow me to administer women's rugby.' Tensions had almost boiled over ahead of RugbyFest in August, when the organisers threatened to split from the men's union. The women's committee had already recommended that New Zealand accept its invitation to the women's World Cup, but that decision needed NZRFU approval. O'Reilly felt that if that was not forthcoming then a separate women's union would be the natural next step.

Regardless, he had reservations about the structure of the tournament. Both his standing in the women's game and his confidence in advocating for what he believed was right were in evidence as he pitched an alternative format to Griffin and Forsyth. O'Reilly felt that more guaranteed games were needed to make the cost of travelling to Cardiff worthwhile. He therefore lobbied for an additional pool stage to be added before the semi-finals to give the eight teams which qualified for it an extra three matches each. It was never likely to sway the organising committee given the tight eight-day timeframe they were working within. However, they did consider the proposal and as a result added a plate competition for the teams which didn't qualify for the last four.

Crisis and a breakaway were averted on 8 November when the NZRFU approved, in principle, the idea of participating in the women's World Cup. However, while this was communicated to Forsyth by Dowling on the day of the meeting, it took another five weeks for official confirmation to arrive in London. The reason for that, it seems, was that the women's committee needed time to weigh up the benefits of sending a team almost 12,000 miles round the world against the cost of doing so. O'Reilly had been right to be sceptical about the prospect of funding from the NZRFU and along with his fellow selectors he would have to find enough players willing and able to pay for their passage to South Wales.

'They chose something like 50 or 60 players from that 1990 World [Rugby] Festival and they sent them letters saying, "Do you want to be involved in the '91 World Cup? If you want to be involved, this is how much you're going to have to pay",' recalls New Zealand great Anna Richards, who played in the first of her five World Cups in South Wales. 'From memory, I think it was something like NZ$5,000. So, it was quite a large amount of money back in those days, and they picked the side from the girls who said yes. So, there would have been girls who just didn't have the money who probably may have made that side.'

Natasha Wong's employers at the Christchurch Academy held a fundraiser to help pay for her trip to the UK, while, at O'Reilly's suggestion, she and a couple of teammates also competed in the gruelling Coast to Coast endurance event. 'I'll never do that again in my entire life, but we did some crazy things for money,' she says. 'Back in those days, it was just expected that you basically had to find your own way. It's quite different now, obviously, but if you didn't have to pay for all of it, there'd be a significant percentage of it that you'd have to pay for, and any money that you got given was a bonus. What that meant, though, was there were a couple of the players that couldn't go because they couldn't afford to go. They were the exception rather than the rule, which was good. Most people found a way to be able to pull the money together.'

On 14 December 1990, the same day that Cory-Wright faxed Forsyth to finally confirm that New Zealand would send a team the following April, NZRFU chairman Eddie Tonks signed a press release confirming the names of the 26 players and five non-playing reserves who would represent the country at the World Cup. Anyone who thought that would be the end of the uncertainty for those players was in for a shock. Although the release had been sent in Tonks' name and the letterhead on the correspondence faxed by Cory-Wright featured the union's emblem, it was not guaranteed that the team would be allowed to play in a jersey featuring the famous fern.

It would be another two months before Tonks confirmed that the team would indeed line up in black jerseys bearing the fern for the first time. 'It's very significant because we don't give them away lightly,' he told the *Herald*. 'They won't have Women All Blacks on their jerseys. There's only one lot of All Blacks.' Hardly an enthusiastic endorsement of the players who were about to make the trip of a lifetime to represent their country. It was, though, an encouraging development. The players would have to wait until the eve of their opening match of the tournament to learn whether they would be granted permission to perform a Haka by Māori elders.

*****

On Monday 28 January 1991, as Griffin neared the end of her maternity leave, she made a now familiar yet gruelling trip west with Victoria. On the agenda in Cardiff were meetings with the WRU and volunteers Lyn Delfosse and Richard Decaux to discuss arrangements for the preliminary stage matches before a trip to the suburb of Ely to visit Glamorgan Wanderers' Memorial Ground. No mean feat when accompanied by a 12-week-old baby.

Delfosse and Decaux's wife Jane had offered their services as local organisers for the tournament, answering a call for assistance in the latest edition of *In Touch*. The WRFU magazine revealed details of a 'World Cup Lottery' which the organisers hoped would raise as much as £15,000 – vital funds as hopes of finding an official sponsor were receding. 'At the end of January all clubs will receive raffle tickets,' the article stated. 'It is very important that all clubs sell their allocation to provide any necessary finance.' Appealing for volunteers, it concluded: 'Please come forward if you are willing to help in any capacity – don't leave it to the usual few!'

The trip to Cardiff clearly came at a delicate time for the inaugural Women's Rugby World Cup. The press launch at the end of November had raised the profile of the tournament, and since then things had progressed still further. New Zealand had confirmed their entry, the USSR were making positive noises, and Griffin had secured five grounds at which to play matches. JTI had also struck a deal with Leyland DAF to supply eight minibuses for use by teams and volunteers during the tournament in return for an executive box at the semi-finals and final, as well as advertising space at the ground and in the official World Cup brochure.

When Cooper sent the tournament brochure to print at the end of March, Leyland DAF's full-page ad would sit alongside plugs for Gilbert, British Gas Wales, the Milk Marketing Board and two hotel chains. However, all were barter deals. By then, the original list of 24 companies to target for sponsorship had swelled to more than 600. While the businesses in the brochure wanted to be associated with the women's World Cup, and in the case of The Celtic Bay Hotel provided rooms for the England team, none was willing to part with any cash for the privilege. As a result, the organising committee's finances were in a far from buoyant state.

Although each competing nation was required to pay a £200 deposit on accepting its invitation, Griffin was more than six weeks late in paying the guarantee for accommodation at the Cardiff Institute of Higher Education. This is not necessarily surprising, considering she gave birth two weeks after the original deadline, but the financial strain she was under is evidenced by the fact that her cheque was made out for £1,000 and not the £1,200 previously agreed. At that time, she remained confident that sponsorship could be found, but as the New Year came and went things began to look less positive. Griffin met Derek Casey at the Sports Council on 15 January and was assured that the tournament's grant application would be discussed four weeks later.

The following day, she wrote to Noriko Kishida in Japan and Evelyn Kirifi in New Zealand and informed them that the organising committee and JTI remained in talks with two potential sponsors. The deals were dependent on satisfactory broadcast coverage, however, something which was undermined by BBC Wales' reluctance to cover the pool-stage matches. Griffin and co. had set the potential commercial partners a deadline of 31 January to strike a deal, and time was clearly running out. Three days before she travelled to South Wales, Griffin wrote to all ten nations that had confirmed their participation, as well as France, to inform them about the progress on the tournament and various arrangements. Again, she insisted that the organising committee was still in contact with potential sponsors, but teams were warned they were likely to have to foot the bill for their accommodation as well as travel.

By the end of January, the organising committee owed more than £1,500 to JTI for time and expenses, and another £1,007.50 to JB Jewellery and Antiques for the World Cup trophy, but money was not their only concern. Griffin and Forsyth both fielded concerns from the USA as a result of escalating tensions in the Middle East. On 17 January, a US-led coalition, of which the UK was part, launched an air offensive in Kuwait in an attempt to expel the occupying Iraqi forces. Following months of posturing, it kicked off what became the First Gulf War and was watched anxiously by those responsible for women's rugby at the USA RFU.

'The USA RFU Board, concerned for obvious reasons about the safety of our Women's World Cup party during the period [of] the Cup, has asked me to inquire as to protective measures that will be taken in this regard,' director of administration Karen Kast wrote in a fax to Forsyth. 'Will there be any security measures in place at the Cardiff Institute of Higher Education, parks where the USA team will be playing, and generally, any protection from a possible terrorist attack? As possible targets of terrorism, we trust you appreciate our concern.'

Consideration had been given to cancelling sporting events in the UK in light of Operation Desert Storm, including the England v Wales and Scotland v France Five Nations Championship matches on 19 January. However, those games had gone ahead on the advice of the UK Minister for Sport Robert Atkins, and there is little evidence to suggest that the organising committee ever considered postponing or cancelling the women's World Cup. 'Cardiff Police are informed of the details of all participating teams in the World Cup tournament as routine,' Griffin replied to Kast, copying a statement which had been prepared by National Sports Centre for Wales principal Gwynne Griffiths. 'They will liaise with Special Branch of Scotland Yard and the various embassies who will advise the appropriate security measures to be taken.

'May I add as a comfort to your concerns that Cardiff regularly hosts major world sporting events, particularly gymnastics, fencing and martial arts. In this respect they have previously hosted teams from Israel and other sensitive areas. As a nation we are also on alert for possible IRA attacks.

'I hope that this allays your concerns and look forward to welcoming you.'

It is not documented whether the inference that the UK was a hotbed of potential terrorist attacks allayed the fears harboured by Kast and her colleague Jami Jordan on the USA RFU women's committee. However, as Griffin headed for Wales, it must have been a relief to be able to focus on rugby rather than money or security. The search for pitches on which to play matches had been a task she had taken on herself from the outset. She had first written to the Cardiff Athletic Club about using the Arms Park in March, although it took until the end of July to accept the offer to host the semi-finals and final there, primarily due to negotiations about the use of perimeter sponsorship boards at the ground. The following month, Griffin began writing to elite clubs in the area enquiring about the availability of their pitches for the pool-stage matches.

The organising committee had agreed to pay a combined £2,500 for use of the Arms Park across the two match days, and so money was tight as they sought other venues. To keep costs down, they proposed holding the opening-day fixtures on 6 April as curtain raisers to men's matches. Four fixtures were scheduled for the first Saturday, meaning Griffin had to find four clubs willing to let the women use their facilities. There was only one issue; the WRU had scheduled the semi-finals of its national competition, the Schweppes Challenge Cup, to be played at the

National Stadium that weekend. This meant the biggest clubs in the region could not be sure of their arrangements for that Saturday until much later in the season. The Schweppes Cup quarter-finals would not be played until 16 March.

Unperturbed, Griffin sent out enquiries to a host of clubs in August, and, fortunately for her, their fixture secretaries had already been hard at work ensuring there would be no gaps in their lists should the first team fail to reach the semi-finals. Bridgend were unable to help as they would be away at Bath if not still in the Schweppes Cup. Pontypridd, meanwhile, put the blame at the door of its landlords, who had been 'most stringent in the use of the pitch, other than for already arranged senior games'. As the letter noted, the club's Sardis Road ground would be used to stage a pool-stage match during the men's Rugby World Cup the following October.

More encouraging replies were received from Neath, Swansea, Pontypool and Glamorgan Wanderers, and so, when Griffin started her maternity leave, she set about firming up that interest. Glamorgan Wanderers had secured a home fixture against London Irish on 6 April and offered the use of their Memorial Ground for all three pool-stage match days. Pontypool and Swansea, scheduled to face Cross Keys and London Welsh respectively if not featuring in the semi-finals, were happy for games to be played on their pitches on the first Saturday. Council approval was needed and received, but the primitive nature of facilities at club grounds at the time was exposed by the fact the opening matches would be double-headers. As the men's teams would be using the only available changing rooms, the women playing at Pontypool Park would have to get ready in the council-owned leisure centre next door, while a school close to the Memorial Ground opened its doors to the squads drawn to open their World Cup campaign at Glamorgan Wanderers.

More pitches were needed, though, and so Griffin sent out

another round of enquiries in October 1990. The following month, Aberavon replied with an offer to use the Talbot Athletic Ground. An historic club, the Wizards found themselves in the second tier as the Welsh league system was initiated ahead of the 1990/91 season. They were not expected to reach the Schweppes Cup semi-finals, and subsequently lost 23–13 to Swansea in the first round on 26 January. Griffin set off to South Wales two days after that defeat, unaware of the problems to come with regards the Port Talbot club.

Certainly, as she arrived in Cardiff, it looked as though things were coming together. As the meeting with Delfosse and Decaux highlighted, much of the scaffolding which would allow the women's World Cup to take shape was now in place. Four grounds had been secured for the opening matches, and rent of the Memorial Ground for the pool-stage matches on Monday and Wednesday was a reasonable £250 with a 50–50 split on gate receipts. With eight matches to be played across those two days, Griffin still needed to find another host, and an answer was provided by Decaux. He lived in Llanharan, a village around 18 miles north west of Cardiff and close to the M4, and suggested contacting the local club. Happy to help, it was onto the club's Dairy Field that the players representing the Netherlands, USSR, England, Italy, Japan, Sweden, New Zealand and Wales would run in April.

Away from the matches, the WRU offered to give the World Cup's participants a guided tour of the National Stadium followed by tea with its president, Gwilym Treharne, on Tuesday 9 April, a designated rest day for the players. The Welsh union also agreed to publicise the tournament with a full-page advert in the Schweppes Cup semi-finals programme and an announcement on the National Stadium's public address system during the matches. Griffin would return to South Wales the following month to meet club officials at each of the pool-stage hosts, but February was momentous for two entirely separate reasons. First, the IRFB finally gave its approval to the new women's World Cup logo, while at the end of the month the tournament draw was made in London. France would ensure it was a fraught occasion.

*****

Not long after her trip to Cardiff, Griffin remembers being summonsed to a second meeting with Keith Rowlands, this time in London. The issue of the logo had hung over the organising committee since that first trip to Bristol and caused Griffin considerable stress as she weighed up the pros and cons of getting it redesigned for a second time. In the end, most likely because of the cost involved and the IRFB's reluctance to cover it, they had made the decision to stick with Young's second design. Promotional materials, from souvenir bookmarks and mugs to official posters and letterheads, had been produced and the women could not afford to start all over again. Moreover, if the Board, or more accurately the organisers of its men's Rugby World Cup, sought financial recompense then the women's tournament would be put at serious risk.

It has to be said that Griffin and her colleagues on the organising committee dealt with the myriad issues hanging over the women's World Cup with supreme equanimity. In mid-January, she described the task of organising the tournament as 'very exciting' in a letter about ticketing to Cardiff secretary John Nelson. This was a time, it should be remembered, when she was fielding questions on broadcast, sponsorship and security from participating teams, attempting to finalise host venue details, searching for outside investment, all while looking after her two-month-old daughter.

Understanding exactly what Rowlands and the IRFB thought

of the women's World Cup in 1991 is difficult because the actions of all parties contain a number of contradictions. Certainly, the Board was not willing to risk its reputation or what money it had on the tournament and did what it felt necessary to safeguard its own competition. Conversely, Rowlands did not appear to want to block the tournament, providing a 'statement of support' ahead of the launch, which, in lieu of official endorsement or funding, Griffin and co. used to give their tournament credibility. That was integral as they sought to convince sponsors, broadcasters and France to sign up.

What cannot be reconciled, though, are the memories of the two women who attended the meetings with the IRFB in November and February. Neither Griffin nor Dorrington recall being welcomed with particularly open arms by the towering Rowlands. 'They were quite stressful,' Griffin says of those conferences. 'Can you imagine being whatever age we were and meeting with these guys and being told "We don't think you should be doing this"? You can imagine what the stress levels of that were.'

'They weren't interested and the whole logo thing, it irritated them,' is Dorrington's verdict. 'It was never make or break in terms of the tournament delivery, that was never on the table for us. We were always ready to deliver the tournament with or without them. So, to have their backing would have been more advantageous and lent weight, particularly to drag a few teams over the line like France ... but it was never "Oh, if we don't have you, we're not going to do it".'

Dorrington adds that she and Griffin went into the meetings with the IRFB 'with nothing to lose' and, following the latter's trip to the Royal Garden Hotel to see Rowlands in February, they would have felt like winners. As Griffin relayed in a fax to Liz Ferguson at the Canadian Rugby Union on 25 February, the organising committee had 'at last received "approval" from the

IRB to use our logo'. As part of the agreement, the Board had to be informed if the logo was to be used as part of a sponsorship deal worth more than £5,000, but otherwise the organisers were free to use it how they saw fit.

A significant hurdle had been overcome, but if there was ever a time when those on the organising committee doubted the World Cup would go ahead it was in the weeks leading up to the official draw, when teams were digesting the news that they would have to pay their own way. Griffin agonised over that decision and worried that teams would struggle to find the extra £5,000 needed to participate in South Wales. 'We didn't think anybody would want to come if they were having to pay,' Griffin says.

That assumption undervalued the hunger of both players and administrators to compete in a World Cup, however, and proved wide of the mark as the USSR became the 11th team to confirm its entry midway through February. However, a presage of trouble to come was contained with the transmission sent to Griffin by Viktor Ermakov, who advised her to 'please advise urgently whether there is possibility of financial assistance'. The addition of the Soviets to the tournament, or more forebodingly the lack of an answer from France, left the organisers in a difficult position as the day of the draw arrived. 'It meant the whole thing was imbalanced,' Cooper recalls. '[We were] poised because everything had to hold while we were waiting to find out.'

No one on the organising committee envisaged the difficulty they would face in attempting to convince France to compete at the inaugural World Cup. Having done so much to promote international women's rugby, including hosting the European Cup in 1988, it was assumed they would be one of the first teams to commit. Since that tournament in Bourg-en-Bresse, France's men's union, the FFR, had assumed responsibility for the female game, though, and it seems there was some confusion about where the invitation needed to be sent. Forsyth faxed information about the tournament to the union's women's committee in late October, while Griffin met with Marcel Martin in January. But as the day of the draw arrived, the tournament was still stuck on 11 entrants.

One explanation for that could have been the relationship between those responsible for the women's game in France and the organisers of the men's tournament. It is unclear whether Martin met Griffin in his capacity as a director of the IRB's Rugby World Cup 1991 or as a representative of the women's game in France. Following their meeting, Griffin wrote to Martin, commending him on his 'very positive attitudes to women's participation in rugby', while outlining the costs entailed in competing in South Wales and enclosing an invite. However, when approached by a British journalist in the days leading up to the draw, French officials pleaded ignorance, claiming to have been unaware they were invited. Whether Martin failed to pass on the information Griffin gave him the previous month is unclear, but what it is irrefutable is that France only came on board once the logo dispute had been resolved.

BBC Wales probably regretted declining their own invitation to film the Women's Rugby World Cup draw on 25 February. That decision convinced Griffin and co. to hold the ceremony in the mundane surroundings of the JTI offices, but also ensured the broadcaster missed out on a great deal of drama. Minutes before the teams were due to be pulled out of the hat, word reached Chiswick that France would take part after all. A collective sigh of relief was quickly followed by a hastily assembled press release.[i]

Events in Chiswick did not garner quite as much attention in the UK press as the launch had, but it did not go unnoticed

---

[i] The organising committee were ready to go ahead with 11 teams and had drawn up a tournament schedule which comprised three groups: two of four and one of three. Each of the pool winners would have progressed to the semi-finals, along with the best runner-up. For the purposes of identifying the best runner-up, the second-placed team in the four-nation groups would have had their result against the bottom team discounted. France's late entry made the equation a lot more straightforward.

elsewhere. Beyond the seeded nations the draw was open, as the organisers reasoned quite understandably that there hadn't been enough international women's rugby to rank those outside the top four. This, though, produced some pools which looked more difficult than others on paper. New Zealand were drawn alongside Canada and Wales in Pool One and were among the teams that sought clarification on how the groups were decided. The fact the draw took place behind closed doors only fed any feeling of resentment from those waiting for information from the other side of the world.

For the organising committee, though, the countdown to the inaugural women's World Cup was beginning to ramp up. Griffin and co. had teams, pitches, accommodation and a fixture list for the tournament, making it more real than ever before. There would be many more bumps on the road to South Wales, but with less than six weeks to go until kick-off it was safe to assume it was going ahead.

*****

Griffin had returned to work three days a week by the time the World Cup draw was made in Chiswick, but as she settled back into office life, another of the organising committee was preparing to start her own maternity leave. Mary Forsyth (née Schofield) had grown up in a large sporty family. The third of eight children, all born within only ten years, her upbringing in suburban Pittsburgh provided her with the ideal preparation for a life in sport. Local kids would congregate outside the Schofields' three-bedroom home, due partly to the fact it sat at the bottom of a big hill, and offered a flat piece of ground big enough to play a game of kickball on, and partly because the number of children living there meant a match was never far from getting underway.

Unsurprisingly, given her father was an insurance broker

and her mother had a master's degree in home economics, her parents were also canny with money. The private Catholic elementary school the siblings attended only charged for the first two children per family, and only the first paid full price. A family membership at the local swimming pool, meanwhile, cost $125 a year, regardless of how many children you had, so that is where the Schofield kids spent much of their free time. 'You took your towels, you took your playing cards, you took something to drink, and you stayed down there all morning, every day,' Forsyth remembers. 'That's where we spent, unless it was raining, every single day of the week. And then on the weekends you'd have swimming matches.'

The stamina she developed swimming and playing kickball for hours on end as a youngster would later ensure that Forsyth was a powerful presence on the rugby pitch from the moment she picked up an oval ball at Penn State University. There was no doubt that she would pack her boots when in 1985 she transferred from Pittsburgh to London for work. Six weeks later, her sister arrived in London on a Fulbright Exchange and fortunately had been provided with a flat in Finchley. The sisters soon learned of the nearby women's rugby club through the local newspaper, and for Forsyth training could not arrive quickly enough.

'They trained on a Sunday, so I wandered up on a Sunday,' Forsyth recalls. 'Simon [Crabb] was our coach for years and years, the whole time I was there, and he was out front with three girls, and they were all practising kicking. The rest of the team had gone in for something to eat and drink or whatever, and I said, "Oh, I'm looking for a rugby club and I saw this dah, dah, dah." He said, "Oh, I'm Simon and this is Jane, Jane and Jane – but your name doesn't have to be Jane to play rugby!"

'They had been trawling bars looking for tall women because I think the tallest player they had was about five-six or five-seven. And he said, "Have you played before?" And I said, "Yes, four years at Penn State and three years in Pittsburgh." "Oh, my word!" So, I came in and they were all over me.'

The following Saturday night, Forsyth put on a turquoise jumpsuit and, having shared some homemade brownies with her new teammates, headed back to the club for her first social at Finchley. It was an enjoyable night and one which resulted in two invitations from members of the club's men's team to watch the rugby league play *Up 'n' Under*. By the time Piers Forsyth tracked down a number for his future wife, she had already watched it with another suitor, but that did not kibosh his chances. The couple got to know each other at a pub in Hampstead, away from prying eyes in Finchley, and their budding romance survived the move by the women's team to Richmond. Mary and Piers were married in September 1987, and just over two years later she finished her playing career prior to starting a family.

Kathryn, the couple's first child, was born on 30 March, just seven days before the women's World Cup was due to kick off in South Wales. Forsyth is typically modest about the role she played in organising the tournament, but documents highlight how involved she was as a point of contact for various unions which were planning their trips to the UK. That was particularly true around the time that Griffin gave birth to Victoria, but continued until the event got under way. When her mother Clementine came to stay with her and Piers ahead of Kathryn's arrival, her sleep was disrupted on more than one occasion as faxes arrived from all over the world. 'I remember my mother going, "You got another one overnight!" because it was up in her room,' Forsyth says.

Forsyth was at home in Ealing when the women's World Cup got under way, but acclimatising to life as a mother and coping with a week-old baby did not prevent her from playing a role in the event. Griffin and Cooper had both been equipped with mobile phones for the tournament; however, the technology was not widespread or particularly trustworthy three decades ago. That meant the organisers needed a personal assistant, and Forsyth dutifully stepped up to the plate. She would take messages on her landline at home in West London, and then volunteers on the ground could phone her to pick them up.

Given the number of plates which both Griffin and Cooper were required to spin across those nine days in Cardiff, it proved a useful system. 'We didn't have any way for people to get in touch with us,' Cooper says. 'It's ridiculous, really, when you think about how used to having mobile phones we are now.' Although they would struggle for a phone signal as they traipsed across South Wales, the women's World Cup received a reception of a different kind in Cardiff. On the eve of the tournament, the players paraded into County Hall as part of a civic opening ceremony, listening excitedly to speeches from Griffin and other dignitaries as the World Cup officially got underway.

11

WINDS OF CHANGE

TIME WAS TICKING until the Women's Rugby World Cup began, but there was much still to do before the teams arrived in Cardiff. There would be no title sponsor, despite the best efforts of the organising committee and JTI. However, there was some good news from a financial perspective at the beginning of March. Having procrastinated for much of the previous year, the Sports Council wrote to Deborah Griffin on 7 March proposing a grant of £5,000. 'In reaching this decision the Panel acknowledged that by staging the event, Britain's WRFU would attract International recognition, domestic participation in the sport would be stimulated and the development of playing standards would be encouraged,' the offer letter stated.

The money was offered on the conditions that an audited set of accounts for the event would be produced, that it would be financially secure and, if the World Cup made a surplus, then a proportion of that profit would be used to repay the grant. The Sports Council also forbade South Africa from competing at the tournament, and the body stipulated that its support for the World Cup should be advertised prominently. Griffin and co. had anticipated any grant would come with such criteria and had organised the tournament to comply with regulations set out by the Sports Council. This meant, among other things, that they had made provision for drug testing in South Wales.

If any part of the offer letter gave the organising committee pause before they typed up their acceptance, then it would have been Clause 3(c). This stated: 'The Sports Council requires the assurance of the WRFU that the grant will result in the event being sufficiently financially secure to enable it to be staged without the possibility of a deficit which the WRFU would find unmanageable.' Griffin had been made aware of the Sports Council's decision prior to receiving the offer, during a phone call with Joe Patton. He soon learned exactly how desperate the organising committee was for cash as Mary Forsyth faxed him a request for an advance on 4 March. Forsyth asked for £4,001.71 to pay five creditors, one of which, JB Jewellery and Antiques, had been waiting since November.

Less than £1,000 remained and the tournament was yet to kick off. With more large invoices expected, including for the hire of the Arms Park, there would have been reason to fear that the women's World Cup was not going to be 'sufficiently financially secure'. Nevertheless, Forsyth replied to R.D. Knowles at the Sports Council on behalf of the organising committee on 12 March to accept the grant. The cheque for £5,000 was subsequently sent to her home in Ealing and was used to pay the unsettled invoices and ensure that the World Cup was kept afloat and on course for Cardiff.

As March progressed, the main focus for Forsyth and Griffin became confirming exactly when and where teams were arriving, and where they were staying. Although the Cardiff Institute of Higher Education had been block-booked, only seven of the squads ended up staying there. Wales, of course, had been offered rooms at the National Sports Centre for Wales, where Griffin, Cooper and key volunteers would also stay. Sue Dorrington had brokered a deal with Rank Hotels, which meant the England squad would stay free of charge at their Celtic Bay Hotel. The USA kept their options open until late in the day but eventually plumped for the Grand Hotel on Westgate Street, where the Cardiff Ladies pioneers had changed 74 years previously. Canada, meanwhile, had found alternative student accommodation in Penarth, and the Netherlands were booked into the Cardiff Youth Hostel.

Chasing that information proved a particularly onerous and time-consuming task as party sizes and flight or hotel details appeared to change on a near daily basis. Meanwhile, Forsyth's pleas to the USA and New Zealand for squad profiles and historic results to be used in the official souvenir brochure, which had originally been requested in October, grew more and more desperate as the mid-March printing deadline drew closer. 'Please don't let us down,' she wrote to Evelyn Kirifi on 11 March. The following day, that had escalated: 'PLEASE, PLEASE, PLEASE reply today,' Forsyth implored. In the end, all 12 teams, including late-comers France and the USSR, supplied enough information to fill the programme, although with contrasting amounts of detail, which created a problem for the printers.

On Friday 15 March, Griffin made one final trip to Cardiff, with Tom Purvis and Deborah James of JTI, to meet representatives of the Sports Council for Wales, Cardiff RFC, the WRU, South Glamorgan County Council and the City of Cardiff. Fittingly, the meeting was held in the Hubert Johnson room, where the photograph of Ma Rosser and the Cardiff Ladies players would be found and digitised more than 25 years later. It is not known exactly how long the picture had hung there, but it is heartening to think that they might have been watching on as Griffin provided her final update on how preparations were proceeding.

There was much to discuss with only three weeks to go until the tournament was scheduled to kick off at the Glamorgan Wanderers ground. Potential national press coverage, including a slot on the BBC's flagship talk show *Wogan*, ticketing and other arrangements for the semi-finals and finals, and the week's hospitality programme were all reviewed and finalised. However, the most pressing issue for Griffin was the uncertainty over where three of the four matches on 6 April were going to be played. She knew that the opening game, between New Zealand and Canada, would take place at the Wanderers' Memorial Ground. Aberavon, Swansea and Pontypool were earmarked as hosts for the other three, but Talbot Athletic Ground did not have 'adequate changing facilities' and the two Premier Division clubs had reached the Cup quarter-finals.

In the last eight, Swansea had been drawn at home to Tondu, a team from the village of Aberkenfig who were enjoying an improbable cup run. 'As a consequence it is likely that they will proceed into the semi final stage,' the City of Swansea's director of leisure services had conveyed to Griffin the previous week. Pontypool had what looked like a tougher assignment against fellow top-flight side Newbridge, but 'Pooler' would also be at home and were fancied to make the last four. The quarter-finals were due to be played the following day, 16 March, and so Griffin and co. conducted some contingency planning. Newport was identified as an alternative venue, while Gwynne Griffiths was sounded out about using the pitch at the National Sports Centre for Wales as a back-up.

Ultimately, both Swansea and Pontypool won the following day, 22–13 and 12–3 respectively, to set up a semi-final clash against each other at the National Stadium the following month. That meant that neither would have a home match on 6 April, but that didn't prove to be the hammer blow to the women's World Cup that Griffin might have expected. Both clubs and their council landlords were happy to keep their offers on the table, meaning the organisers were spared a pretty big headache. That still left the question of Aberavon, and sometime after the tournament brochure was sent to print the following week the decision was made to look elsewhere. It is unclear why Newport declined the approach from Griffin as documents relating to her conversations with the club have not survived. However, Vernon Pugh, the man who had carried out the investigation into Welsh involvement in the centenary tour of South Africa, came to the women's aid. His club, Cardiff Harlequins, stepped in to provide the pitch on which France got their campaign under way against Japan.

Another catastrophe had been averted with only weeks to go until the teams arrived in Cardiff, but the difficulties the organising committee faced had not gone unnoticed among participants. On 19 March, Forsyth wrote to Jeannette Bakker at the Nederlandse Rugby Bond to calm Dutch concerns. 'The rumour that the Women's World Cup will be cancelled is WRONG! We have 12 teams participating and are quite looking forward to seeing everyone when they arrive.'

The organising committee would not have to wait long to welcome those teams, but Forsyth's forthright response to Bakker did not mean they were not experiencing serious problems. In the week leading up to the tournament, Griffin spoke to *Evening Standard* journalist Chris Jones, and suggested she would seek assistance from the IRFB to deal with what the reporter termed the 'latest financial crisis to hit the inaugural women's rugby World Cup'. On 1 April, Viktor Ermakov had sent a fax to Forsyth revealing that the Soviet women had 'met with unforeseen difficulties connected with the provision of hard currency .... We ask you to consider urgently the possibility to accommodate our team at lowest possible cost.'

'The Soviet women are members of the USSR Rugby Federation and the International Board is, therefore, responsible,'

Griffin told Jones. 'I will ask the International Board to cover the £6,000 the Soviet team needs because we cannot afford to take this bill on board.' Griffin knew her appeal to the Board was the administrative equivalent of a 60m drop-goal on her wrong foot, but such was the dire financial straits the tournament found itself in. What she did not realise, though, was that this would not be the most severe headache the USSR team would induce over the next week and beyond.

*****

Unsurprisingly, the IRFB did not reach out to Griffin or the organising committee with an offer of help. More unexpected perhaps was the letter sent from the office of IRFB secretary Keith Rowlands to Deborah James at JTI, accepting an invitation of hospitality at the Women's Rugby World Cup final. The offer had been extended on behalf of Griffin and the organising committee, and, as teams began to arrive in the UK, it was their job now to put the struggles to one side and deliver the best tournament they possibly could. Obviously, Forsyth's focus was on daughter Kathryn (although she sent a fax to Ermakov less than two days after giving birth) while Dorrington, having earned her place in the England squad, was excused administrative duties for the nine days in South Wales. That left Griffin and Cooper to oversee operations, assisted by Tom Purvis and Deborah James from JTI as well as a team of organisers, team chaperones, match managers and other volunteers from the women's rugby community.

Participating nations had started to arrive in the UK from the beginning of the week. Some, like New Zealand and Canada, played warm-up matches on their way to Cardiff. Others, the USA included, headed directly for the Welsh capital. Once there, each delegation was required to register at the Institute, and it was when doing so that England number eight Gill Burns first discovered she was the tournament's cover star.

Having picked up her ID badge, Burns was handed a copy of the souvenir publication and was shocked to see a picture of herself in action splashed across the front page. 'I remember being absolutely gobsmacked,' she recalls. 'I couldn't believe it, not that it was very recognisable. But I realised that this is big, this is a world event. And I couldn't believe that my picture was on the front of the thing!'

However difficult it had been to get to this point, there was no turning back now. By Friday 5 April, players representing all 12 nations were in South Wales and waiting for the tournament to get under way.[i] Griffin had been drawn to Cardiff as a host city, in part because of the enthusiasm for the tournament she encountered among officials at the Sports Council for Wales, South Glamorgan County Council and the City of Cardiff. From early on in those negotiations, the promise had been made to open the World Cup with an official civic ceremony.

County Hall, which sits on Atlantic Wharf in Cardiff's docklands and was designed as a symbol of regeneration in the area, would welcome players, coaches and team managers as well as dignitaries and members of the press for the event that Friday evening. However, there was one important person absent. Dorrington was back at the Celtic Bay Hotel, England's base for the tournament, where she had quite literally been left holding the baby. As chair of the organising committee, Griffin had agreed to make a speech at the opening ceremony, but as husband Chris was not due in Cardiff until the following day, she needed someone to look after Victoria. Step forward Dorrington. 'It sounds awful, but it was just such a hectic week,' Griffin admits.

---

[i] Only half of the USSR squad had arrived in Cardiff by 5 April. The remaining players and delegates would touch down in London the following day.

Dorrington had been the first member of the England squad to arrive in Cardiff, primarily to check on arrangements at the hotel, which she had secured. She approached looking after Victoria as her final act for the organising committee before she could concentrate on playing in the World Cup, beginning with England's opening match against Spain the following day. 'I had a five-month old in my room playing, babysitting, the night before the tournament kicked off,' Dorrington recalls. 'So, I maintained my responsibility. The minute that we kicked off I was done. I had to be. I wanted to focus, I was not going to let anything disrupt me. I didn't speak to them, I didn't see them. I wanted nothing to do with them.'

Had Dorrington opened the window to her room, she would have been able to hear the hum of people arriving for the opening ceremony at County Hall, which was only a short stroll from the Celtic Bay Hotel. It was the first time that so many female players from so many different countries had been in such close proximity. Some of those present knew each other from past international matches or club tours, but the novelty of the occasion only added to the air of nervous excitement as the teams waited for the festivities to begin.

The guests were soon ushered into the County Hall reception area, which at least offered respite from the gathering wind outside. Events at Atlantic Wharf had been scheduled to run on a tight schedule. Each of the 12 competing squads would be led into the civic building's central courtyard by members of the Royal Regiment of Wales, the team captains following slightly behind holding their country's flag. The organising committee has then set aside 25 minutes for speeches from Griffin and the chairman of South Glamorgan County Council, William J. Bowen, the raising of the tournament flag (which featured the recently approved logo) and an affirmation of spirit and fair play from the captains of England and Wales.

Players had been asked to attend the ceremony 'dressed in track suits [sic] or team jumpers' and every nation had complied with that request. Only the USA, who would wow crowds with their free-flowing back play, had veered even slightly off-script. They arrived wearing jeans and zip-up jackets, their training tops concealing more formal red team jumpers that the players recall with horror to this day. There was a roughly 50–50 split between squads assembled in formal wear and those looking slightly more relaxed in tracksuits. Among the latter were New Zealand, whose players beamed with pride as they discussed what was to come while wearing black-and-white shell suits embossed with the unmistakeable and hard-earned fern.

The England and Wales squads meanwhile were kitted out in almost identical tracksuits, donated to them by Cotton Oxford ahead of their meeting earlier in the season. Wales' were red and black, which each player had teamed with a daffodil flower; England's were a mix of dark and light blue. 'I remember the tracksuits because we thought, at the time, they were quite flash,' England captain Karen Almond recalls. 'I mean, looking back now, they probably weren't at all but at the time we thought we looked pretty smart.'

Inside County Hall, the foyer reverberated to the sound of chatter as around 350 members of the international women's rugby community swapped pleasantries and compared stories about their journey to Cardiff, both literally and metaphorically. Some guests had to search for a common language, but their shared passion for the oval-ball game soon broke down any cultural barriers.

A Japanese player stood on the stairs above the crowd, recording the scene for posterity. As her lens scanned the room, women who would soon become rivals on the pitch and friends off it posed and waved for the camera. Two members of the Japan squad originally picked for the World Cup had been forced to withdraw due to work commitments, and Paula George took the opportunity to record a message for those absent players. 'Pity you're not here. It's going to be a good time,' George, a 22-year-old Wales winger and future England captain, said into the camera. She then added sheepishly: 'OK, that's it.'

Welsh and Japanese players would strike up an unlikely bond, which was initiated as they waited for the ceremony to begin. 'Barely a word between us in terms of understanding, but they were fabulous,' Wales fly half and vice-captain Amanda Bennett remembers. 'The key to it was shared excitement. It wasn't just "We're Japan and we're coming to a World Cup and we're gonna try to win it." Or "We're Wales, we're the hosts, we need to win it." Or 'We're England, we're one of the top teams, we're gonna win it." It was, I use the phrase, "We're all in this together, we're doing something very special here." It was a shared excitement.'

In the building's internal courtyard, just a few yards from where the players were waiting patiently, the finishing touches were being applied to the space which would welcome them. A brass band was preparing as TV cameras were set up, photographers took their places, and bunting was fixed to the sides of a raised stage. As women's rugby prepared to take a momentous step into the unknown, council workers crowded the windows which overlook the quad in a bid to get an unobstructed view of the historic events unfolding below.

*****

Outside County Hall, where the teams were being corralled into single-file units, anxious excitable smiles abounded as the clock edged towards 7.00 pm. Players from New Zealand and Spain sang songs and exchanged dance moves as they waited to be called into the ceremony. The Japanese posed for pictures with Dutch winger Annelies Sleuthel, who towered over her new friends at 1.88 m (6 ft 2 in) tall. Above her, the grey clouds had begun to disperse, making way for a blue sky. But the wind continued to build, flags fluttering in the sky a harbinger of what was to come in less than 24 hours.

At approximately 6.50 pm, Griffin watched on as Canada led the 12 teams through to the courtyard, where the brass band heralded their arrival. Each team paraded past the stage, being filmed and snapped as they passed, before turning right and arcing their entrance to line up in alphabetical order, facing the stage. For the first time since agreeing to chair the organising committee, the size of the task was laid out in front of Griffin. Her eyes scanned from Canada on her right all the way down to Wales at the far end of the courtyard.

Councillor Bill Bowen, chairman of South Glamorgan County Council, wearing a black suit and ceremonial medallion, stepped towards a microphone stand. A stout bespectacled man, with an almost fully receded hairline, Bowen had a baritone voice. 'It's my very great pleasure, and I mean that, a very great pleasure indeed', he beamed, 'on behalf of the people of Wales, to welcome all of you today to this ceremony to mark the opening of the first Women's World Rugby Cup.

'In Wales, and I'm sure you're all aware, rugby is the national game. It is the pastime. It is the religion. In a country where sport is taken very, very seriously indeed. The Welsh people, I can assure you, are therefore delighted that this first-ever world tournament for women should take place in the true home of rugby.' Adding a touch of levity to proceedings, Bowen added: 'Hear that, England?' Laughter, cheers and some boos erupted from those watching on.

Griffin stood at the back of the stage, alongside WRFU secretary Rosie Golby, as Bowen continued his speech. She wore a wide grin, the sleepless nights and stress of the past few months receding into the distance as the significance of what she and the organising committee had achieved hit her. Only 13 years after she first picked up a rugby ball, just nine since the first match of international women's rugby had been played in Utrecht, they had organised a World Cup. 'This in itself is proof, if proof was needed, that women's rugby is now firmly established on a worldwide basis and this first international championship is the forerunner of many to follow,' Bowen continued. 'It took the men 100 years to get a World Cup. It's only taken you 20 years.'

It was a crowd-pleasing way for Bowen to conclude his welcome, and as Griffin headed towards the microphone, more cheers echoed round the quad. As the organising committee chair placed her notes onto the lectern, the scaffolding on the side of the stage strained to hold onto the bunting which seemed determined to escape into the wind. Concerns over the weather had to wait until the morning, though.

'When Great Britain agreed to host the 1991 European Cup back in 1988, we could never have anticipated that it would grow into this inaugural Women's Rugby World Cup,' Griffin said from the stage, her dark hair staying impressively still in the breeze. 'As Councillor Bowen has said, it seems appropriate to be staging this event in Wales with its inherent love of rugby. It has been a delight while organising this event to find so many willing hands and be encouraged by so many quarters in Wales.

'The warmth of this Welsh hospitality is something I hope you will all come to know and enjoy during the next ten days. While the World Cup will serve to put women's rugby not only on the map but allow it to take its rightful place alongside all other international sports, its success will set the standard for the future. This event is, after all, the first of many Women's Rugby World Cups. I now declare open the first Women's Rugby World Cup.' Whoops, cheers and a rendition of 'Oggy, Oggy, Oggy' greeted the conclusion of Griffin's speech. A few formalities remained, and it would be a long night for Griffin, Cooper and their team of volunteers, but they had done it. The first ever Women's Rugby World Cup was up and running.

12

A PERFECT DAY FOR RUGBY

ALICE COOPER HAD watched the Women's Rugby World Cup opening ceremony from the side of the stage. As head of press, it had been her job to welcome reporters, direct camera crews to their positions and generally ensure that the jostling photographers did not inhibit proceedings. Like every volunteer who was working in an operational role that week in South Wales, Cooper had been given a laminated badge. It had her job title and the official tournament logo printed on it. On the underside, the tall second row had written, 'Don't quote me.' 'The journalists thought this was hilarious,' she remembers. Cooper, the conduit between the organising committee and the press, would of course be quoted in print and on TV and radio across the next week-and-a-half. In doing so, she helped to propagate an apocryphal tale that endures to this day. More on that later, though.

For now, as her friend, teammate and colleague Deborah Griffin finished her speech and accepted the warm applause of those in attendance, Cooper knew she had a long night ahead of her. The teams retired to a room within County Hall for a brief drinks reception. Inside, players swapped songs, teaching the uninitiated lyrics and actions as they enjoyed a communal sing-song while sipping red wine and munching on nibbles. Tara Flanagan and Tam Breckenridge, the USA 'Locks from Hell', weaved through the crowd, seeking out second rows to have their picture taken with. By this time, though, Cooper, a lock herself, had already made the trip back to the National Sports Centre for Wales at Sophia Gardens. At 9.00 pm she met key volunteers, including JTI and Isla Nicholson, who had taken over from Mary Forsyth as financial controller for the ten days in Cardiff.

With only 16 hours to go until the first Women's Rugby World Cup match, between Canada and New Zealand, kicked off at the Glamorgan Wanderers ground in Ely, West Cardiff, there was much to discuss. The logistics of transporting eight teams from six different locations to four grounds, one of which was almost 50 miles away in Swansea, was only one item on the agenda. Isla Nicholson (now Meek), a Bath number eight good enough to represent the South West regional XV and the South of England, had been recommended to Griffin by WRFU committee member Sue Eakers. Despite having no previous experience in finance, other than being a club treasurer, she was tasked with looking after the money on arrival with husband Chris.

This primarily entailed overseeing the merchandise stalls which were set up at games, making sure each had enough float money, counting the profits at the end of every match day, finding a secure place to store the cash and delivering stock to where it was needed. Forsyth had typed up instructions for Nicholson on her work computer and used the fax machine which had been installed in her spare room at home to send the document to the tournament's makeshift headquarters at Sophia Gardens. For Nicholson, who had not interacted with the WRFU prior to volunteering for the first women's World Cup, it was a daunting undertaking.

'I was just told to report to the sports centre in Cardiff and got given this massive task. I remember being really impressed with how well they had set it all up. I suppose I was a bit jealous that I hadn't been involved a bit sooner. I would have liked to have helped from the beginning, but it was great fun and very, very well organised,' Nicholson says.

'Alice Cooper, I remember, spending the most amount of time with really, getting lifts backwards and forwards to games because, like her, my role didn't really involve much watching of the game. She was busy organising the press, I was making sure that stock got there to be sold and that money got collected. So, I don't remember watching a lot of rugby, I remember doing a lot of counting money and trying to get money hidden somewhere safe.'

Before Cooper and Nicholson could hit the road the following morning, however, the former still had lots more work to do. Following the meeting, Cooper retired to her temporary press office at the National Sports Centre. Gwynne Griffiths, the National Sports Council for Wales principal, had agreed to arrange for one to be set up on the site the previous month. He had ensured the room had access to a phone line, a fax and a photocopier, all of which would be integral to Cooper's hopes of producing the official match programmes. What Griffiths had not been able to provide, however, was a window. More than 30 years on, the thought of the 'hot little room' she referred to as the 'bunker' evokes in Cooper a mixture of nostalgia and despair.

It was in the bunker that Cooper would spend the early hours of the opening day of the women's World Cup. The programmes produced for the pool stage matches were simple, four-page A5 affairs. The front page featured the names of the teams competing, the day, time of kick-off, venue and price (50p), while the disputed World Cup logo took pride of place in the top-right corner. The team line-ups were printed on the two inside pages, along with the name of the referee and a line to say that the balls being used had been donated by Gilbert. On the back page was printed the tournament's fixture list.

Although more rudimentary than the colour A4 souvenir brochure Cooper had sent to the printers a month before the tournament and which would be sold for the first time at Saturday's matches, the programmes still required a fiddly amount of work. Cooper was at the mercy of team managers when it came to supplying the line-ups on time and in a legible format. It was her job to type up the team lists for the printer, who would arrive at 7.00 am sharp to pick them up, so any spelling queries had to be settled by then. 'Quite often it would arrive on a handwritten piece of paper, and you couldn't read the handwriting,' Cooper recalls. 'You then had to go and find the coach or the selector and say, "How do you spell this name?"'

The finished programmes would be delivered back to the bunker before midday, at which point Cooper needed to get them to the match manager before they left for the ground. If they had already started their journey, then it was her job to get them there. The opening day provided a particular logistical challenge as the first match kicked off at 1.00 pm, albeit only four miles away at Glamorgan Wanderers' Memorial Ground. The other matches, though, were all scheduled to get under way at 2.30 pm, and with Pontypool Park 22 miles to the north east, and Swansea's St Helen's 43 miles to the west, time was tight.

'This is all pre-digital age, so I've got a dot matrix printer that I'm typing the programmes on,' Cooper says. 'A local printer would come and collect them at 7 o'clock in the morning, so I'd be up and doing it by then. The phone would start ringing at 7 o'clock … just endlessly, the press calling all the time.' Following the matches, Cooper would return to the bunker to type up match reports and phone them into news wires. 'You're not so much on a learning curve as [being] vertical, falling over backwards, you know. A lot of stuff we didn't know how to do at all, but blithely assumed we could.'

*****

Stuck in her windowless office, Cooper would have been oblivious to the gathering storm outside. For much of the morning, though, it would have been reasonable to question whether the matches she was producing programmes for would even go ahead. Statistically, 1991 was a dry year. According to the Met. Office's rainfall report, it was the 'driest since 1975 and the eighth driest [at that time] this century'. April, however, was not a dry month. On the contrary, it was 'unsettled, generally dull and wet'.

Nowhere in the UK was this more pronounced than in Wales. On the first day of the month, 96 mm of rain had fallen in 24 hours in Llanymaddwy in the north west of the country, and the wet weather barely let up. Over the next 30 days, South Wales experienced around 150 per cent of its average monthly rainfall. The organising committee had selected the dates for the tournament to maximise their chances of finding cheap and affordable university accommodation for the competing teams, during what was the Easter break. A wise decision, but one that put the tournament's opening matches on a collision course with some bleak weather.

It is apocryphal to suggest that no men's matches took place in Wales on 6 April. Aberavon, Ebbw Vale, Newport, Pontypridd and Glamorgan Wanderers, where Canada and New Zealand contested the first ever women's World Cup game, all hosted matches on what was a wet and bitterly cold Saturday. But three of those matches were abandoned, each when less than 61 minutes had been played. Aberavon's clash with Cheltenham at Talbot

Athletic Ground, where France had originally been scheduled to meet Japan before a late switch to Cardiff Harlequins, lasted only 55 minutes before the men succumbed to the weather.

Postponing was simply not an option for the women's World Cup. Theoretically, the Sunday and Tuesday were rest days as there was no rugby being played, but that does not mean they were free days. The following day, injured England flanker and WRFU development officer Carol Isherwood was due to facilitate a coaching conference which many of the coaching and management teams would have been expected to attend. Moreover, tickets for the Schweppes Cup semi-finals at the National Stadium had been provided by the WRU, which had also agreed with organisers to hold a parade of participating nations in the break between the two matches. On Tuesday, a second conference, titled 'The Way Forward', was scheduled to take place at the Celtic Bay Hotel, while teams had also been invited for a tour of the National Stadium and tea with WRU president Gwilym Treharne. Postponing matches would have proved extremely disruptive to the tournament's hospitality programme.

Griffin and Cooper do not remember fretting too much over whether the matches could be played, simply because there was no other option. In the England hotel, though, Dorrington and her teammates were less certain. 'I was playing at 10–11 per cent body fat. I had no body fat, and it was the coldest I've ever been in my life,' she says. 'We kept checking the weather, checking the weather, checking the weather. Are we going to play? Aren't we going to play? But we had to stay on schedule.'

Ultimately, it was left to the individual referee at each match to decide whether they thought the pitch was safe enough to play on. Fortunately for Griffin, Cooper, Dorrington and the players, Dave Morgan, David Swift, Laurel Lockett and Andy Evans all deemed that their playing surfaces were OK. 'We would have left it, as always, up to the referee to determine whether the pitch was playable or not,' Griffin recalls. 'Perhaps we should have taken a different view on it as it was a World Cup. But, like all games that we played then, it was the referee that determined whether the pitch was playable or not.' The final unforeseen obstacle had been overcome. History was about to be made.

*****

New Zealand's squad had made a confident entrance to Friday's opening ceremony in Atlantic Wharf. As they paraded through the quad, a group of the women's All Blacks (and whether Eddie Tonks liked it or not, that was exactly what they became known as in South Wales) turned heads for more than their new official tracksuits. Half a dozen or so players (including front rowers Tracey Lemon and Nicky Inwood, half back Anna Richards and centre Natasha Wong) had enjoyed a short stroll to the Errol Willy salon in Roath earlier in the day to get a fresh trim ahead of the World Cup. However, they were not after a perm or blow dry. Instead, the players requested the initials 'NZ' be shaved into the sides of their heads.

'We're doing this because it's good fun and we like to get the team spirit flowing before a game,' Inwood told the *South Wales Echo* at the time. 'It was lucky that some people were watching because I think the person that was going to [do it], she was going to shave it wrong. It was going to be "NS" or it was going to be something,' Wong recalls. 'Someone said, "Whoa, whoa, that's not right. It's actually a 'Z'". So, we all went and got that done as a group and that was a lot of fun.'

Wong cannot remember who tipped off the press about their trip to the hairdressers, but she is certain it would not have been the players themselves. 'Back then we weren't that media savvy, so we wouldn't even have thought to,' she insists, laughing at the thought. As Inwood had informed the *Echo*'s reporter Rhian Beynon, the excursion was the latest in a series of successful attempts to bond the players during what was a long trip away from home. New Zealand's players had already been on the road for ten days by the time they arrived in Cardiff, having enjoyed a stopover in Los Angeles, where they played a warm-up match, on their way to the UK. The squad landed at Gatwick on 28 March and played several games, including one against Richmond, before jumping on a coach to South Wales six days later.

Squad morale would clearly be tested during the four-week expedition, and so coach Laurie O'Reilly did his utmost to keep spirits high. 'Laurie was very into us singing post matches,' Richards remembers. 'So, we had a few Maori songs. One of the ones he loved was "Pōkarekare Ana", so he always used to love us singing that after we played teams and socialising with the other teams and just spreading the love of rugby.'

Those inter-squad singing sessions would take on another dimension on the eve of the tournament when word reached Cardiff that Māori leaders back home had for the first time given the team permission to perform a Haka, a traditional war dance, ahead of their Women's Rugby World Cup matches. The links between the Haka and rugby date from at least 1888, when New Zealand Natives toured the UK and performed one before matches. Seventeen years later, when the first All Blacks 'Originals' made the same voyage, they began games with a rendition of 'Ka Mate', which would remain the Haka of choice for the men's team for the next 100 years. Today, New Zealand's women's team, the Black Ferns, have their own Haka, 'Ko Uhia Mai', but back in 1991, there was no time for the players to do anything other than practise 'Ka Mate'. So, that is what they did.

By the time the team arrived at the Memorial Ground on Saturday 6 April, the players who had been selected for the historic match knew exactly what they needed to do. At approximately 12.55 pm on the outskirts of Cardiff, New Zealand centre Debbie Chase stood on the halfway line and looked through a crowd of photographers towards her opponents, Canada. Behind her, 13 of her teammates were arranged in a semi-circle, steely-eyed and ready for Chase to give them the signal to begin.[i]

'The Haka was pretty special, obviously, to most of us, but more so to the Maori girls in the team,' captain Helen Littleworth recalls. Richards adds, 'You grow up watching the All Blacks and it's a big tradition with them and we were only so new to being a team that we picked up our own traditions along the way, but it was very big. That sort of heritage is very important to New Zealanders.'

For Wong, the moment encapsulated the journey the players had been on to get to the point where they could compete on the international stage. 'It was pretty cool. Even just that first time hearing the national anthem, even thinking about it now, you can think about how emotional it was,' she says. 'I think also because it had taken so much to get there as well, it was almost like, "Oh my God, we've made it! We're here, we're doing it and how cool is this?"'

New Zealand harnessed the energy of that moment to score the first try in Women's Rugby World Cup history, as police officer Helen Mahon crossed the whitewash. Although the following day's *Observer* suggested 'the All Black women were pushed around in the set-piece', Canada had no answer in any other area of the match. O'Reilly had been told prior to the tournament that, in line with IRFB regulations, on-pitch coaching would not be allowed at half-time, and it certainly wasn't necessary at the Memorial Ground. New Zealand had a comfortable 16–0 lead by the break, which they converted into a 24–8 win as Mahon

---

[i] Nina Sio and Elsie Paiti were of Samoan and Cook Island heritage respectively and had not been given permission to perform the Haka. Sio had been selected to start in the second row at the Memorial Ground and therefore waited patiently on the sidelines as her 14 teammates performed the ritual.

completed her hat-trick, Haka leader Chase added two tries, and Geri Paul notched the other.

Both the World Cup and New Zealand were on their way, but clouds were gathering overhead. The opening match in Ely had been the only one to be played as a curtain raiser to a men's match as had been planned, which meant the teams avoided the worst of that day's weather. Players elsewhere, particularly those lining up for England, Spain, the USA and the Netherlands would not be so lucky.

*****

As the women All Blacks applied the finishing touches to their win against Canada in Ely, the three other seeded teams were preparing to make their World Cup debuts. France would do so a few miles up the road against Japan at Cardiff Harlequins, while the USA had been drawn to play the Netherlands at Pontypool Park, and England would take on Spain in Swansea. All three matches were scheduled to kick off at 2.30 pm, and in Pontypool and Swansea in particular, the weather would play havoc with proceedings.

St Helen's Rugby and Cricket Ground is an iconic stadium, its beachfront location the setting for many famous afternoons and evenings for supporters of Swansea and Wales. The most recent of those had come only three weeks previously when Robert Jones captained the All Whites to victory over Tondu and a place in the Schweppes Cup semi-finals. It is not, though, somewhere you would necessarily want to play when wind and rain are whipping in off the Bristol Channel. St Helen's sits on reclaimed sandbanks, separated from Swansea Bay only by Mumbles Road. Moreover, the uneasy truce made between oval- and red-ball games over space has left sections of the rugby pitch open to the elements.

It was not only the lean Dorrington, selected at hooker for England with Ponsford among the replacements, who found conditions tough going as the storm intensified. The weather was also taking a toll on the usually unflappable Karen Almond. Less than 15 minutes into the match against Spain, the England captain, fly half and general talisman had to ask her half-back partner Emma Mitchell to stop passing her the ball so much. 'She was putting out her hands mainly just for a static sort of pass directly to her because she was having to kick so much,' Mitchell recalls.

'I was hitting her hands, which is what I'd usually do, and I'd be proud of that, but it was just hitting her hands and going on the floor. She came over to me and she said, "I can't feel my hands." And I've got this lovely picture where I'm just rubbing her hands and she's just stood there, and she ended up saying to me, "You can't pass to me. You're just gonna have to keep running back-row moves or pick and go yourself or go blind to find the winger", because she said, "I can't catch." And this was 15 minutes in, so, I was like, "Oh my God, our best player, our game-changer, decision-maker and I can't pass to her!"'

'It was freezing,' Almond remembers three decades on, 'absolutely freezing!' Fortunately for their skipper, the joint-favourites were able to get the job done in Swansea as Cheryl Stennett, Claire Williets and Gill Burns scored unconverted tries. 'It was just a case of getting through that first game because it was horrendous,' try-scoring winger Stennett admits. 'Not very pleasant at all. Not a day for a winger.'

'A lot of the backs were pretty much suffering from hypothermia at the end of the game. They just got into the showers in all their kit for about 20 minutes and they couldn't even move, they were like penguins starting to turn the other way,' Mitchell adds. 'Bless, one of our wingers, three times she went over the line and rather than diving, she tried to put the ball down and dropped it. So, the score, actually should have been a really quite comfortable win for us. But the conditions and our lack of experience in perhaps just putting a game to bed or putting the ball down or diving with it, it was a real challenge.'

It was a similar story 50 or so miles to the east at Pontypool Park, where the USA, tipped by many to win the World Cup, struggled as much against the conditions as against their Dutch opponents. Disaster struck for the Americans less than six minutes into the match when scrum half Barbara Fugate suffered a knee injury and left the pitch on a stretcher. Her replacement Patty Connell set up the opening, and ultimately only, try of the game five minutes later, putting Patty Jervey into space on the blind-side wing to score an unconverted try. Andrea Morrell added a penalty before half-time. However, despite spending much of the 80 minutes camped deep inside the Netherlands half, the USA were not able to breach the committed Dutch defence again. 'Their 7–0 margin against Holland was seen as a shock result,' the *Observer* reported on Sunday.

One big reason why the USA's dominance did not translate onto the scoreboard was the icy rain which hit the players in horizontal sheets. Flanker Cathy Seabaugh, more used to the heat and humidity of Texas, became so disoriented by the deluge that she attempted to bind onto one scrum facing in the wrong direction. 'Somebody had to go over and grab her and bring her over to the other side of the scrum', Kathy Flores, who had watched on from the safety of the stands as a non-playing reserve that day, remembers. 'She got in kind of not knowing what she was doing. I think she was hypothermic.'

Seabaugh was soon taken off for her own safety, but it took her replacement Tara Flanagan several attempts to get her to leave the pitch. 'She was quite a thin person and if anybody had hardly any body fat, it was her,' Flanagan says. 'She wasn't getting the message. I was saying, "Go down, you're hurt" because you could only make a replacement for an injured player, and she was like, "Uh, what?"'

Back in the changing rooms after the match, Flanagan and her fellow replacements began ferrying cups of tea to players in the showers. In lieu of hot water coming out of the pipes, some resorted to throwing the drinks over themselves in an attempt to get warm.

'It was something to remember for sure, the fact that we all survived to me was amazing. Usually, when the conditions are kind of rough, you figure, "Well, once I get out there in the field and start playing, I won't even think about it." You couldn't stop thinking about it,' lock Tam Breckenridge recalls. 'It was tough, and then a few minutes in to lose our most experienced scrum half, it kind of added a sense we all had to step it up …. I was really worried for the safety of some of the players. It was just horrible, the conditions.

'The Netherlands, they were a strong team, they were a good team, they were an experienced team, and there was no give in them at all. It was something I think we survived. I never felt like we were going to lose the game, I was just worried we might lose some players …. I just remember afterwards, going to the showers and just standing and I couldn't stop shivering. I couldn't untie my shoes.'

Breckenridge had suffered a head injury during the match but was unable to clean the wound sufficiently for a doctor to look at it until she was back at the team's base in Cardiff. 'I had a cut on my head, and it was so muddy at the field, even with the shower that I had they wouldn't look at it until I got back to the hotel and by then it had closed up,' she adds. 'I couldn't talk, and I think most of us were in that situation. We were just shaking. People would bring tea and we were shaking so hard we were spilling it all over ourselves. I remember being glad afterwards that I brought extra shoelaces because they cut my laces off my shoes to get them off. It was happy times!'

Back in Cardiff, things were a lot more routine for the fourth and final seeds France. The match was momentous for the fact that it was the first World Cup game to be refereed by a female official. Floridian Laurel Lockett, who had travelled to the UK with the USA squad, could not have hoped for an easier afternoon as the French, with future Les Bleues coach Annick Hayraud on the bench, eased to a 62–0 win. Winger Fabienne Saudin ran in three of France's 11 tries at the Diamond Ground, while fly half Juliette Dalbarco contributed 12 points. A tough 80 minutes for Japan was compounded when they lost scrum half Ayako Horikita with a broken collarbone.

As Cooper headed back to the bunker to type up her match reports and begin the arduous task of ringing round news wires and sports editors, she would have been forgiven for feeling a little euphoric. The day had not been without its problems, the weather chief among them, while Horikita and Fugate were not the only players nursing injuries as they got into bed that night. Cooper, of course, had no time to pat herself on the back. The challenges would keep coming, only growing in size as the Soviet squad dunked Griffin in an Olympic-sized pool of hot water. It is also true that the organising committee had achieved what it set out to do. Griffin, Cooper, Dorrington and Forsyth had organised a World Cup and the women's rugby community had responded to their efforts. There would be dark days ahead, but on Saturday night it must have been tempting to crack open a celebratory beer and raise a glass to all those who had doubted them.

13

RESOURCEFUL RUSSIANS

SUNDAY 7 APRIL was a rest day for the teams competing at the Women's Rugby World Cup in South Wales, but having navigated the inclement weather of the previous day, storm clouds of a different kind were gathering for the organising committee.

Although there were no matches scheduled, the hospitality programme was packed with a coaching conference at Cardiff Institute of Higher Education and an excursion to the National Stadium to watch the Schweppes Cup semi-finals. Organised by Carol Isherwood, who had missed England's opening match as she continued her rehabilitation from a dislocated shoulder, the conference was the first to bring together coaches from across the international women's game. An England and Great Britain flanker, and former flatmate of Deborah Griffin and Chris Brown, Isherwood was one of her country's best players, but she was as important to the community for her work off the pitch as on it.

Isherwood, a former WRFU secretary, had initially committed her thoughts on the future of women's rugby to paper in

1988, the same year she agreed to become the female union's first development officer. Working with Rosie Golby, she had updated the proposal the previous September as they sought up to £12,000 in funding from the RFU, as well as a similar amount from the Sports Council and sponsorship, to make the role permanent. The coaching conference in Cardiff was, therefore, the first opportunity Isherwood had had to present those ideas to a wider audience. She was joined in delivering talks by Helen Ames, England coach Steve Dowling, her international teammate Sam Robson and their team manager Val Moore. Topics discussed inside the Institute's lecture hall included 'Improving Standards of Play', 'Youth Development', 'How to Tap Existing Resources' and 'Fitness for Rugby'.

Although the forum had a focus on the game within the UK, all interested coaches, administrators, team managers and players were invited to attend. 'You look back and you think, "Gosh, how did we manage all that?"' Isherwood says of organising the coaching conference while a member of the England squad. 'Now we'd be going, "Well, wait a minute, you should be focusing on your game." But for the '91 World Cup, before I even got to report in, I had to drive one of the minibuses to pick the Russians up at Heathrow and take them down to the event down in Cardiff. So, everybody was mucking in, I guess.'

The conference lasted all day, from 10.00 am until 4.00 pm, meaning those who attended were not able to take the WRU up on its offer of tickets to the day's Cup semi-finals at the National Stadium. Pontypool and Swansea had of course made it through to the last four and were drawn together in a de facto women's World Cup host derby, while Llanelli and Neath would compete to face the winner of that match in the final. It was a line-up that would usually have been expected to draw a big crowd to Cardiff. However, the decision to hold the event on a Sunday had received a huge backlash from fans. The debate raged for much of the season, and traditionalists from each club decided to boycott the match, insistent that rugby, men's rugby at least, should not be played on the Sabbath.[i]

If there was one thing that Welsh rugby fans detested more than watching matches on a Sunday, though, it was being confronted by players from England while doing so. Alongside its offer of tickets, and the ad placed in the match programme, the WRU had arranged for a group of players representing each nation to parade round the National Stadium to promote the women's tournament. So, when the women embarked on their journey along the narrow running track which encircled the pitch, the few wearing their dark blue Cotton Oxford tracksuits attracted the most attention.

Watching on from the stands, Emma Mitchell quickly realised she had made the right decision to stay put. 'Off they went, and they were spat at and shouted at,' she remembers. 'It was really quite unpleasant. It was a crowd that had had a fair few beers. It was more against the English than the fact it was women playing rugby, but I remember a couple of them coming back in tears, really upset by it.' Mitchell's half-back partner and England captain Karen Almond had been part of the parade. 'The Welsh crowd obviously didn't like the English players, so we got booed the whole way round,' she recalls. 'It was possibly a little bit more than boos, too, but I just ignored it, I mean tried to ignore it as much as I could.'

However much the unsavoury incident affected individual players, Almond and her teammates were not able to dwell on it too much. They had a crucial match to prepare for the following evening, against Pool Four rivals Italy in Llanharan. Win it and England were through to the semi-finals. They would take to the Dairy Field pitch once the Pool Three match

---

[i] WRU committee-meeting minutes record that the union considered the attendance at the semi-finals 'disappointing' and attributed it to the fact that a 'substantial number of supporters in Neath, Llanelli and Swansea objected to matches being played on a Sunday'.

between the Netherlands and the USSR had finished, but it was not their performance on the pitch which had people chatting about the Soviets.

It was amazing the Soviet squad had made it to South Wales at all, such was the destitute state they arrived in. Griffin had not exaggerated their financial plight when talking to Chris Jones earlier in the week. If anything, she had undersold it. When Isherwood and Ames collected the first Soviet delegation from Heathrow, they had been astounded to find that the team's luggage contained more items to sell or barter than actual playing equipment. It later emerged that much of the kit they had packed, albeit most of it intended for sale, had been stolen at Moscow Airport. The 'unforeseen difficulties connected with the provision of hard currency' which Viktor Ermakov had alerted Mary Forsyth to the previous Monday were so severe that Soviet players could not afford the bus fare from their base at the Institute to the National Stadium to watch the Schweppes Cup semi-finals. The players instead walked the four miles into Cardiff city centre: the lap of the pitch must have seemed a breeze by comparison.

Ermakov, coach Vladimir Kobsev and the players had an entrepreneurial solution to their cash crisis. However, thanks to press coverage in Monday's papers, their plan would not go unnoticed by those in authority. It was a headache Griffin could have done without as she continued to look for a way to solve the tournament's own financial struggles.

*****

Griffin remembers being woken very early on Monday 8 April as the big plastic brick she had been lent, which doubled as a mobile phone, began ringing. That morning, several articles appeared in the local and national press relating to the USSR squad and their penniless state. Speaking to journalists, Ermakov and Kobsev had laid out the financial challenges facing their team, who within two days had eaten all the salami and cucumbers they had brought with them for subsistence and now had to survive on nothing more than the free breakfast provided at the Institute. Some of the uneaten food, theirs and other people's, had been shovelled into bags for later in the day. 'We have no money and nothing to eat,' Kobsev told reporters through an interpreter. 'It is a desperate situation. The girls love rugby and are determined to play well.

'But the danger is that they will be too weak to provide serious opposition. It is tragic, they have all the heart in the world and have saved everything to come to Wales.'

The problem for Griffin, Cooper and the Soviet team was that the officials had also divulged their plan to make enough money to pay for their board and meals while in Cardiff – and it was not legal. Ermakov and Kobsev, perhaps naively, stated that they had brought with them enough cheap vodka, caviar, *shampanskoye* (Russian champagne) and souvenir watches to sell to punters in South Wales. 'Booze is one of the few things still plentiful and cheap in Russia,' Kobsev reasoned. The squad had also intended to bring enough Soviet-branded sportswear to trade, but most of that had gone missing at Moscow Airport and they needed what remained to get through the games.

Griffin had been made aware that the squad hoped to sell some souvenirs at their matches prior to their arrival in the UK. Viktor Svirisou had written to her in March seeking permission to hawk 'advertising materials such as booklets, calendars, watches' on the sidelines. In reply, Griffin stated that the organising committee had 'no objection' to that. However, Kobsev's current proposal was on a much bigger scale to what she had previously envisaged. One of the articles which appeared on Monday, in the *South Wales Echo*, reported that the Soviets hoped to sell the watches for £50 apiece. It was no surprise that the media coverage caught the attention of local customs officials.

When Griffin answered her gigantic mobile, she was informed that two representatives of Her Majesty's Customs and Excise were on their way to the Institute to talk to the Soviets. It is unclear whether Ermakov and Kobsev thought they could trade goods on the streets of Cardiff without a permit or licence, or assumed the authorities would not read the articles or take them seriously, but they were wrong either way. Griffin and Cooper immediately made their way from Sophia Gardens to the Institute and were there by the time the customs officers arrived on campus. 'I had to go and speak to them [the Soviets] and say, "Look, you can't do this I'm afraid",' Griffin recalls.

As the pair travelled the four miles or so to the Cyncoed Campus, almost certainly not on foot, the myriad legal implications of what the Soviet officials had allowed into the public domain would have been whirling round their heads. However, if they feared an outcome which would sink the tournament, such as a large fine they could not pay, then those concerns were quickly allayed when they arrived at the Institute. The squad was warned about trying to sell the goods which had been brought into the country; however, following what was described in the next day's papers as a friendly chat, the customs officials left without taking any further action.

'We accepted assurances that the alcohol imported into this country was within legal limits and would not be for sale,' a spokesman said at the time. 'As far as we are concerned, there is no problem.' Cooper, in her role as World Cup spokeswoman, told reporters, 'The customs men were extremely reasonable, but in the event all the publicity has led to several offers of help with food during their stay.'

It is a fair assumption that Ermakov and Kobsev spoke to the press in the hope of raising awareness of their plight, and perhaps some cash to help them during their stay, although members of the organising committee remain sceptical that they ever intended to pay up. The magnitude of the support must have surprised them, though, as the local community rallied to their aid. The following day, the squad was treated to a three-course lunch of leek and potato soup, chili con carne and cheesecake at The Bank café-bar on St Mary Street, having been taken on a complimentary trolley-dash at Marks & Spencer. The management at The Bank promised the Soviets a free meal every day for the duration of their stay in Cardiff. Clothes vouchers worth £1,800 were also provided by Cardiff Marketing Ltd, while Industrial Cladding Systems Ltd paid for the hire of a minibus for the party. There were offers of pizzas, food and accommodation from elsewhere too. An unnamed male Welsh international was reported to have donated £1,200 to their cause, and the mother of Bess Evans, a hooker in the Wales women's World Cup squad, pledged £100.

'I remember taking them to places like Marks & Spencer, where I think they gave them something like £50 or £100 each to spend on clothes,' Isla Meek (formerly Nicholson) says. 'I remember taking them down there. They were miserable as sin. You wouldn't think they were being given anything. It was obviously terribly political. I don't think we ever really got to the bottom of it all.'

Cooper and Griffin might have been cursing the Soviets on Monday, but the incident only increased the amount of coverage the tournament received, and not only in the broadsheets and local papers that had covered it up until this point. Suddenly, the tabloids were interested too, and the *Daily Mirror* was one red top that created some space for the women's World Cup, finding a few inches for the Soviet story and then sending women's editor Carole Malone to Llanharan to take in some of the action first hand. 'What it *did* do was give an edge to the publicity as that was the story that all the papers picked up,' Cooper says.

'Ironically, the tournament gained some traction and exposure because of it.'

*****

A considerable crisis had been averted thanks to the understanding customs officers, but while the Soviet squad and newspaper reporters were happy, and the organising committee relieved, not everyone shared their euphoria. Every team that had made it to South Wales had had to scrimp, save and scale countless other obstacles in order to do so, and there were those who felt those sacrifices were being taken for granted. It is also understandable that some members of the Wales squad would question why the businesses lining up to help the Soviets had not been interested in giving the Welsh players similar support for the tournament.

The tone of some articles was not helpful in this regard, either. One report which appeared in the *Western Mail* decried the plight of the Soviet players 'while the wealthy American and English girls are staying at luxury hotels'. This was easy journalistic shorthand at the end of the Cold War, and it is true that there were players in both squads who lived comfortably. There were many more, though, who had racked up credit-card and other debt to play the game they loved and envied the offers of food, shopping trips and money being sent the Soviets' way. That feeling only intensified as a result of the squad's alleged behaviour at the Institute. Kobsev told one reporter that his players were 'collecting unused food from the breakfast table', but according to some who were there at the time the bread and cornflakes they were storing away were very much in use.

This behaviour was not a surprise to the New Zealand squad, who had welcomed the Soviets to Canterbury for RugbyFest the previous August and now lined up alongside them at the Institute's breakfast buffet. 'They got to New Zealand literally with no money. I don't know how they got here. They literally had nothing, no money or anything like that and Laurie [O'Reilly] would have come to their rescue, I would say. We ended up having to organise accommodation for them,' says Natasha Wong, one of the RugbyFest organisers. 'We all, just as a team, sort of did what we needed to do to support them. So, I think they literally came over on the smell of an oily rag and yeah, pretty much we had to organise and fund a lot of their stuff.'

Although the organising committee was aware of the struggles the Soviets had faced the previous year, Cooper telling journalist Henry Winter ahead of February's draw that they appeared in New Zealand 'with little kit and extremely hungry', few involved with the World Cup could have understood just how tough life was for them back home. This was a time when the Soviet Union was crumbling. Following the fall of the Berlin Wall, a number of uprisings, both peaceful and violent, weakened its grip over Eastern Europe, while nationalist feeling in satellite states such as Estonia, Lithuania and Ukraine would push those nations, too, towards independence. The financial impact of the Era of Stagnation, moreover, and the move away from the planned economy under Mikhail Gorbachev were crippling for the general public.

Long queues were a common sight in Soviet towns and cities as people lined up for food and other essentials. Once they got to the front there was no guarantee that what they had waited patiently for would be there, as supermarket shelves, fridges and freezers regularly ran empty. Moscow, where the majority of the squad had been drawn from, was not immune to food queues despite being the capital. When the first McDonald's opened in the USSR in 1990, on Moscow's Pushkin Square, the queue to get in stretched for kilometres and contained as many as 30,000 people. As a Big Mac, fries and drink cost the equivalent of half a day's wages, though, it was only an extremely rare treat for most.

As the shelves became emptier and the queues grew longer, there was of course one way to make sure your family got to the front quicker or had that piece of meat put to one side by a friendly government official: bribery. And, as the willingness of Muscovites to queue for hours on end for a hamburger showed, there was a premium placed on goods from the West. That is most likely why, when let loose in Marks & Spencer, the Soviet players did not fill their baskets with stuff for themselves. Instead, their trolleys were piled high with trousers, shirts and shoes that would look good on family members back home, but also, possibly, could be used to secure that last piece of bread. If they looked miserable as they navigated the aisles of M&S, it might have been because they were resigned to shopping for others, unable to escape the struggles back home even when thousands of miles away.

Eileen Langsley worked at the World Cup as its official photographer and had travelled extensively through the Soviet bloc covering gymnastics and ice-skating events. She was not shocked by the state the squad arrived in or the methods they used to get by, only that they had been allowed to leave the USSR in the first place. 'If anything, I was surprised that other people were put out by it,' Langsley says. 'But they had no idea what conditions people were living in in the Soviet Union and how the chance to come to Britain and buy something from the West or get Western currency, you know, would have been a huge thing for them.

'They were great at pushing teams out here, there and everywhere when they knew they were going to win. I mean, if I'd got a fiver every time I heard the Soviet national anthem played for a gold medal I'd be a rich woman now. But I was a bit surprised they got out for rugby because they weren't going to win, and they were coming out for experience more than anything.... They didn't seem to have much of a KGB entourage with them, whereas I'd worked around the Soviets so much, and particularly in gymnastics, you knew who of the delegation was KGB. I knew a lot of the Russian [gymnastics] coaches really well, some of them are still really good friends, but we always knew we'd never even look at each other if somebody from the KGB was around. But I don't remember the rugby having a big KGB presence. Maybe it was a sign of the times, politically.'

*****

Whether the Soviet secret police reasoned the rugby players were a low flight risk, or just required more agents elsewhere, is not known, but the squad soon had to switch its attention to on-pitch matters. Only a few hours after the UK's customs officers had departed the Institute, Kobsev and his team set off on the 17-mile journey to the Dairy Field in Llanharan where they were scheduled to make their World Cup debut against the Netherlands.

Kobsev's fears that his players' sporadic diet would render them too weak to provide strong opposition on the Monday afternoon proved unfounded, at least from a disciplinary point of view. Referee Les Peard warned two Soviet forwards about violent conduct during the match in Llanharan. Ultimately, neither was sent off but, even with a full complement of players, the Russians were no match for the Dutch, who secured their first World Cup victory with a 28–0 win.

Two days later, the Soviets were back in action, this time at Glamorgan Wanderers' Memorial Ground, where they took on the USA. The USA coaches Kevin O'Brien and Chris Leach made wholesale changes to their starting line-up, and the dry conditions suited the running game they wanted to play. However, it was two survivors from the downpour in Pontypool who caught the eye. Winger Patty Jervey continued her try-scoring form with a hat-trick, while centre and stuntwoman Candi Orsini touched down twice. In total, the USA ran in nine tries to secure a 46–0 win and seal their passage to the semi-finals in style.

Orsini's mother Bette, a Pulitzer Prize-winning journalist, had accompanied the USA squad to South Wales and took an interest in her daughter's opponents on that Wednesday in Ely. 'My mom was hanging out with them. She just thought it was incredible that they were there,' Orsini recalls. 'She's always finding the story within the story, and so she thought it was incredible how they were selling goods in the stands and everything. She bought a police hat. I think I still have it to this day – a Russian police hat. I mean, they were doing what they had to do to be there. Really, you know, they were good players. They were great players, but they had this …. It was cumbersome for 'em, right? They couldn't just focus on their game. They had to do all this other stuff, you know, to help pay for the trip and stuff like that.'

MA Sorenson, who lined up at prop for the USA at the Memorial Ground, remembers some of the USA squad trying to trade the 'hideous' warm-up tracksuits they had been given by their union with their Soviet counterparts. 'They didn't even want 'em!' she says. Sorenson does still have a chocolate bar she bought from them in Cardiff ('It's wrapped up and I have it in a bookcase at home') and a number of her teammates returned after the tournament with Russian dolls, number plates and other knick-knacks from their Soviet opponents.

'We saw that their coaches were so passionate, and the players were so passionate to play rugby and to be part of it,' US second row Tam Breckenridge says. 'They were so passionate and so friendly and so excited to be there that you felt for 'em and didn't want to see anything bad. So, I helped. I was glad to hear that people stepped up, local people stepped up to help them out. Coming from Russia, you know, in those times, it was just amazing that they could come and be there and that they went through all the hoops and did whatever it took to get there and put together a team that wanted to take the field.'

It is perhaps unsurprising that Breckenridge and her fellow 'Lock from Hell' Tara Flanagan were impressed with the entrepreneurial spirit displayed by the Soviet squad. The Belmont Shore clubmates had brought a suitcase full of confectionary, cereal and protein bars to the World Cup from California. It was too much for two women to eat, and so their room at the Grand Hotel became an unofficial tuck shop. 'We did have a lot of stuff because we didn't know what the food supply would be,' Flanagan admitted.

'It was actually good forward-thinking because we had no time, and it wasn't like the team had team meals like they do nowadays or available food. So, yeah, we had a ton of food, Tam and I, and I don't recall actually selling much of it. People would tip us occasionally. I think we had a tip jar, but we would give it to people. People were like, "I missed breakfast. I didn't have a chance …", and we were like, "Oh, well, here's cereal." We had all kinds of things.

'So, that was fun, too, for us, because then everybody would come to our room, and then we'd get to socialise with people or get to know them better. Also, Tam had arranged a sponsorship through PowerBar … that was when they were in their early stages, so we had cases of PowerBars in our rooms. Some people on our team, if you offer them a PowerBar to this day, they'll sort of gag because we ate so many!'

Unlike the 'Locks from Hell', though, Griffin and Cooper do not retain fond memories of the Soviet squad. The problem for the organising committee was that the donations which were made did not filter through to them despite the Russians' accommodation tab standing at more than £5,000. It was even left up to a World Cup volunteer to remove the sponsorship message from the minibus Industrial Cladding Systems provided for the Soviet squad before it was returned first thing on Monday morning. 'The signmaker advises us that should the letters not come off easily a hairdryer will remove them,' the cladding company's owner John Lewis, assured Isla Nicholson in a fax sent on Friday. By the time the Soviet squad departed Cardiff, the size of their unpaid bill had swelled by the cost of the broken sink discovered in one of the player's rooms.

'I kind of got the impression that they were in some ways taking us for the capitalists who needed to be taken down a peg and laughing in our faces,' Cooper says. Griffin is even more succinct: 'I wouldn't care if I never saw them again.'

TIME'S UP FOR WALES

AS AMANDA BENNETT and Liza Burgess took to the stage at the Women's Rugby World Cup opening ceremony, they hoped to use their time at the lectern to remind those gathered in the County Hall courtyard that they were in Wales. Burgess as Wales captain and Bennett, a fluent Welsh speaker, had been asked by the organising committee to read an affirmation of spirit and fair play alongside the England skipper Karen Almond. 'This is our opportunity,' Bennett remembers future Welsh Women's Rugby Union chair Delyth Morgan telling her. 'We've got to make sure that people know it's not a UK World Cup. You're in Wales and we start with this.'

That is not to say that there was any ill feeling between Bennett or Burgess and the London-based organising committee – far from it. Both lived and worked in England and played their club rugby for Richmond's city rivals Saracens. They had also represented Great Britain multiple times, training and playing alongside most of the England squad, including the World Cup's commercial manager Sue Dorrington. The pair had been at the vanguard of the growth of the women's game and had witnessed the sacrifices which had been made to get it to this point. Bennett and Burgess, with a daffodil pinned onto each of their Cotton Oxford tracksuits, just wanted to make sure a nod was given to the host country.

'We were really privileged,' Bennett says of participating in the ceremony. Burgess remembers: 'I suppose looking back at it, you don't really think about "Oh, we're making history". But it was just we realised the occasion was a huge occasion, and [there was] a huge sense of responsibility. So it was incredibly exciting but also a huge honour to be part of it. Looking back, it was just exceptional.'

The feeling that the World Cup offered Wales an opportunity to assert itself as a women's rugby nation certainly fits with events which were rumbling in the background at this time. On 4 April 1991, as teams continued to arrive in South Wales and Bennett and Burgess prepared to make their contribution to the opening ceremony, a bid for change within the WRFU was being typed up in Swansea. The proposal, signed by Swansea Uplands WRFC secretary Maddie Austin, concerned the structure of the women's union and argued for greater autonomy for both Wales and Scotland.

Since its creation in 1987, the WRFU's Welsh committee had been responsible for the running of the game in the country. This included, but was not restricted to, overseeing the Wales national team which contested test matches and the Welsh Counties side which competed in regional competition, as well as the East and West select XVs which met annually. The committee selected a representative on the WRFU committee, who for the season leading into the World Cup was Dahne Gammon. This set-up put the Welsh committee on the same rung of the union's organisational chart as the regional committees in England.

As women's international rugby began to take on more importance, an increasing amount of the Welsh committee's work started to focus on the national team, in terms of securing fixtures and selecting the side. Gammon first requested a meeting with WRFU officers in March 1990 to discuss the union's structure. These talks resulted in the appointment of team managers for both the Wales and England teams, but did not sate the Welsh committee's appetite for change. Securing funding from outside sources such as the WRU or Sports Council for Wales was difficult while the WRFU retained overall control of the women's game in the country.

This was the basis of Austin's plan, whose proposed structure would create three national committees for England, Scotland and Wales operating under the umbrella of the WRFU. In her view, this would 'allow the further expansion of the WRFU into a more cohesive and workable structure, ensuring an equal and balanced approach to the needs of individual countries within the WRFU.' Under the proposal, each national committee would supply a representative to the overall board, with voting power resting solely with those three delegates. The document was seconded by Newport WRFC on 5 April, the day of the World Cup opening ceremony, and supported by a further 13 clubs before it was sent to the WRFU secretary Rosie Golby.

It is unclear when Golby received her copy of the proposal, but she certainly didn't have time to consider its implications until after the World Cup had concluded.[i] Concerns over the structure of the WRFU and whether it could support further growth were not only held by Austin and her peers in Wales, however. There was also scepticism as to whether the men's home unions would be willing to support them. The debate would rage during the ensuing months, and in January 1992 a special conference was held on the matter with input from the Sports Council. These steps ultimately led to the dissolution of the WRFU in 1994

[i] When Golby did consider the plan, her concerns about it contained a slight echo of the attitude the RFU had taken to their fellow home unions' attempts to set up the IRFB more than 100 years earlier. 'There is no proportional representation, i.e. Wales with 25 clubs has as much say as England with 90 clubs,' she wrote to Griffin.

as each nation went its own way. For now, though, Bennett, Burgess and their Wales teammates were determined to assert themselves on the pitch.

*****

Wales would have to sit and wait to make their Women's Rugby World Cup debut, though, forced to watch on as Pool One rivals Canada and New Zealand took to the pitch at the Memorial Ground on the opening day. Not that the players were necessarily unhappy to do so. As guests of the National Sports Centre for Wales in Sophia Gardens, the squad had lots of ways to entertain themselves as the clock ticked down to their opening match against Canada on Monday 8 April. The players had free access to all the amenities on site, the only restriction being a request from their management not to use the swimming pool too close to matches.

'For us, to be staying in the rooms there and having all the facilities and whatever, that was something on its own actually,' says Bee Davies, who practised judo at the Sports Centre and so knew her way round Sophia Gardens. 'We felt that we'd been recognised that we were allowed to stay there, [although] we had to pay for it.'

Confidence was high as Monday arrived and the players prepared to take on Canada at Glamorgan Wanderers. Since playing their first women's test against England at Pontypool Park in March 1987, Wales had played seven matches. They were yet to taste victory, losing to both the Netherlands and Catalonia in that run. However, with only the pool winners progressing to the semi-finals, they knew that they needed to beat a similarly winless Canada if they were to have the impact on the tournament they craved.

Burgess had represented Great Britain at the European Cup in 1988 and was recognised as one of the best players in the country, having also been a founding member of Saracens WRFC and helping to turn it into a top-division club. Nothing she had previously achieved, however, came close to the feeling of captaining her country in a World Cup. 'Words really can't describe that sense of emotion that you get,' she says. 'Being selected to play for your country is massive and then to get that honour as well was just … you just feel incredibly proud, overwhelmed. You just want to do the best you can as a captain and lead the team in the best way you can.'

Burgess had her great friend and Saracens teammate Bennett to lean on when making decisions during matches, and as the game against Canada progressed, things were going according to plan. Fly half Bennett had slotted a first-half penalty to give her side a 3–0 lead at the break, which became 9–0 in the second period after Philippa Evans profited from a Burgess interception to score her side's first World Cup try. However, Canada soon hit back through Corinne Skrobot, who touched down following a dominant scrum from the North Americans. Micheline Green converted to cut the Canadian deficit to just three points, but with time running out it looked as though Wales had done enough.

The problem for Wales was time never seemed to run out. As the game continued deep into injury time, Burgess and her teammates assumed the next stoppage would signal the end of the match. Each time, though, referee Andy Evans waved play on until a tired Kate Richards, usually 'safe as houses' under the high ball, dropped one and as Canadian players homed in on the scene, a red jersey picked up possession in an offside position. 'We're all going "Noooo!"' Bennett remembers. '"Don't touch that ball", but she did.' Evans blew his whistle to give Green the opportunity to level the score from in front of the posts. She made no mistake, securing an improbable draw which kept both teams winless and did neither any good in terms of reaching the last four.

'We thought we should beat them, and we should have beaten them,' Bennett adds. 'We made mistakes, but that should never have happened. We were winning, the game should have finished, including injury time.' Bennett and others who played for Wales that day remember referee Evans telling them later: 'I lost track of time, I was enjoying myself so much.' Whether that was true or not, it provided the squad with scant consolation as the magnitude of the result sank in.

'We'd worked really hard, and we were always a good team, but not quite good enough,' says Kate Eaves, who lined up in the second row against Canada. 'I think we felt like we should have won that one. We put ourselves in a position to win it and just didn't quite have that killer instinct, really. And, you know, we had a couple of games like that previously where we'd been really close to victory, but it just wasn't quite our day. Funnily enough, that's the only match my mother has ever watched me play.'

Qualifying for the semi-finals was always going to be a tall order in a pool which contained New Zealand, but the nature of the draw against Canada made the task seem almost insurmountable. That was certainly the tone of the coverage which appeared in the Welsh press, which had suddenly begun to show an interest in the women's game as the World Cup was being played in its backyard. The match report in the following day's *Western Mail* spelt out the equation facing the tournament's home nation. 'Now they must concentrate on the job in hand – beating New Zealand tomorrow to go through to the semi-finals,' Cat Whiteaway wrote.

It was indeed a daunting task. New Zealand's women might not have had as fearsome a reputation as the male All Blacks but their defeat of the USA at RugbyFest the previous year marked them out as contenders at the World Cup. The relative ease with which they had beaten Canada in the opening match had further underlined the team's quality. Although the Welsh players were aware of the increased media interest in them during the tournament, they didn't need anyone to tell them they would need to be at their absolute best to secure their place in the semi-finals. Reflecting on the Canada draw three decades later, Jackie Morgan says, 'In the end, it didn't really make any difference to our journey.'

The team's voyage would take them to Llanharan on the afternoon of 10 April, and there were hopes within the squad that the venue might give them the edge they desperately needed. Wales had trained numerous times on the Dairy Field pitch as it was their physio's home club, a fact which guaranteed they would receive a warm welcome and the support of a small but vociferous crowd. Before the match could get under way, though, New Zealand first had to perform their Haka. But as the Welsh players linked arms and prepared to face it, a swarm of photographers and cameramen appeared like a solar eclipse to block their view.

'The media were all over it,' Bennett recalls. 'In front of us were probably a dozen photographers and people filming it, to the extent where in some cases you couldn't actually see it.' Incensed, Wales team manager Dawn Barnett rushed onto the pitch in an attempt to clear the phalanx of snappers so her players could enjoy one of the game's most special rituals. 'I said, "You have to move. You cannot stand in front. The teams have got to be facing each other." And they just went, "No, this is where we're standing." I said, "This is absolutely shocking. This is so disgraceful and disrespectful to the Welsh and the New Zealand teams."'

Once Debbie Chase had led her teammates through the Haka, and the photographers and cameramen had finally left the pitch, Wales did their best to cause the upset they needed. Much to the delight of the 1,000-strong crowd standing on the sidelines, the Welsh pack was more than a match for their opponents. The problem came, as it often did, when they opened up and tried to play with width. The Welsh backs were sadly no match for those wearing black. 'A confident New Zealand set out to prove their superiority over Wales but didn't find it as easy a job as they expected,' Alice Cooper would later type in the bunker. 'The Welsh forwards dominated the Kiwi pack throughout the game but the New Zealand backs proved again and again that their swift running and slick handling was all that was needed.'

New Zealand scored twice in an absorbing first half, both finished by winger Lesley Brett, but the hosts remained in touch at half-time, trailing 10–6, thanks to a pair of Bennett penalties. Wales' work-rate never let up in the second period and, according to Steve Jones in the *South Wales Echo*, 'with a fraction more luck and judgement, the backs could well have opened up the Kiwi defence'. From the moment Anna Richards scored New Zealand's third try, though, there was only going to be one winner, and Brett completed her hat-trick in the final quarter before Amanda Ford put the seal on a 24–6 win and a place in the semi-finals.

According to the *Western Mail* reporter Whiteaway, the set-piece manoeuvre which put Ford over in injury time was 'one of the most complicated penalty moves surely to exist'. Wales fly half Bennett certainly found it hard to do anything other than sit back and watch. 'We knew playing New Zealand was gonna be incredibly tough and that was a lesson. Oh, boy was that a lesson in how to play rugby,' she says. 'I wish I was a spectator because it was a joy to watch. You're not supposed to say that when you're playing opposite, but it was a joy to watch, and they had a particular penalty move (and I just thought "Oh, that's beautiful!") which was a double pivot that left us really scattered.'

'The physicality and the skills were just way above what we were used to,' remembers Morgan, who was able to watch the match unfold as a replacement. 'They were just obviously head and shoulders above. They were regimented, they were physical, their skills at passing, their kicking game, everything was just way above what we were used to. But the girls really, really stuck in, especially the forwards. They really stuck in and gave them a physical game. But, you know, in the end, they were just so much more powerful and so much faster.'

Following the match, the teams retired to the clubhouse where the New Zealand players pulled out a guitar for a sing-song with their opponents and Llanharan members. 'The club afterwards was buzzing,' Morgan recalls. 'We had a brilliant time.' Victory had put the women's All Blacks through to a semi-final against the USA at the Arms Park in two days' time. In the final on Sunday, the winner of that match would face either France or England, who had topped Pool Two and Pool Four respectively. For Wales, there was a much tighter turnaround, as a match against the Netherlands in the Plate competition awaited at Cardiff Institute of Higher Education the following day.

However, the press reaction to the defeat to New Zealand was positive, predicting better results to come. 'For although the host nation are now left to turn their attention to today's Plate Competition,' Steve Jones wrote in Thursday's *South Wales Echo*, 'they can do so with justifiable optimism.' There was also evidence of the progressive impact the World Cup was having on the clubs which hosted matches. 'In the old days, the men would have thought it diabolical to see women playing rugby and knocking back pints,' Llanharan chairman Malcolm Hall told reporter Helen Weathers. 'But it's great, absolutely wonderful, to see ladies playing here. Myself, I think it's done a lot of good for rugby. We are not living in the dark ages.'

Wales coaches Les Hill and Jim Pearce also got swept up in the upbeat afterglow of their side's performance, telling the *Pontypridd Observer* that 'the team is starting to improve and shape up as they hoped'. Angela Griffiths' article would not be published in the weekly paper until the following Thursday, by which time the World Cup was done and dusted and the co-coaches' words rang hollow. Less than 24 hours after their committed display against the women's All Blacks, the Welsh bubble had well and truly burst, and Hill and Pearce found themselves in the firing line.

*****

Although some Wales players woke up on the Thursday morning with a heavy head, there was an expectation that a first test win was only a few hours away. Whether the demanding schedule forced the coaches' hands, or they felt compelled to make an example of players who had defied their alcohol ban the previous evening (or they simply wanted to give squad members who had paid money and trained hard a taste of World Cup action) is unclear. What we do know is Hill and Pearce elected to rest a number of senior players for the Plate quarter-final against the Netherlands, and the decision backfired.

Fly half Bennett, who retained her place from the New Zealand match, kicked a penalty, but it wasn't enough as the Dutch secured a 6–3 victory on one of the Institute's training pitches. It wasn't where many of the squad had hoped their World Cup journey would end. Already knocked out of the main draw, it meant that Wales' involvement in their home tournament was over within three days of it beginning. In the minutes and hours after the final whistle sounded, the frustration that some of the players felt began to turn to anger.

'We were really just hoping to win our pool games and see where we got,' captain Burgess remembers. 'But then we got to the Plate and our coaches decided they were going to rest some players, and then we ended up losing to Holland. It was just a ridiculous thing to rest players. It wasn't the days when you could rest players, because our squad wasn't big enough.

We didn't have enough depth in our squad. That was a decision that wasn't great.'

Morgan was one of the players who benefited from the decision to rotate, coming into a pack which had impressed in the opening two matches. She does not remember her second cap with much fondness. 'It was really, really disappointing because our coaching team, they were dedicated and committed and good, but they kind of took the attitude that everybody wanted to get a game,' she explains. 'But we didn't have a strong enough squad to justify that, and we should have put out our best possible team and gone all out to win that game. I think it was an important game to win and I think the attitude on the coaching staff was people who've put in the effort deserve to have a game in the World Cup, which ... I mean, it's arguable, but to me, it wasn't the right thing to do, and we put out a weak team.'

'I was never very impressed by them,' prop Davies insists. 'I played in various teams and had various coaches and I knew that they weren't up to scratch. We had better ones for Wales. I would like to think I didn't actively revolt with the others, but I certainly wouldn't have been sad to see them go.'

As the mood in the squad became more mutinous, team manager Barnett sought out WRFU secretary Rosie Golby to discuss the situation and inform her that a group of players were keen to get rid of Hill and Pearce. 'I met with Rosie, and I said, "Look, I've got a real problem in the Welsh camp at the moment. The players want to sack the coaches",' Barnett recalls. 'Rosie is going, "Well, this isn't good. This isn't a good image for Wales women to sack their coach three-quarters of the way through the World Cup. It's just not going to look good. It's not professional." She said, "You need to go back to them and speak to them and tell them you've just got to suck it up. You're out of the World Cup. You've got to move on and keep with it, and then we'll discuss it after the World Cup."'

That is the message Barnett took back to her players, and without any competitive matches left to play, it seems it was enough to ensure the heat was taken out of the situation. The passage of time has certainly cooled Bennett's opinion of the 1991 World Cup coaching ticket. 'I think the mood in the camp had shifted. In that game, we knew we should have beaten them. No question, we were better than the Netherlands,' the fly half says. 'We're amateurs, people have trained hard, they've paid a lot of money, they've taken time off work and to say to them "You're not going to play in the World Cup" …. There is an argument for it [rotation], and you could say, "Well, we lost, so it's their fault." That's rubbish.

'As far as I'm concerned, when you pull on a Welsh team shirt, when you put on a Saracens team shirt, if you are in that team then you're in the team and you must demonstrate that you're good enough to wear it. There is personal responsibility. There's also collective [responsibility]. I think the night before, something had happened and we'd got back a little bit late. We hadn't properly prepared, took it for granted, were complacent. Even with the changes in the team, we possibly didn't take it as seriously as we had done Canada and New Zealand. So, I think that that defeat is all on us.'

*****

By the time that Barnett caught up with Golby at the Institute, a BBQ and disco for the teams and volunteers was getting started. It offered everyone involved with the World Cup an opportunity to relax with a cold beer and chat to those they might previously have met only on a rugby pitch, if at all. Those four teams whose tournament was over could enjoy themselves a little more than those who had a match to think about the following day. One person on her way to Cyncoed Campus for a hard-earned drink was Deborah Griffin.

It had been a long week for the organising committee chair. Having managed the fall-out from the Soviet revelations on Monday and helped to deliver the squad to Marks & Spencer for their trolley dash, she spent the rest of Tuesday at the Celtic Bay Hotel where the first ever international women's rugby conference took place. Titled 'Women's Rugby – The Way Forward', it had been organised by Golby primarily to give attendees an insight into how women's unions in the UK and USA operated, to debate the need for an international body, to discuss lessons from the current World Cup and begin the process to identify the host of the next one. Griffin gave a presentation on her experience heading up the organising committee, while there were also contributions from Golby, USA RFU women's committee member Jami Jordan and Sallie Barker from the Sports Council. Keith Rowlands and Denis Evans of the WRU were both invited to the conference, although neither was able to make it.

'It was focused on the game and what was happening worldwide. There was reference at that time to "Can we organise ourselves so that we have a women's IRFB?" Jordan recalls. 'It was becoming clearer that, "Wow, you have a lot more social structures here that would support women in sport than we do in the US." So that was, I felt, a bit obvious, even though we were all struggling with the same things, trying to grow the sport, and trying to do it while fighting with a lot of men, quite frankly.'

Jordan was particularly envious of the Sports Council and the support it was willing to give women's rugby in the UK. 'There are so many sports in the US that the men couldn't even compete for money, much less the women,' she explains. 'We don't have anything like that in the US. It still is every dog for themselves … Infrastructure to support the game or women playing the game was just not something that we were gonna have in the US, and teams that were going to have that were going to benefit, definitely.'

Rowlands might have been particularly interested to listen into the deliberations about the merits or otherwise of an international women's rugby body. France had attempted to set one up in 1988, and the WRFU had initially been receptive to the idea. However, after Fiona Barnett attended a meeting of the organisation in Paris, which she reported was 'run and organised by the French for the French', that interest waned. In truth, the 1,000 francs annual membership fee proved prohibitive, while there were also concerns that joining could cause friction with the RFU as the body was affiliated to the FIRA. Interestingly, France were one of the two nations that did not send a delegation to the Celtic Bay Hotel. They were not in the room, therefore, when it was decided a second World Cup should be held in 1994, and that a conference to elect the host nation would take place in Madrid in September.

Griffin had agreed to compile a list of requirements for the potential host nation, but the 1994 tournament would have been far from her thoughts as the current World Cup continued apace. On Thursday evening, Griffin accompanied Golby, Cooper, Sue Dorrington, Tom Purvis and Deborah James, as well as the captains and team managers of each participating nation, to a civic reception with the lord mayor of Cardiff, John Smith, at Mansion House. The end of an arduous week was coming into view, and it was an opportunity to toast what had been achieved to date and look ahead to an exciting weekend to come.

It also gave her an opportunity to catch up with people she hadn't seen all week as she raced from ground to ground, crisis to crisis. As the function came to an end, and with husband Chris looking after Victoria back at Sophia Gardens, Griffin decided to continue her night at the Institute, where the rather less-formal disco was in full swing. It was there that she bumped into Gwynne Griffiths who, as principal of the National Sports

Centre for Wales, had been a key ally to the organising committee on the road to Cardiff.

The pair had each worked incredibly hard to make the World Cup a reality, but while there was plenty to celebrate, Griffiths was in no mood for pleasantries. 'He started having a go at me about how I was only doing it for my ego .... I'm probably the least egocentric person you'll find. I don't do it for me,' Griffin recalls. 'I was just doing it to make sure that we had a World Cup, and I certainly didn't put myself forward in any way to lord it. So, that was quite hurtful because it was suggesting something that just wasn't true.

'He'd done an awful lot as well. I mean, he was the person who got the dinner done, he was the one who got the opening ceremony done. He had worked really, really hard. I think even at the time, I thought, "Well, actually, I think this is because we're not making enough of you." And that's probably the case, you know. I probably should have made more of people like him as well, but it wasn't that I was making something of myself. It was just that we were all getting on and organising it.' Griffin left the disco in tears, but as she returned to Chris and Victoria, she knew there was still much to get on and do.

15

'HARDER, STRONGER, FASTER'

AS ASSISTANT COACH Chris Leach watched his USA players train on the eve of their women's World Cup semi-final against New Zealand, he detected a nervousness in them he had not noticed before. Having beaten both the Netherlands and the elements in Pontypool on Saturday, the Americans roared into the last four with a nine-try defeat of the USSR in the Cardiff suburbs on Wednesday evening. The USA were yet to concede a point, but in truth the team had not been tested, by their opposition at least, and that is exactly what they expected from the women's All Blacks the following evening.

By the time their victorious players had walked off the Memorial Ground pitch a little more than 12 hours previously, Leach and head coach Kevin O'Brien had already switched their focus to the challenge that awaited at the Arms Park. The identity of their opponents on Friday was no surprise. Before a ball had even been kicked in South Wales, the pair had reasoned New Zealand would provide the biggest obstacle to their hopes of World Cup success. They didn't underestimate England or

France on the other side of the draw, they just believed that beating the women's All Blacks would provide the squad with a surge of confidence going into the showpiece match.

'Chris and I talked about this, that if we got by the New Zealand game, we were in good shape,' O'Brien explained. 'We had to get by that New Zealand game, and that was our mindset. We didn't think about the Sunday. We were just thinking about the New Zealand game, because what was going to happen on the Sunday was going to happen, but if we didn't get through the New Zealand game, it didn't matter.'

O'Brien and Leach had been coaching the USA squad in tandem for almost two years and enjoyed working together. Both had grown up in traditional rugby countries, the head coach in Wales and his assistant in South Africa, where O'Brien also spent time. The Welshman had enjoyed a nomadic existence since qualifying as a PE teacher in London in the late 1960s, travelling extensively through the rugby-playing world. In 1977, he hitch-hiked his way through New Zealand and Australia in pursuit of the 1977 British and Irish Lions and stayed long enough in the latter to enrol on the country's first coaching course.

Unable to find regular work in Wales, O'Brien then embarked on short stints coaching and supply teaching in Boston, Massachusetts. It was while on one of these trips that he was persuaded to share his knowledge with female players by USA great Karen Onufry. 'My response was, "Women don't play rugby",' he admits, 'and they've never allowed me to forget it!' The Welshman was soon won over by the players' enthusiasm and dedication, and following another spell back home, where he completed a WRU coaching course, he agreed to return to coach Beantown, one of the USA's premier sides. Supposed to be a season-long stopover as he made his way back to Australia, that year turned into two, then three, then four, and, as the national titles began to stack up, he never left. The World Cup offered an opportunity to return home and introduce his partner and newborn baby daughter to his family and friends in Cardiff.

Leach's own journey to the States was rather more straightforward. Born in Zambia, he finished his education in South Africa and went on to play rugby at the University of Witwatersrand in Johannesburg. It was during this time that a friend asked him to help out coaching at a local school, which proved a 'real buzz'. When, due to security concerns in Johannesburg, he relocated to Minnesota with his US wife in 1985, Leach used rugby to acclimatise to his new surroundings, coaching both men's and women's sides. He found working with women much more rewarding and fun, however, and after leading the University of Minnesota to national success, he came to the attention of the USA RFU's women's committee.

One of the things the coaches shared was an old-school fondness for hard training sessions. During his time as a player in Johannesburg, Leach would drink in the same pub as members of the revered Diggers club after Thursday night training sessions. Talking to provincial stars and potential Springboks as they dripped sweat onto the dusty floor instilled within him a belief that effort outweighed everything else in preparation. 'The thing that I learnt was them saying, "You know what? We look forward to the game because we know it's not going to be as hard as the practice",' Leach says. 'There's a lesson in that.'

In O'Brien, Leach had found a kindred spirit and, having identified the scrum as a key battleground against New Zealand, the former devised a gruelling training plan for his forwards. It was O'Brien, a wizened former front row from his globe-trotting playing days, who had responsibility for the pack. On that Thursday, barely 24 hours out from the biggest match of their careers, he put the USA pack through scrum after scrum after scrum, each at match intensity. 'I believed in scrummaging and rucking, and basically that's what I was going to do. If they could survive the scrummaging sessions, they could survive the game,' the Welshman recalls.

'For me, that was one of the worst practices of the whole tournament because we just kept scrummaging and scrummaging,' prop MA Sorenson, who emerged from the session with a black eye, suggests. 'The back row was like, "Oh, please don't make us do anymore", you know? That's the flankers, come on! And then when you walked away, you could see the steam coming off us … it was crazy.' Second row Tam Breckenridge concurred that training intensified as the week wore on. 'Scrummages were much harder, line-outs were heavily contested,' she says. 'There was no touch or tag. Everybody was going for it. We knew starting positions, roster spots were on the line. We knew we had a very fierce opponent …. We knew we were in for a fight. We knew we were in for a very physical dogfight against New Zealand. And you could tell we picked it up in practice at that point.'

It was an approach which created more steam than just that rising from the backs of the forwards as they hit yet another scrum. Winger Krista McFarren remembers Leach taking her to task for a lacklustre showing in one training session. 'He got in my face,' she recounts, 'and he said, pretty much, "Get your shit together." I've told my daughter since then, you know, sometimes it takes somebody jolting you a little bit to kind of go, "OK, all right. I'm going to show you I'm better than this," you know, or you can implode. So, I went out on that field, and I was like, "I'm playing, I am *playing*. Chris is going to see what I got here."'

The air of anxiety which Leach had picked up on round the squad had nothing to do with the intensity of the training session or uncertainty about who was going to be picked the following evening, however. Neither was it a fear of New Zealand, who had inflicted on the USA their only defeat to date: 9–3 during

RugbyFest the previous August. O'Brien had not been able to afford to take the time off work to travel to Canterbury, so hadn't been with the squad, while Sorenson had missed the trip to get married. Other players, such as second row Tara Flanagan, had come into the team since then and there was a feeling they were in better shape. No, what had created the tense atmosphere within the playing group was the uncertainty about how they should face their opponents' Haka.

It was something the USA players hadn't had to think about at RugbyFest, because New Zealand did not have permission to perform one then. That of course, had changed ahead of the World Cup, and there were those within the USA squad who believed it could give their opponents a psychological advantage in what would be a close match. 'I have the utmost respect for the nation of New Zealand, for their indigenous peoples, for their culture and their rugby tradition. Utmost respect,' Flanagan says. 'But my understanding of what the Haka is, is a message. A message of, "We're gonna kick your arse" and I don't know any sport where I would sit and listen to somebody before the whistle blew, somebody telling me they're gonna kick my arse, pardon my bad language.''

Unsurprisingly, given his background and the amount of time he spent thinking about the game, Leach had a solution. He had seen how different men's teams had chosen to face the All Blacks' Haka, or not, and had his own ideas about what the Americans should do at the Arms Park. Leach would come to regret the advice he gave the players.

******

As the Arms Park stadium clock ticked towards 6.00 pm on 12 April, Debbie Chase stood on the halfway line and prepared to start only the third rendition of 'Ka Mate' at a women's rugby match. Behind her, 13 women dressed all in black waited for their cue to join her in the ceremonial war dance. And waited. Referee Gareth Simmonds waited too. Beyond the row of cameramen crouching, ready to capture the scene, the USA team remained in its pre-match huddle, arms linked, chanting in unison 'Harder, Stronger, Faster'. That had been the USA squad's mantra since they congregated in Cardiff, and they continued to repeat those words after Chase had belatedly got the New Zealand Haka under way, not breaking off until their opponents had finished.

'I have to, with embarrassment, stick my hand up and say I was the one who said, "OK, here's what we're gonna do. You're in a huddle, stay in your huddle, talk to each other",' Leach admits. 'I took a couple of individuals aside and I said, "What are you going to say in the huddle? OK, good. How about this? How about that? " It was me that made that decision. I say I'm embarrassed because, at the time, to me, it was what I saw as a required and necessary tactic to defuse the power of the Haka for my people, but not to disrespect the nation.'

Three decades ago, the Haka did not have quite the same resonance as it does today. 'I don't think that we were as bound by this tradition of: you need to face the Haka and that's just how it's done,' Barb Bond, who captained the USA in the semi-final, insists. 'We decided what would be the best thing for us in terms of the competition and we just stayed tight together. I think that was the right thing to do, honestly. From the perspective of winning the match.'

That being so, Leach remembers speaking to a couple of women's All Blacks following the match: 'I said, "Listen guys, I apologise. It wasn't meant disrespectfully. It's just that our guys were so scared of you guys and your power in that sense, that I just had to do something and that's what I chose to do, but please forgive me.' The New Zealand players were really nice people, and they may not have forgiven me, but they say they did, and we had drinks afterwards and we had a really good party.'

New Zealand captain Helen Littleworth admits that her 'understanding of the Maori culture back then was limited', but 'for some of the women it was very offensive. I didn't understand the full ramifications of it. I sort of turned it round and added it to extra spice on the field, really. But I do know that some of the women were pretty upset.' Scrum half Anna Richards, though, believes the incident stemmed from a misconception of what the Haka means. 'I didn't see it as disrespectful,' she says. 'If you look at the Black Ferns' Haka today, it is just a story about us. And so, it tells you where we're from and we've come together and we're looking forward to the contest. So, I think some people don't understand what it's actually about.'

Once the Americans had broken from their huddle, referee Simmonds blew his whistle and the match unfolded exactly how O'Brien and Leach envisaged. An arm-wrestle of a match was decided by a pushover try from skipper Bond and a Chris Harju penalty. 'That was a huge moment,' Bond recalls. 'We had been training with one of the men's clubs in Cardiff and we had been working on that, and in training I had knocked the ball on! So, there we were in this moment, and it was a very tight game, and it was just textbook as I remember it. That's the moment that still brings chills to me, that pack try that we scored.'

Not that the forwards had all the fun on the Arms Park pitch. Patty Jervey almost scored a second try for the USA that would have gone down in the annals as one of the best ever scored in a World Cup. 'Jen Crawford made a break, fed it to Candi Orsini. Candi did her usual sidestep and gave it to Patty Jervey, who sidestepped three people in 15 yards and was diving over the line,' O'Brien says, reliving the moment as if etched on his brain. 'A marvellous bit of defence, I think it was from one of the centres from New Zealand, just dislodged the ball from her hand as she was going over. My mates who were there were just applauding because it was great defence but also great attack.'

'That's an interesting game for me. I was completely in the zone the entire game,' centre Orsini recalls. 'I remember being in the locker room before the game and I remember being in the locker room after the game. It was like it was a complete game in the zone and we won by a pushover try. It was beautiful. It was just the most beautiful thing. They probably expected us to take it to 'em in the backs because our backs were pretty well known, but, yeah, that pushover try was amazing.'

For the women's All Blacks, it was a crushing way to bow out of a tournament they had sacrificed so much to attend. 'It's never fun to lose,' Richards concedes. 'I was so disappointed I didn't ring my mum and dad for two or three days to tell them what happened. But, yeah, it was a hugely physical game, and the Americans always play like that. I remember we had quite a few injuries after that game as well, so it would have been interesting if we had made the final with the injuries we did have. They were a very good side, the Americans. They had a lot of experience in the right places, and it was a good contest.'

New Zealand's frustrations crystalised round the draw, and a belief that the organising committee had engineered it so that England would make the final. Accusations that the schedule had been modified during the World Cup week itself, which persist to this day, are demonstrably wide of the mark, though, as the schedule was published in the official tournament brochure, which was printed in March. 'We were just gutted to lose with a pushover try because it just felt like we weren't strong enough,' captain Littleworth says. 'That really hurt us, you know, especially as a forward pack.'

As the jubilant USA players headed up to the Arms Park's Airspace Lounge to enjoy some well-earned refreshment and take in the second semi-final, they knew a considerable hurdle had been overcome. 'To me, the New Zealand match was the final,' was Flanagan's verdict. 'They were so good.'

For O'Brien and Leach, the win served as vindication for their pre-match tactics. The Welshman, a World Rugby coach educator, admits he would no longer subject players to such an intense scrummaging session on the eve of a match, but says 'times were different' then. 'I wouldn't have done it if I didn't think they could do it,' he adds. 'Chris and I had long discussions about how we should approach the training and we knew that, forwards-wise, we were up against it. So, we had to be good at what we did and the backs we knew could run and we just needed to win 'em ball and let them go and support. But we weren't gonna do that ... without a front five.'

*****

Almost as soon as New Zealand and the USA had left the Arms Park pitch, players representing England and France were out and ready for their national anthems.[i] There was no pre-match Haka, but the rivalry between the sides was no less intense. Officially, the semi-final was the first time the two teams had met in a test. However, the enmity between them dated to the first Great Britain match at Richmond in 1986. France had won that encounter 14–8 and repeated the trick twice more, including at the European Cup in 1988, before the British secured victory in Jim Greenwood's final match in charge a year later. The tension between the two nations at an administrative level, and the fact France made the organising committee sweat before confirming their World Cup entry, only added to the occasion.

Carol Isherwood had recovered from her shoulder injury to take her place in the England back row for their match against

---

[i] Griffin requested the first semi-final kick off at 5.00 pm, but due to 'contract car parking difficulties' Cardiff's secretary insisted there was 'no way the first game on the Friday evening could start before 6.00 pm.'

Italy at Llanharan on Monday, where the pre-tournament bookies' favourites had found themselves in an unfamiliar position. Although England took the lead through a Sarah Wenn try, a mammoth Carla Negri drop-goal flipped the momentum. 'We were like, "Oh my God, I can't believe that!"' Isherwood admits. According to Michela Tondinelli, the 16-year-old scrum half who assisted Negri, it wasn't only the England players scratching their heads as she dropped the ball onto her foot. 'We played in the same club in Rome, and we often found ourselves kicking together, but she had never dropped a goal in a game before,' Tondinelli says. 'When she called to me for the ball against England I thought, "Now she does it?" And so it was: pure madness and magic.'

Steve Dowling's side were momentarily dazed and had to contend with losing Jane Mangham to injury as Nicky Ponsford came on for her first-ever appearance at loose-head prop. The Italians took full advantage, and two Lorena Nave penalties ensured the Azzurre turned round 9–4 in front. Dowling was not able to talk to the team at half-time as in-game coaching was banned in line with IRFB regulations at the time, but the players found a way to turn things about. A Gill Burns penalty early in the second half cut the deficit before Cheryl Stennett put England into the lead with a little less than 20 minutes remaining. Karen Almond crossed shortly afterwards before Stennett completed her hat-trick with two late tries that confirmed a 25–9 win. 'We really had to dig in to even get that win,' Isherwood recalls. 'It could have all been very different I guess.'

Isherwood retained the number-seven jersey for Friday's semi-final and was one of five players who had featured in that first Great Britain match against France at the Athletic Ground five years previously. Unlike Jayne Watts, Karen Almond, Debbie Francis and Sam Robson, though, she had missed the win at Roehampton in 1989 and so had yet to taste victory against the French. Due to a quirk of the fixture schedule, both England and

France, who secured their passage to the last four with a routine seven-try 37–0 defeat of Sweden at the Memorial Ground on Monday, had four days to prepare for their last-four showdown.

England's week had not been without incident, though. Midway through it, the Celtic Bay Hotel where the team was staying realised they were overbooked and, favouring their paying customers, requested the squad make alternative arrangements. Sue Dorrington, having organised the rooms, managed to keep hers, but her teammates were faced with the choice of finding other accommodation or sleeping on the floor of a conference room downstairs. 'Because I was one of the organisers and the hotel knew me, I stayed in my room,' Dorrington admits. 'A number of women had to sleep on cots downstairs, so I wasn't majorly affected by that because I was the contact and selfishly I stayed.'

Some players, Emma Mitchell included, elected to club together to pay for a room at a local bed and breakfast. 'It was one of those with the nylon sheets that you'd get stuck in,' she recalls. 'We had three or four in the room, so with just one bed, you know, two people were on the floor and two in the bed.' Number eight Gill Burns decided to stay put at the hotel, and instead tested one of the pull-out beds that had been hastily arranged in the conference room. 'In my early 20s, I could sleep anywhere,' she insists. 'You just did it and there was no point in getting stressed about things, I've always felt like that. You just look at what's in front of you and get on with it. Don't moan, never moan, always be thankful for the opportunities you've got, is my philosophy.'

Fortunately, England were safely back in their hotel by the time that Friday arrived. The question facing the teams now, though, was how best to prepare for an 8.00 pm kick-off. Both teams had experienced later matches for the first time four days previously, England taking on Italy at 5.45 pm in Llanharan and

France playing Sweden at 7.00 pm in Ely. But the concept of a night match was still an alien one to them. What should they do to keep focused with a long empty day between them and such a momentous match? Dorrington did what she did every day while at the Celtic Bay Hotel and headed out to the car park with a couple of teammates to practise throwing.

'My sports psychologist had spoken to [Dowling] and said, "Sue needs to stay focused. Keep her throwing." And that worked, because I didn't throw not straight throughout the tournament. I felt so good.' Others drifted into Cardiff or went bowling, taking out their rising stress on a Whac-A-Mole machine in the adjoining arcade. 'All I can remember is being really nervous and really excited,' Mitchell says. 'It was the first time we'd played an international in the evening, and the day seemed incredibly long, and I was just so eager to get the game going.'

Some of those nerves were evident on the pitch as England struggled to turn their dominance under the floodlights into points during the opening 40 minutes. Burns got her side on the scoreboard with a penalty, the number eight's booming toe-pokes often used to intimidate opponents early in matches. 'I had a toe-end kick like Mal Meninga and having big powerful legs I used to kick goals for England,' Burns explains. 'The fly-halves were always accurate, mine either went over or (one in five, I'd say) would go off at a 45° angle, but they went a long way. It was actually a tactic early on in an England game: if we got a penalty anywhere in the opposition half, I would attempt a toe-end goal because I could kick further than other girls could. So, it was to warn the opposition, "You slow us down, we've got a goal-kicker who can kick the distance."'

England could have turned round with a lead bigger than 3–0 had centres Robson and Claire Williets made better decisions when they had overlaps in attack, or had Almond converted one of her two drop-goal attempts. Robson remembers being on the receiving end of a sly headbutt, and, as tension rose, Dorrington attempted to land a more metaphorical blow on her opposite number Nathalie Francoise. 'There were two tactics I took into those tournaments, from two hookers I'd met along my journeys, and one was a dirty tactic that when the opposition hooker gets her [line-out] call, call back to her. Look at her in the face and call back to her,' she explains. 'I'd be in her face calling it back to her. I broke the French hooker, she was sobbing and I knew I had her.'

It was Burns who made the telling contribution early in the second half as she charged down an attempted clearance from Myriam Supice and then dived on the loose ball to notch the crucial first try. Burns added an impressive touchline conversion after Francis had finished off a flowing team move to put the seal on England's 13–0 victory. 'I can't remember the actual try but I remember it being a great night, and knowing that I'd had a good game,' Burns says modestly. 'I was pleased with my performance and couldn't wait for the big final, because we were playing the team everyone was talking about.'

Much like the USA two hours previously, victory was a momentous one for the England players and helped convince them that they were good enough to win the World Cup. 'I can remember it being an incredibly physical game and a very close game, and Debbie was so exceptional in scoring her try,' Mitchell says. 'That was huge for us. In many ways, once we got to that stage, every game obviously was a final. But to beat France as England and not as GB was huge.'

However, there was a warning at the end of the following day's match report in the *South Wales Echo*: 'England know they can expect a much tougher challenge from the USA tomorrow.' Would it be one they could rise to?

*****

As the post-match function started to wind down, Emma Mitchell and her twin sister Jane had more to celebrate than merely making the inaugural Women's Rugby World Cup final. The siblings would turn 25 on Saturday and, with a busy day of training now ahead of them, this was their chance to mark the occasion. So, the Mitchells and a couple of teammates, including try-scorer Francis, headed across Westgate Street to the bar at the Grand Hotel, where the Americans were toasting Jane Thompson and Krista McFarren, whose own birthdays were on Sunday and Monday respectively, as well as their defeat of New Zealand.

'We passed midnight in the pub with the American team. So, it was about at least five of us having a couple of refreshing drinks,' Mitchell admits. 'It was still those days when you'd finish and look to have a good few drinks of water, but if we wanted we could have a pint and you see that through some of the coverage of the tournament, too. There was still definitely a social element to the way the game was played and how teams mingled afterwards. The New Zealanders would have their guitars out playing, you know, the Welsh would be singing, and there was definitely that element of it's still to be enjoyed.'

Certainly, those members of the USA squad who were in the bar at that time were more than ready to entertain their final rivals. 'The English side, they were in a little bit more of a structured environment with a little more lockdown going on,' McFarren explains. 'So, they were pretty happy to come over our way for a little bit. I mean, we were kinda like, "Yeah, come have fun", and they came, and we had fun, and then they snuck right back on over where they needed to be. But they were kind of like, "What, you guys get to do all this?" And we were like, "Nobody's telling us not to, so we're gonna do it!" No, that was a ton of fun.'

The Americans potentially landed an early psychological blow ahead of the teams' final meeting, however, when a bag of bright orange nibbles was offered to their English counterparts. 'They had these snacks that were shaped as goldfish, and they'd teased us and said they were some sort of superfood,' Mitchell concedes, laughing. 'We thought we were eating goldfish, which is naïve but there was a good bit of banter.' If Mitchell's anecdote betrays a lack of street smarts within members of the England squad, then that is something the USA would target at the Arms Park around 15 hours later.

16

'DON'T QUOTE ME'

IN SPITE OF her tongue-in-cheek plea for a quiet week in South Wales, Alice Cooper had indeed been quoted and quoted heavily as the Women's Rugby World Cup unfolded. Whether stuck in her windowless bunker in Sophia Gardens or on the road in Llanharan or Ely, the tournament's official spokeswoman had been on hand to provide comment at every turn. Cooper had satisfied reporters' appetites for a line on Soviet vodka sellers, intrigued customs officials, guitar-wielding New Zealanders and, of course, the perilous state of the organising committee's finances.

Every time she did so, Cooper attempted to bring a touch of levity to her responsibility, but even she grew weary at the angle some, primarily male, journalists persisted in taking. Broadcast reporter Paul Wade received a particularly stony-faced rebuke as he interviewed the head of press on the touchline of the Dairy Field on Monday afternoon. 'So, basically, the appeal of rugby for women is exactly the same as it is for men?' Wade asked Cooper. 'Yes,' she replied, barely attempting to conceal her contempt as she stared back at her interrogator. 'Well, it's not surprising. It's the same game.'

'He was so surprised that I'd come back straight with that answer that he went "That's probably the end of that, isn't it?" Yes, it is, but durgh!' Cooper remembers. 'I can see myself thinking "What a stupid question that is. You play for the same reason as the men – it's the same game! Why would you not?"'

In truth, it was off-pitch events that piqued national press interest rather than anything unfolding on the playing surfaces at Glamorgan Wanderers or the Arms Park. The escapades of the impoverished Soviet squad had obviously cut through. Newspaper editors in South Wales, London and on regional titles reserved column inches on pages towards the front as well as the back of their publications for updates on the Soviets' fate and the public reaction to their plight. However, the World Cup and rugby in general had been an addendum, colour that made the protagonists seem even more exotic and unusual. One tabloid, the *Mirror*, did send its women's editor to a match in Llanharan, but Carole Malone's copy could have been phoned in from home, offering only a caricature of life in a Welsh village rugby club.

Moreover, Malone's assertion that 'men who once dug coal' and were 'frightened that once more upheaval was being forced upon them' ran at odds with the experiences of the players who ran out at the Dairy Field that week. 'Their lifeblood had been taken from them 30 years ago. Now it was their sport that was being stolen,' Malone added. 'And as if to rub salt in the wound, a pretty blonde clutching a pint of beer strode past them – flaunting her rugby boots! In that single moment the elders of Llanharen [sic] realised they were going to have to let go of their sporting history.'

Of course, there was some reticence about watching women play rugby from a handful of members, but as chairman Malcolm

Hall told Helen Weathers, many thought it was 'great, absolutely wonderful' to see the teams line up in Llanharan. Certainly, once Cooper had managed to locate the ground, she found the locals to be enthusiastic and appreciative. 'I ended halfway up the bloody Rhondda Valley before I found Llanharan. And the whole of Llanharan turned out and they would turn out for whoever England was playing to cheer for them,' she reminisces. 'One of the best renditions of "Hen Wlad Fy Nhadau" that I've ever heard, though, [came] from the Welsh girls. That was incredibly moving, I remember that really clearly.'

That is not to say that the women's World Cup was welcomed with open arms everywhere it went. One of its most vocal opponents was *Wales on Sunday* columnist Michael Boon. Ahead of the tournament, Boon wrote in the weekly newspaper that he 'would not cross the road to watch five minutes of a physical contact sport that should be EXCLUSIVELY for men', something which he admitted himself 'aroused a furious retaliation'. His ridiculous comments led to a heated debate on BBC Radio Wales between Boon and Sue Dorrington and Wales team manager Dawn Barnett.

Answering a challenge from presenter Steve Taylor, Boon attended Wales' opening match against Canada but was not impressed with what he saw. 'The women's rugby World Cup has been a success, no doubt about that. But not for me,' he wrote the following Sunday. 'It was everything I feared that it would be – women grappling with each other. They enjoyed it, and so did most of the spectators. I didn't.' Even Philippa Evans' length-of-the-field break to score the Welsh try elicited nothing more than a shrug from the scribe. 'In the National Sports Centre several days later, I saw some of the Welsh players. There was a vivid black eye and other scars of battle,' Boon concluded. 'I am sure they wore their wounds with pride. Whether the dignity of womanhood was enhanced is something else again.'

It must have been hard for Cooper and those who had volunteered their time, to read such misogynistic bile from a generally respected source. That Dorrington and Barnett found the energy to debate those opinions on live radio is impressive. Unfortunately, though, Boon was most likely not the only newspaperman to make such an assessment of the women's World Cup. As the business end of the tournament approached, coverage in the national titles was thin on the ground. The *Daily Mail* had run a preview on the semi-finals on Friday, but the focus of Peter Jackson's article was the furore which surrounded New Zealand's Haka rather than what would happen on the pitch after the ritual had been completed. On Saturday, the *Independent* ran a report of the previous night's action, while the *Daily Telegraph* and *Guardian* took agency copy which erroneously described Gill Burns' try as a pushover, rather than resulting from a charge down.

The weekend of 13 April 1991 was a busy one, as Bath secured the Courage League title, Ian Woosnam chased Masters glory and Gazza scored an outrageous free-kick at Wembley to lead Spurs to the FA Cup final. Although some of the biggest names in rugby writing were expected at the Arms Park on Sunday, the on-pitch action at the World Cup was relegated to news-in-brief status in comparison. A pulsating final would be rewarded with the space it deserved in most of Monday's editions, but editors were not ready to give a women's team sport top billing. Three decades on and while change has occurred, it has been glacial. The British media, it seems, have held on tighter to their 'sporting history' than the patronised elders of Llanháran.

*****

One story that *did* attract considerable interest, whether from newspapers, TV or radio, was that concerning the tournament's finances and whether the World Cup would make enough money to cover its costs. Griffin had laid out the cash problems facing the organising committee the previous week, in the wake of the revelation that the Soviets would not be able to settle their accommodation bill. This had saddled the World Cup with a £6,000 debt before a ball had been kicked and forced the organisers to cut their cloth accordingly. 'We wanted to give every player a commemorative medal but that was £1,000 we just could not guarantee finding,' Griffin told the *Evening Standard*.

It was during that interview, printed two days before the World Cup was officially opened on Atlantic Wharf, that Griffin first raised the possibility of re-mortgaging her house should the tournament run into serious financial difficulty. 'We have a budget of £29,000 and that means we have to get 6,000 people through the turnstiles on those two days (semi-finals and final). If we don't achieve that target then I suppose re-mortgaging my home is one option! It is very frightening and I will probably be counting heads on the Friday and Sunday in Cardiff.'

As the New Zealand and USA teams warmed up at the Arms Park the following Friday, there was no need to count heads. Ticket sales for the semi-finals had been far from brisk and the two cavernous concrete stands which ran the length of each touchline were sparsely populated. A cursory glance round would confirm that considerably fewer than the 3,000 fans required had walked through the turnstiles. The Friday evening kick-off time, a novelty not only for the players, had not helped, and there was hope that a more family-friendly Sunday afternoon slot would help sales for the final.

However, there was no getting away from the fact that the crowd needed to break even was unprecedented for the women's game. Indeed, at a time when rugby still resolutely saw itself as a participation rather than spectator sport, attracting between 5,000 and 6,000 fans through the turnstiles would have been considered a success by any of the men's teams hosting Heineken League or Courage Clubs Championship matches that weekend. When asked in an interview for *Rugby Special* what would happen if the size of the gate for the final was not big enough to break even, Cooper replied: 'If not, I'll probably have to re-mortgage my house.'

It was a claim she repeated in conversation with newspaper reporters ahead of the showpiece match. On the morning of the final, Chris Dighton wrote in the *Sunday Times* that 'a valiant attempt to prove that the female of the species is capable of storming the traditional chauvinistic bastion of rugby could result in the organisers of the inaugural women's World Cup having to take out second mortgages on their homes because of tournament losses which could amount to as much as £30,000.' According to Cooper, the dilemma had been christened the 'Tracy Edwards situation', a reference to the sailor who skippered the first all-female crew in the Whitbread Round the World Yacht Race.

'No one will put their faith in a woman who ventures into a traditional male sport until, like Tracey [sic], they prove they can do it,' Cooper told Dighton. 'No money was forthcoming, and it was decided that the teams would pay for themselves ... but that left us £30,000 to find. We expected to raise this through merchandising, television rights and ticket sales. But these have not been up to expectations. The aspect which really niggles is that the women have been playing great rugby, and the press have been generous in their plaudits.'

Edwards had mortgaged her house to help buy the boat on which she sailed round the world, but her venture was propelled by the backing of King Hussein bin Talal and Royal Jordanian Airlines as well as her sacrifice and dedication. As time ticked down towards the final, there was little sign that such a benefactor was about to bail out the World Cup. There were reports and rumours that a group of businessmen would step in to save the day, but nothing concrete. On the day of the final, the organising committee's best chance of breaking even remained a late surge at the turnstiles.

*****

On the Sunday morning, cold by the standards they were used to back home in California, Tam Breckenridge and Tara Flanagan stood with USA teammate Annie Flavin outside the Grand Hotel. The forwards were waiting for one of the tournament minibuses to pick them up and ferry them to the outskirts of Cardiff, where they had been booked to appear on BBC Wales. Three England players would join them for the interview, the women lining up facing each other in one last push to raise awareness and sell tickets for the final.

Both Breckenridge and Flanagan were used to doing media – they had played college basketball before turning their attention to a different shaped ball. Flanagan had been talented enough to be picked in the first round of the inaugural Women's National Basketball Association draft, while Breckenridge, whose career was cut short by injury, worked in the Athletic Department at University of California, Los Angeles (UCLA). However, neither particularly wanted to be in the Leyland DAF as it trundled through the deserted city centre. 'That's the last thing you want to see on the day of the final, is your opponents,' Flanagan admits.

'I remember that morning going, "Why did we agree to do this?"' Breckenridge says. 'It was something you do, something that's kind of part of it. I think working in the Athletic Department at UCLA, I was used to athletes being asked to do interviews before games and knowing that even when it's not necessarily comfortable or optimal, that's something you do and you give interviews after you lose, you give them before games.

So, I think it was something we saw as an opportunity to talk about the US and to represent ourselves and our team .... We just had fun with the guy that was doing the interview a little bit, but I just saw it as part of the tournament, part of the fun part, creating a bit of a buzz and helping out.'

Breckenridge certainly made her second-row partner Flanagan laugh when the interviewer mistook her surname for a ski resort in Colorado. 'The newscaster guy went down the row and, you know, asked us silly questions, asked us to introduce ourselves,' Flanagan recalls. 'Something really funny that happened is that I introduced myself, "I'm Tara Flanagan from Los Angeles. I'm a lock," and then the guy would make some little banter with you and then he'd move to the next person. Tam was on my other side, and she says, "Hi, I'm Tam Breckenridge" and the guy interrupted and goes, "Oh, Breckenridge, that's a ski area in America, it's quite well known." Tam goes, "Yes, I own it" and he believed her! I was just like busting up over here, like out of screenshot, just like ... Tam has a very dry sense of humour.'

Once Flanagan had composed herself and the presenter had completed his interviews, the players filed back into their minibuses and headed back to their respective hotels to rest ahead of the big match. There was much to ponder for players on both sides as time ticked towards 3.00 pm. England centre Sam Robson, who doubled as the tournament's merchandise co-ordinator, had not necessarily admitted it to herself yet, but she was heading towards the end of her playing career. She was determined to put on a show for those who turned up at the Arms Park on that sunny Sunday afternoon.

'I remember the night before, talking with Stephen Jones from the *Sunday Times* about the game and saying to him that I wanted the game to be kind of a pinnacle of good-quality women's rugby. I wanted it to be a real showcase to show women playing at their best, and to me that was almost more important than winning,' she says. 'Because women's rugby was going to be judged for the next five years on that game and if it was a dire game of everybody dropping it and being absolutely rubbish it would be really bad for the game.

'Don't get me wrong, I absolutely wanted to win ... but I was also conscious in my Women's Rugby Football Union hat, and as a player, of trying to get the two things together. We wanted England to win but we also wanted it to be a huge spectacle. And so, as I say, I think we were all pretty nervous because at this stage we kind of knew, it wasn't like the start of the tournament when it was a bit of an unknown what was going to happen. This was a case of right, now the chips are really down, this is going to be a game. And we knew it was going to be a tough game. We knew that really we weren't the favourites and that we were going to have to play our heart out to be able to win that."

WHEN EAGLES SOARED

AT AROUND 1.20 pm on Sunday 14 April, the USA squad gathered in the bar area of the Grand Hotel, the 'living room' as it had been christened by the players, and prepared to make the short stroll to the Arms Park as a group. In crossing Westgate Street and walking the 300 or so yards to the ground they followed in the footsteps the trailblazing Cardiff Ladies team had taken 74 years before, just as they had done on Friday evening. Once again, they intended to achieve what Ms Kirton and her pioneering teammates had been unable to do against Newport during the Great War and return to the Grand as winners.

It should have taken the USA players minutes to reach the ground, where they would be directed to the changing rooms. However, dressed in their 'number ones', the squad caught the attention of locals going about their Sunday afternoon business as well as supporters who had arrived early. 'People that were on the streets, they stopped and people that saw us from their buildings, they opened their windows and they yelled … and they clapped for us,' Tara Flanagan says, her eyes filling with tears as she recalls the emotion of the moment.

'They said, "Beat the English. Beat the bloody English." … To come from America, where rugby wasn't a recognised sport, to have people stop in the street as you're walking over. At the end, we were walking down the middle of the road. Cars stopped and people were clapping us. People were really behind us, and you felt it. It was so powerful.'

Barb Bond remembers being stopped for autographs ('It was always little boys and old men!'), but that moment was incredibly bittersweet for the squad's captain. As she made the short walk across the street to the stadium, she did so knowing that she was unlikely to play any part in the Women's Rugby World Cup final. Despite scoring the winning try in the defeat of New Zealand that got her side there, Bond had been dropped to the replacements' bench. Barring an injury to one of her teammates, that is where she would stay as the match unfolded.

'It was, of course, heart-breaking to me, but I think, you know, that was the decision that got made and you just have to be ready and suck it up,' she admits three decades later. 'The Dutch match had been really depleting, the New Zealand match had been really depleting, and in a certain way, these days it wouldn't be a big thing and it isn't at all uncommon for the freshest players to be going in but, yeah …'

There were rumours that senior players had been to see coaches Kevin O'Brien and Chris Leach to suggest a change at the base of the scrum and that some felt the move was political, with Bond being collateral damage in a power struggle between East and West Coast factions within the squad. The captain plied her trade in San Francisco at a time when the majority of the squad were still drawn from teams on the opposite side of the country. The truth, though, is much more mundane; if Bond was the victim of anything, it was the strength of the USA squad. She had been picked for the semi-final for her physicality, but the selection committee reasoned that a more agile back row was needed to beat England, and that was where Kathy Flores had the edge.

Losing out on a place in the team to Flores, moreover, was no embarrassment. The Florida State University number eight was shorter than Bond, but what she lacked in height she made up for in fight and game knowledge. Flores had captained the women's Eagles in their first-ever match, against Canada in 1987, leading the walkout, and according to her long-time teammate she was 'a person you'd jump off a cliff for'. 'Quite honestly, it was horses for courses as far as I was concerned. It was no reflection on people,' O'Brien insists. 'Kathy Flores' leadership is outstanding. She's not only a brilliant player, but she's a marvellous leader and that's what we wanted.'

'We were in that sense the luckiest coaches-stroke-selectors in the world, because we had two world-class number eights that had different strengths, quite distinctive strengths,' Leach says. 'It was clear that we needed Barb's strengths in the semi-final and not Kathy's. But it was also clear (and it was a little bit of a gamble, no one's going to deny that) that Kathy's strengths would play really well in the final.'

What is certain is that there was no ill-feeling between the two women who went head-to-head for the place at the base of the USA scrum. 'I don't remember it as being disruptive at all, although I'm sure Barb Bond suffered a lot from that, emotionally, at the time. However, we all have to put our personal needs aside to win a World Cup and we all have to sacrifice,' Flanagan says. 'I wasn't in that situation to be dropped, I imagine I would be gutted like a fish on the one hand, but I'd have to say you deal with that later. You deal with that when you get home to America.

'Right now, you do everything you can to facilitate the win. I remember us having unequivocal faith in our coaches' selections for that final. I remember having unequivocal faith that they knew what is best and they are doing what is best, and that's what you have to do .... And Kathy is, to say a great rugby player that's not stating it well enough, but also a leader. And people would follow Kathy Flores through a wildfire. Not because we're a bunch of lackeys, but some people have that leadership, and you need your loosies and you need your eight to be driving the pack. And I think the coaches made the right decision.'

In later years, O'Brien and Leach would discuss whether they should have found a way to field Bond and Flores together in the same back row. 'Maybe we should have played Barb as a number eight and Kathy as a flanker,' the head coach reflects, 'but that would have been unfair to the other flankers.' For now, the focus for the players, and the coaches as they gave out their final instructions before heading up to the stands, was finding a way to beat England and win the World Cup.

Pinned on the USA changing room wall, metaphorically at least, was a belief that they were being underestimated. England and the USA each came into the final on the back of wins which were hugely significant to them psychologically. France had dominated Great Britain in the teams' early showdowns and so for England to beat them at the first time of asking, and relatively comfortably too, was a massive confidence boost. On the other hand, the women's Eagles had proven to themselves that they could win 'ugly', emerging from an arm wrestle against New Zealand. It is understandable, therefore, that the two teams would each feel they were in shape to take the final step.

It seems local bookmakers, though, had stuck their necks on the line and made England favourites. This was not something that went down well with the inhabitants of the Grand Hotel. 'I know for both the New Zealand game and the England game, we were heavy underdogs,' Tam Breckenridge recalls. 'On the way back, either from getting something to eat or from that (BBC) interview, we went by some pub or bar where they were taking bets on the game and US were huge underdogs. Tara and I were like, "Do we do it? Do we put any money on?" We didn't put money on [but] boy, if we'd have done that, we could have paid for our entire trip, we were that big an underdog.'

If the USA were not already a fearsome proposition, the players now had a perceived injustice to fight.

*****

USA players clearly hadn't read the *Observer* on the morning of the final if they felt British papers and bookies had already unilaterally handed the trophy to England. Although there were certainly those in the press who discounted the USA on the basis that it wasn't a 'traditional' rugby nation, Norman Harris was not one of them. In the weekly *Rugby Review* that Sunday, Harris had devoted his final three paragraphs to a review of the World Cup to date. In conclusion, he wrote: 'What of England, who contest today's final? They appear, at least to Welsh eyes, to play to a set pattern that doesn't allow for much flair and variety. On the other hand, their opponents at the Arms Park, the United States, have impressed all with their strong forwards and imaginative attacking play focused on a stuntwoman, Candi Orsini, in the centre.

'Who knows what the consequences might be of a rugby World Cup won by the US. If their women have arrived, can the men be far behind?'

Now, you could argue that a national team bereft of 'flair and variety' was completely on-brand for England as a rugby nation, especially at a time when the mercurial talents of Stuart Barnes were being consistently ignored by the selectors of the men's XV. It was a summation that did a couple of the players, not least the supremely talented half backs Emma Mitchell and Karen Almond, a disservice, but it also succinctly hit the nail on the head when it came to the two finalists' polarising difference in style. While the USA were an all-court maelstrom of attacking talent, England were much more pragmatic, playing for territory, percentages and to a strict game plan.

It is interesting to think how an England team coached by Jim Greenwood might have approached the World Cup, but his decision to step down in 1989 precipitated a change in direction. His successor Steve Dowling had played under the great Scot at Loughborough in the early 1970s, but he was not a devoted disciple of 'Total Rugby'. Having represented Saracens after leaving university, Dowling's playing career was ended at the age of 34 by a heart problem which required an aortic valve replacement. He turned his hand to coaching and, after some success, was persuaded to take on the London and South East women's side by a teaching colleague, England winger Cheryl Stennett. His involvement in the female regional game gave him a seat on the selection committee for the England and Great Britain squads, and therefore when Jeff Williams, Greenwood's original replacement, stepped aside, he was well placed to answer the WRFU's SOS.

The first and most significant change Dowling made when taking on the England job was to ask Almond to stand flatter, acting as a pivot rather than taking the ball at full pace. 'I'm not sure how much Jim would have appreciated that,' he admits. 'I think he would have sat there and thought, "What are you doing with this side, Steve?"' Although he might not have shared his former coach's commitment to a 15-player game, Dowling still wanted every one of his players to know exactly what their roles were on the pitch, and, crucially, why they mattered.

To this end, Dowling would often take the full squad, up to 30 players at a time, on pitch walks, running through various game scenarios and what he wanted from each player at any given time. 'So, I'd say, "OK, we've got a scrum here, five yards out. What's your role? What's the role of the prop?" And we would actually try to get people to understand their individual responsibilities in these key positions so that there was an understanding about what we're trying to do across the whole squad. So, we'd spend some of the weekends doing that sort of thing, which is something they'd not done a lot of before,' Dowling explains. 'One of the things I wanted to do with all my coaching, men and women, was to get people to understand the totality; if you call a move, everyone's now got a role. What is it? Do they know what it is?'

Unsurprisingly, given the level of detail the squad was exposed to by Dowling and his coaching staff, England became an extremely well-drilled side. 'Steve Dowling as coach was incredibly calm and measured and thoughtful in terms of how he delivered game plans to us, how we would break out into mini-units and talk about what we were going to be looking to do,' Mitchell says. 'We'd go out in the (Celtic Bay Hotel) car park and go through the line-out calls and make sure we knew what we were doing, you know, for each of those, and just do a general sort of walk through to get our brains thinking through how we were looking to play the game.'

However, as Harris had inadvertently noted, the problem with rote learning is its potential to stifle creativity and the ability of its students to problem-solve on the fly. To beat the USA to the inaugural women's World Cup, England would need to unscramble equations they had never encountered before on the pitch, either in a match or on a training walk. 'We went in feeling as though if we played well, we could win it,' Mitchell adds.

'The press had made us favourites just because traditionally no one thought America knew anything about rugby. So, you know, that probably in some ways didn't help us because I think you always prefer to be the underdog in anyone's eyes and especially even in your own eyes. It sort of keeps the focus going.' Both sets of players had their sights trained firmly on the antique silver cup.

*****

By the time the England and USA players arrived at the Arms Park at 1.30 pm, Deborah Griffin, Alice Cooper and the other volunteers were already following an extremely tight schedule. They had been at the ground since around midday as they got various changing rooms ready for the match officials, brass band and ball boys as well as the two teams, and made sure they had access to the pitch and balls. At 2.00 pm, dignitaries and members of the press began to arrive for a VIP reception in the Airspace lounge.[i]

The organising committee had made a point of inviting the women's game's detractors as well as its supporters to the showpiece match. Stephen Townley, whose legal firm had threatened action over the World Cup logo, and male England fly half Rob Andrew, reportedly 'mystified' that women would want to play, were among those who politely declined invitations. Keith Rowlands accepted and the duplicity of doing so when sitting on a board that attempted to tie the tournament up in legal red tape was rightly skewered in the following day's *Independent*. 'Various rugby dignitaries put in an appearance at Cardiff Arms Park (the club ground) yesterday and in some cases this was not wholly appropriate,' Steve Bale wrote. 'The inaugural Women's Rugby World Cup … was a success despite, rather than because of, the attitude of officialdom.'

---

[i] Cardiff RFC had made a donation of £200 to the organising committee to be put towards hospitality costs on the day of the final.

Some of those who had helped the World Cup get to this point, such as Helen Ames and Kim Rowland, who had spent the week looking after the teams at the Cardiff Institute of Higher Education, and Stephanie Bowyer, whose London home doubled as the tournament ticket office, were able to enjoy a drink in the executive box as they watched the band trooping out onto the pitch. Below, girls and boys from local junior clubs lined up to play an exhibition of Dragon Rugby, a mixed version of the game for children under the age of 11 which was being trialled in Wales. The display had been the WRU's idea, and it therefore would have been tempting to presume there was a bright future ahead for female players.

Mary Forsyth had also made it to Cardiff, with newborn daughter Kathryn and husband Piers. Her mother Clementine had come along for the trip, keen to spend as much time as possible with her first grandchild. Clementine spent the early afternoon visiting an old friend in Barry, though, meaning Kathryn would get an early exposure to live women's rugby. 'It was chaos,' Forsyth admits. 'I can remember sitting up in the stands, and there was a bit of a cover, with this swaddled up 2-week-old baby .... We weren't going to miss it; it was the final!'

Kathryn was not the only baby at the Arms Park that day. Griffin had Victoria in tow, but trying to juggle childcare commitments with making sure the final went smoothly did not always prove easy. 'In actual fact, Stephen Jones held her for most of the final as I was running around trying to do things,' Griffin recalls. 'It was really tough. I look back on it, everybody will look back on those things in a different way. If you were a player, you will look on it in a different way. I mean, I didn't sleep the whole week.'

Sunday Times journalist Jones had just become a father himself, and was more than happy to lighten Griffin's load, however temporarily. 'I just think I held her baby because I liked babies at the time,' he remembers. 'I think she was a bit panicky that I'd drop the baby, but I didn't because I was used to handling them. It was really nice.'

Beneath the Airspace lounge, where guests discussed the week's events and debated how the final would go, the brass band was now in full flow as fans filed into the ground. Inside the changing rooms, Steve Dowling, Steve Peters, Kevin O'Brien and Chris Leach were giving out their final instructions. Ahead of the semi-final against New Zealand, injured USA scrum half Barb Fugate had delivered a rousing speech to the 15 players selected. 'When you're tired and feeling all alone,' she told them, 'remember, there are 20 others with you. Take some energy from us … we have a score to settle.'

That energy was needed again on Sunday. The message coming from coach O'Brien was very simple: they would have to be better than they were on Friday. 'Think of who you are playing with,' the Welshman urged his team. 'You will have to dig very, very deep. They will come out very, very hard. Dig deeper today than you've ever dug before.' When O'Brien was finished, Leach stepped in to offer some final words of wisdom: 'They will never give up. The only way to beat them is to score points … over and over again. The match will belong to the team with the least mistakes.'

'I don't think you're completely confident when you're playing against an opponent that you've never played,' USA centre Candi Orsini says. 'That's what gave more stress to the situation – we'd never played them. I mean, sure, the Wiverns tour but that's different. That was playing, you know, regional sides and everything, and we recognised that, and we recognised it was a different year. They'd come a long way, right. So, I think it was very tense. It was very stressful.'

As 3.00 pm and kick-off approached, however, the Wiverns tour was playing on the minds of those England players who had encountered the all-conquering team six years previously. 'They were pretty amazing players,' England captain Almond says. 'The American backs were awesome. I must admit in that first World Cup in '91, we were, I think, a little bit in awe of those girls and that didn't help with the way we played in the final.' For some in the England team, their pre-match nerves became too much to hold in.

Confronted by the sound of studs clattering towards the toilets and retching from within the cubicles, Dorrington thought to herself, '"Oh, for Christ's sake … Why aren't you ready for this?" I had spent one year mentally, physically, emotionally getting ready for this moment. I remember sort of feeling angry with them and disappointed and like, "Get out of the loo, you know, woman up!"'

*****

At 2.55 pm, the teams emerged from the changing rooms and walked slowly out onto the Arms Park pitch. Sitting up in the main stand, Griffin and Cooper would have known they had not hit their ticket target, but the repercussions of that were for another day. The attendance for the inaugural Women's Rugby World Cup final would later be variously reported at somewhere between 2,000 and 3,000. Perhaps not enough to cover the financial cost of the tournament, but still comfortably the biggest gathering of paying fans for a women's fixture in the UK at that time.

'It was a bit nerve-wracking,' USA number eight Flores admits. 'We'd never really played in front of crowds before, you know, and though it may not seem much to other people, if you never have people at your games and you have 3,000 people there all of a sudden, that's a lot. Then, the fact that you're in a stadium and the sound kind of travels, so when something happens, and as we start playing, something happens and it's like "Aaaah" – it's really loud in comparison to what you've been used to … At one moment of the game, I remember being like, "Oh, my God!" and then snapping out of it, like, "I can't do this, I can't." You know, "I can't think like this, I'm just playing a game. Just playing a game. Nobody's here," you know?'

For now, that extra volume was used to amplify the national anthems, and, as the teams lined up either side of the match officials, facing the South Stand, it was a special moment for Dorrington. Not only had the Minnesota-born hooker dedicated hour upon hour of the previous year to make sure that the tournament went ahead but this was the moment she had been visualising with her personal trainer and sports psychologist. She had always thought that the USA would be the team standing in England's way, and when she looked down the line and past referee Les Peard there were members of the opposition whom she had played with and against when taking her first steps in the game a decade before.

'That was a bit tearful. I got pretty emotional,' Dorrington recalls. 'I literally remember looking left going, "Oh, there's Mary and there's …" you know, and looking at these women that I had played with or against in the United States. But, you know, putting on that white shirt and singing the national anthem at the first-ever Women's Rugby World Cup, it just took over and took over your emotion, and you were so proud, and you were so [full of] anticipation that you couldn't even imagine what was going to happen next. All we wanted to do was start playing.'

Once referee Peard blew his whistle, the USA players must have had their coach's pre-match team-talk ringing in their ears as England started as brightly as their fresh white jerseys. The USA, further ingratiating themselves with locals by wearing red shirts, were being beaten in the scrum and could have fallen behind had Gill Burns converted one of two early penalty attempts.

The women's Eagles were yet to concede a point during the tournament, but that changed on the quarter-hour when flanker Claire Godwin pulled down a USA scrum as it reversed towards the line, and England were awarded a penalty try. Burns stroked the conversion through the posts to give her side a 6–0 lead.

A Chris Harju penalty halved the USA's deficit, but as the teams turned round, it was England who were in the ascendancy. No one on the losing side was panicked, though, as they devoured their half-time oranges on the Arms Park pitch. O'Brien and Leach had used 26 players in their side's opening two pool matches, sharing the workload and ensuring each had an opportunity to stake their claim for a place in the starting line-up at the business end of the World Cup. Flores' inclusion in place of Bond was the only change from the semi-final for Sunday's showpiece match, meaning only four players had started all four matches, albeit a fifth, Patty Connell had featured in all but five minutes of the competition due to Barb Fugate's early injury against the Netherlands.

By contrast, Dowling had made only two changes in the entirety of the tournament. Carol Isherwood had missed the opening game, while the injury prop Jane Mangham picked up against Italy had subsequently ruled her out of the semi-final against France. She was fit enough for a place on the replacements' bench by Sunday, but England elected to stick with Sandy Ewing and Jayne Watt in the front row. That meant that the final was the fourth game in eight days for 13 of the starting line-up, and both teams expected them to tire as the contest wore on. 'I think our coaches learnt the lesson from that World Cup and certainly by the next World Cup they were much more focused on managing the whole squad and using the whole squad where they could,' Isherwood says. 'No matter how fit you are, four games in eight days is just not right.'

Isherwood, Burns and Janis Ross were locked in a crucial

back-row battle against Godwin, Whitehead and Flores, and as the match wore on, the more mobile USA trio began to gain the upper hand. The momentum of the match swung decisively the USA's way in the three second-half minutes it took Godwin to make amends for her earlier misdemeanour and score two tries. Both came from line-outs, the first a training-ground move which had been devised during Thursday's marathon session.

'That try came from Tara Flanagan,' O'Brien explains. 'We'd been working on line-out peels, which I was big on at the time, and it just wasn't working, and I couldn't figure it out. Tara made a suggestion about maybe going to a different part of the line-out and utilising a different support runner. So, I said, "Oh, let's give it a shot." It worked and then in the final that was a try we scored because an intelligent rugby player, an intelligent athlete had figured out, "Hey Kev, this isn't working out. How about we try that?" and it worked.'

Godwin's second try was much more opportunistic as the Americans caught their opponents napping to take a quick throw and saunter over the goal line almost unopposed. 'In the middle of the game when it was a line-out, people were looking at our team and had sort of switched off a little bit,' Isherwood recalls. 'I was going "Watch out, they're going to take a quick line-out" and I remember running in and before we knew it, they'd thrown the ball in, and they'd scored and that was sort of the end of our opportunity … We got a fair amount of ball but our ability to try and deal with the speed of thinking of their team just wasn't quite there.'

Things went from bad to worse for England as Jane Mitchell went down injured. Following a short wait as Mitchell made her way off the pitch on a stretcher, Giselle Prangnell (now Mather) came on to take her place at full back. The replacement's first act was to field a high ball and get taken out late. She remembers 'lying on my back, looking at the sky, going "Wow!"' As she did so, her tormentor leaned over her prone body and snarled: 'Welcome to the game.' 'I loved that!' Mather assures me three decades later, laughing at the memory. The impetus was all with the USA now and soon after they added a third try through scrum half Patty Connell to help sew up a 19–6 victory.

Moments after Peard blew his whistle to signal the end of the match, Bond and Mary Sullivan, who had captained the team on the pitch in her absence, led the USA squad up into the South Stand to receive the World Cup from WRFU secretary Rosie Golby. Putting her disappointment at not playing in the final to one side, Bond made sure that she and Sullivan performed a suitable trophy hoist once the antique silver cup was handed over.

'Being the rugby nerd that I was and am, I said: "When we get it, we have to lift it up!" So, we did,' she told me in an interview for *World Rugby* in 2020. 'I was just hyper-aware of the moment, that it was an historic moment and we needed to respond in that way, you know. I was really proud. Speaking in the broader sense, I felt like we were on our way. Like this wasn't going to be the last World Cup, it was only the first.'

For a number of the USA players, scaling those steps to get their winner's medal was the culmination of a long and arduous voyage. 'Going up in the stands and getting the trophy, that was really amazing. And then I remember the champagne and the pictures on the field and everything, and then after we left the field, I kind of broke down. I probably cried for three days, I think, because we had done it, but the goal was over. The quest, the journey had come to an end and, yeah, I was exhausted. Never been so tired in my life ... You became aware of everything all of a sudden, you know, at the journey's end.'

'We didn't deserve to win,' Emma Mitchell admits. 'They played the better game on the day, they were more switched on to opportunities as they arose and, you know, all credit to them.

They also, in some ways, they led the women's international game in those early decades. So, I think it's some credit to them that they did win and that they actually made the '94 and '98 finals as well with, you know, very little infrastructure in place in the US.'

*****

As the USA proceeded up the stairs to get their medals, England captain Karen Almond brought her teammates into a huddle. She was determined that she would never experience that disappointment again. '[I had] the feeling after the final that we were never going to lose again. The next time we got to the Women's World Cup final, we were not going to lose to America.' Looking at her dejected teammates, she told them: 'Come on, heads up. We've got to go and shake hands.'

'I remember people were pretty gutted,' Isherwood says. '[Almond's speech was] immediate and you just go "Right, this is the game" and then seeing them pick up the trophy you're just like "Damn it!" But I think it was then that you get through that and you have a big party that night and you have a chance to chat to people more on their own and you look and think "Well, that's been a pretty amazing week and look at what we did."'

One person who wasn't quite ready to party was Dorrington. She had helped to organise the tournament, she had earned her place in the England team, but her ultimate goal, to lift the World Cup trophy had eluded her. 'Personally, I thought we were ready, but I don't think some of the players were ready mentally for that big game,' she concedes. 'I don't think everybody was ready mentally for raising their level because we'd never run out in a stadium with that many people before.'

It was not just on the pitch that Dorrington's life had changed in the previous year. As she had walked towards the touchline at the final whistle, she had been confronted by the two men in her life, husband Mark and personal trainer David Crottie, approaching to console her. 'Mark came onto the pitch to hug me, and I went to my fitness coach first for a hug,' she says, tearful at the recollection. 'That's how much the relationship dynamic had changed. I hadn't spent the year with him, I'd spent the year with *him* [Crottie]. And it wasn't, you know, there was nothing between me and my fitness coach, it was just that was who I'd shared all my aspirations and goals and dreams with. It wasn't Mark.'

By the time Dorrington made it to Sophia Gardens for the official closing dinner, she was at least ready to forgo the diet she had been on while chasing World Cup glory. 'I had chocolate in front of me and I ate for the first time in a year,' she recalls. 'I suddenly thought, "I can change my diet!"' Alongside Griffin, Cooper and Forsyth, Dorrington received a standing ovation from the assembled players, teams and dignitaries for their efforts in making sure the tournament had gone ahead and been a success. Thanks to WRFU secretary Golby, and donations from tournament volunteers, the four women were presented with commemorative bowls to honour their hard work and dedication.

It was glassware of a different shape that had proved popular with the teams assembled in the large main hall at the National Sports Centre for Wales, though. Each table had been stocked with several bottles of wine bearing the World Cup logo. However, when Cooper was finally able to clock off, every single one inside Sophia Gardens appeared to have vanished. 'I was in charge of looking after the referees and their blazers and that kind of stuff, making sure everything was going all right and no one was behaving badly, because again the rugby girls didn't understand that this wasn't a club dinner, this was a formal dinner,' Cooper recalls.

'Most of them arrived absolutely shitfaced because they were just having a great time. So, there was quite a lot of that, quite a lot of speechifying. Then I'd planned to get drunk and it just didn't happen. We ran out of booze. We had all these nice bottles which had the logo on, special dinner and blah, blah that we got printed. Well, they all got nicked because everybody wanted the bottle. So, they were emptied and gone, so even the empties weren't there!'

As the night wound down and the lubricated teams sauntered away from Sophia Gardens and ultimately Cardiff and the inaugural Women's Rugby World Cup, Griffin was able to finally relax, if only for a second. 'It was relief that we'd done it and got there', she says. 'I mean absolute relief. I think I'd run myself into the ground. I think I was probably ill, although I didn't really realise it, because it was just so exhausting and so it'd taken over my life for a year, and I'd had a baby in the middle of that as well. So, I think the whole thing was just quite exhausting.'

That was a sizeable understatement, however. The organising committee chair could not put her feet up just yet. As the following day's papers would make clear, the World Cup, a roaring success from a purely sporting standpoint, was facing significant losses. The final whistle might have blown, but Griffin's work on the tournament finances was set to go into extra time.

18

PUSHED TO THE BRINK

THE HEADLINE ON the back of Monday's *Daily Telegraph* read 'A dream that became reality', and, although it was placed under a picture of a celebrating Ian Woosnam on Augusta's 14th green, it applied just as neatly to the Women's Rugby World Cup. Deborah Griffin, Alice Cooper, Sue Dorrington and Mary Forsyth had achieved what many, especially those in charge of the men's game, assumed was impossible. They had brought together teams from across the globe and, against what presenter Chris Rea on the previous evening's *Rugby Special* described as 'insuperable odds', had hosted a festival of rugby.

Plaudits had rained down on the organisers from all angles, even devout critic Michael Boon had deemed the World Cup a success. However, what Griffin and co. needed more than platitudes was cold hard cash. Reports of the USA's final victory carried in newspapers on Monday morning invariably noted the committee's losses alongside the names of the try-scorers, putting the figure at somewhere between £10,000 and £30,000. It was hoped that the attendance of around 3,000 at the the Arms Park, of which north of 2,000 were paying customers, would reduce that debt considerably.

However, those calculations had been done on the fly, based on the fact that tickets had been priced at £5 and £2 for concessions. Neither did they include the leaving present left to the Cardiff Institute of Higher Education, and ultimately the organising committee, by the departing Soviet squad. As competing teams, with heavy heads from the VIP dinner the night before, packed up and checked out of the accommodation, it became apparent that the sink in one of the rooms assigned to the USSR delegation needed repair. It was an extra cost Griffin could have done without and would have been particularly galling as she then had to drive a minibus full of Soviet players, coaches and other delegates to Heathrow. No wonder she was exhausted, physically and mentally, by the time she reached home. 'I was quite relieved to get back to normality,' she admits.

Remarkably, by the time that Griffin waved goodbye to her Russian passengers at Heathrow, her organising committee colleague Cooper was already back at her desk and getting on with her day job. As she admits, missing out on the opportunity to get 'completely shitfaced' turned out to be a blessing the following morning as she got up early and drove back to London on a mere three hours' sleep. 'We were just so beyond tired by then,' she recalls. 'I had no voice at all. It's a bit like being jet-lagged. The next week I have no recollection of. I remember my colleagues going "Oh, I saw you on *News at Ten*" or "I saw you on the news" and chuckling.'

One group who were keen to make more memories were the victorious Americans, and three players in particular had made plans to embark on a 'victory march' across Europe. 'Locks from Hell' Tam Breckenridge and Tara Flanagan had devised a short trip with Chris Harju to celebrate becoming world champions. The three women stayed with England scrum half Emma

Mitchell in London before heading to Paris, where they were put up by members of the France squad. The French would have had something to toast, too, having beaten a New Zealand XV in an unofficial third-place play-off on Sunday.

Perhaps unsurprisingly, given they were in an understandably celebratory mood, the trio's first port of call was The Mayflower pub in Rotherhithe. The sight of the three women clutching pints and singing heartily as they commandeered the jukebox might have been jarring for the crowd of midweek drinkers who lined the bar, but it was their insistence on playing Queen's 'We are the Champions' on repeat that landed them in trouble with management.

'It's supposedly where the Mayflower ship set sail from, where the pilgrims went off and found America,' Flanagan explains. 'The bartender guy, after we probably played it like ten times, he came and unplugged the jukebox. He was like, "That's enough, we can't take it anymore. Who are you?" We were like, "Well, we're the world champions, of course!"'

Later, Breckenridge suffered a bout of seasickness as the World Cup winners crossed the Channel and continued their voyage to France. 'It was a good way to unwind,' she insists. 'We were totally exhausted.' What Griffin would have given for a chance to decompress. As she went back to work that week, she was no closer to finding an answer to the tournament's financial problems.

*****

There was some positive news for Griffin as she returned to normality. As Chris Jones relayed to readers of London's *Evening Standard* on Monday, the Sports Council had made encouraging noises about stepping in to 'save four of the organisers from personal financial loss'. Griffin also received some timely correspondence which offered support as she attempted to steel herself for the fight ahead. One, from Ian Walker, congratulated Griffin and the organising committee on 'staging a memorable occasion'. A teacher, Walker had enjoyed the semi-finals on Friday so much that he returned for the showpiece match two days later, with his daughter and her boyfriend in tow. Enclosed with his letter was a 'token contribution to the World Cup expenses'.[i]

Walker's cheque was unlikely to make much of a dent in the organising committee's debt, but it was a welcome sign that what they had done was worthwhile. A couple of days after the letter arrived, Forsyth received one from Howard M. Thomas alerting her to a 'potential opportunity where we may be able to mitigate these losses or even get them totally repaid, via a scheme I wish to pursue with the RFU'. It is unclear whether the organising committee took Howard up on his offer, as lines of communication with the RFU had already been established, but it would have been helpful to know such avenues existed.

The first thing Griffin needed to do as she sat down to balance the World Cup's books was to ascertain exactly how much the organising committee owed and to whom. Before she did that, though, she found time to write to each of the chaperones to thank them for their help in South Wales. These volunteers had been crucial to the (relatively) smooth running of the event, making sure their assigned team arrived where they needed to be on time and acting as the main point of contact for other tournament officials. It was a particularly time-consuming role for student Julia Griffiths, who spent the week clearing up after the Soviet squad.

'After 3 weeks I think I have recovered from the World Cup. The hassles and the pain are beginning to fade and the enjoyable parts are now starting to dominate my memory,' Griffin wrote to Griffiths. 'Of all the chaperones you had the hardest task but I was impressed by your commitment and effectiveness. It is a

---

[i] This was not the only such donation. Ahead of the tournament, on 3 March, former Wales and British and Irish Lions fly half Cliff Morgan had sent Griffin the fee he had been paid, 'minus a drink or too', for a speaking engagement with a large company.

cliché, but true, that we could not have achieved what we did without you.'

Having typed the last of the letters, Griffin turned her attention to compiling the World Cup's draft accounts. She would not receive the final invoice from some of the tournament's creditors for several months, while income from merchandise and ticket sales remained an estimate. However, they presented a fairly accurate summation of the situation. The nationwide raffle had failed to raise the funds hoped for, being predicted to bring in only £2,116, while merchandising receipts totalled less than 50 per cent of the income budgeted. The souvenir brochure did outperform expectations, but when combined with advertising income and programme sales, still produced a £1,123 deficit on the cost of printing.

As of 2 May, the total revenue of the World Cup was £14,475. Placed against expenditure of £32,042, which included the unpaid Soviet accommodation bill of £4,410, this left Griffin to find around £17,567 (equivalent to £32,627 in 2021) to break even. The following day, Griffin wrote to her contacts at the Sports Council, National Sports Centre for Wales and the RFU, enclosing a set of the draft accounts and asking for help. On 7 May, RFU secretary Dudley Wood replied, extending the offer of a meeting at Twickenham 'as soon as you feel sure of the final outcome', and raising a potential area where the organising committee could make a considerable saving.

JTI had been hired for an initial fee of £5,000 with the same sum due at the end of the tournament, while the organising committee were also responsible for the expenses of Tom Purvis and Deborah James when working on the World Cup. Had they been able to secure any sponsorship or other tie-ins, the company would have taken 20 per cent of the income. The agreement meant that in Griffin's draft accounts, JTI accounted for £13,723 of the total expenditure. 'Incidentally, the JTI fee and expenses is a fairly major item,' Wood noted. 'I would have thought that, in the circumstances, they might have been persuaded to make some reduction?'

The Sports Council concurred with Wood, which was perhaps unsurprising given its chairman Peter Yarranton was in the process of becoming the RFU president. Either way, their responses gave Griffin the confidence to approach John Taylor about reducing his company's fee. 'As you know I appreciate the amount of time spent by Tom and Deborah on our account. However most of Tom's time was spent on the Television rights, meetings with Albert Frances of Cardiff regarding hospitality and perimeter board advertising and sponsorship. We have not received any revenues from these sources which would also have paid JTI a 20 per cent fee,' she wrote on 22 May.

'The expenditure on hotels and train fares within the invoiced amounts were also much more than we budgeted. As we were without sponsorship, as an organisation we were extremely frugal – using cheaper hotels and driving where this was cheaper than train fares. Whilst I understand your requirements as a professional company I hope you will understand that should it be necessary I will have to reduce our deficit by the amount of £5,000 in my discussions with these two bodies.'

Taylor insisted that his company had 'endeavoured to keep our expenses to a minimum' while he defended the fee, pointing to the fact that James had worked three days a week on the account between January and April. Ultimately, though, he agreed to the reduction in order to help Griffin in her negotiations with the Sports Council and the RFU. 'I'm afraid a combination of the recession and apathy to women's sports defeated us in the end. But we gave it our best shot,' he wrote. 'The event was such a magnificent effort by you and your team that I am hopeful this will be recognised in your discussion on financial support.'

It was about this time that the Sports Council confirmed that it would supply the organising committee with an additional grant of £5,000, on the same terms as the original funding. Together with the reduction in JTI's fee this would knock £10,000 off the World Cup's financial deficit, but by Griffin's earlier draft accounts, she would still need to find more than £7,000. A cheque from the WRU would have been appreciated, but when it arrived it was with the apologies of Peter Owens. The Welsh union had been given 1,000 tickets, 500 for each of the semi-finals and final, to sell through its box office but had raised only £128. 'I am sorry that we were not able to sell more tickets for you,' Owens wrote to Rosie Golby on 17 June.

Griffin kept Wood updated on her progress and at the end of June was able to let him know that the picture was 'slightly rosier than when I last wrote to you'. The following week, the RFU secretary replied to confirm his willingness to help. What that help would look like hinged on the final tournament accounts, which Griffin compiled on 15 August. These had been improved by increased merchandise revenue and donations of £2,562 as well as the increase in grant funding and reduction in JTI's fee but still showed a total deficit of £6,756. Would the RFU make good on Wood's promise of assistance?

*****

In Griffin's memory, what happened next is worthy of a blockbuster movie script. Having sent the final accounts to Wood on the last day of August, his secretary Celia phoned her up and summonsed the organising committee chair to Twickenham. Sat behind an imposing desk in his office at the citadel of English men's rugby, Wood listened to Griffin as she went through the figures line by line. When she got to the end, he double-checked the outstanding deficit. 'Then he pulled out a cheque book and wrote a cheque for the £6,000,' Griffin says.

It is a lovely image and the perfect ending to the story, but unfortunately it is not true. Griffin did speak with Wood in person at Twickenham, and Celia was doubtlessly the conduit, but she did not leave HQ with any money. The funds instead arrived at 224A Camden Road in the post sometime in the middle of September. 'With reference to your letter of 31 August and the attached draft accounts for the Women's Rugby World Cup, I have pleasure in enclosing our cheque for £6,756.00 which I trust you find satisfactory,' Wood wrote to Griffin. 'Whilst we would not want it to form a precedent, we are delighted to help out and my Committee would wish me to convey our congratulations upon running a very successful event.'

That the cheque was delivered by an anonymous postman and not with a flourish in a Twickenham boardroom does not make its importance, or indeed Griffin's recollection of it, any less significant. Wood was an unlikely poster boy for progress.[ii] He was an ardent supporter of the amateur ideal and as RFU secretary did his utmost to stem the unstoppable tide of professionalism. In the face of the IRFB's increasingly diluted regulations surrounding amateurism, Wood and the RFU refused to bend and implement the changes in England. It put him on a collision course with the country's best male players, the tense stand-off boiling over after a 25–6 win against Wales in Cardiff at the start of the 1991 Five Nations Championship when the England team refused to do any post-match interviews, including with the host broadcaster BBC, unless they were paid.

It is only natural to wonder whether Wood was driven, in part, by a sense that stepping in to help the Women's Rugby World Cup would reflect terribly on his sparring partners at the IRFB. Griffin, it must be said, does not ascribe to this theory. 'I love him. I still see him now,' she says, 'and I always want to hug him and kiss him. He's my favourite man of all time because

---

[ii] During the men's Rugby World Cup in October, Wood expressed his support for the women's game in a conversation with Rosie Golby 'as a separate entity not affiliated to the RFU but with their support'.

he didn't have to do that, and it was a lovely thing to do. Just humane in a sense.'

When Griffin opened that letter, the relief must have been palpable. 'A cause for great joy,' she admits. If that had been the only stressful thing in her life it would have been enough to crush most people, living with the constant anxiety that she was going to come up short. At a time when she was adjusting to motherhood and making sure that her daughter got the care she needed, it is almost inconceivable how she coped. Especially, given that she shouldered the responsibility of balancing the books post-World Cup alone, shielding her colleagues on the organising committee from the worry.

'I have to say it almost destroyed me,' Griffin told me when we first spoke, for a World Rugby profile, in April 2019. 'I think I had a breakdown virtually afterwards. I didn't speak to anybody for about six months.'

'I was just exhausted, just exhausted,' she added at a subsequent interview, almost exactly three years later. 'I didn't recognise it at the time, but, well, you've been doing nothing else for what, 15, 16 months? And had a child as well, and I didn't want to speak to people, I didn't want to see people. I didn't go to the Richmond dinner that year. I went to work and came home and that sort of thing.

'So, I think it was tough. It probably wasn't until I started playing again in sort of September/October that it started to become a little bit more likely I'd get over that. But I got some lovely letters from people, you know, and those things are … because you're not in it, you don't see the press. These days, you'd get a list of the press every morning. We didn't know that, we didn't know what the impact was. We didn't see it on the television, we didn't have any of that. So, you know, you work. You don't know what the impact is, and it wasn't until we started getting letters saying "Thank you so much" and "It meant so much" that you really realise what you've done.

'I don't think that was the worst bit of it for me. I think it was just that it was over and, you know, I'd done nothing else for 18 months and I felt exhausted. And I felt that whole thing of: you put your heart and soul into something, and then it's finished and it's like, "Well, what do I do now?" And I remember being concerned about the money, but I don't remember being desperate.'

By signing the cheque for £6,756, Wood saved the members of the organising committee from more drastic means of raising the funds. It is impossible to say whether one, two or all four would have been happy to re-mortgage their homes had it come to that because the Sports Council and RFU ultimately ensured they didn't have to. Only the four women know how close they came to taking that option, but, given everything they had poured into the tournament over the previous 18 months, it is likely to have been something that was discussed at least. 'Quite honestly, I probably would have re-mortgaged if that had been the case,' Griffin suggests.

Therein, essentially, lies the reason why the notion that they used their properties to finance the tournament has not only been accepted as fact but has become part of women's rugby folklore. In researching this book, I interviewed scores of people who contributed to that first World Cup, whether as volunteers, players, team managers, coaches, administrators, supporters or a combination. When asked about the organising committee, the overwhelming majority referenced them re-mortgaging their homes as a sign of the sacrifice that went into making sure the tournament was not only staged but left behind a successful legacy. 'There's nothing like starting an urban legend,' Cooper joked when we chatted in early 2022.

Whether the anecdote is true or not is frankly irrelevant. It is shorthand which accurately describes the serious bind that the women found themselves in, and the pluck they displayed to get themselves out of it. What makes it such an enduring part of the story of the first Women's Rugby World Cup, despite it being apocryphal, is that each member of the organising committee experienced hardship in the course of making the tournament dream become reality.

Griffin and Forsyth were adjusting to motherhood, the former fitting in trips to the hospital with baby Victoria in-between meetings down the M4 at the IRFB or WRU. Dorrington ploughed so much of herself into winning the World Cup that her marriage began to unravel once it had finished. Cooper, meanwhile, came home from a Christmas trip to Australia and was promptly sacked for taking too much time off. It was the first holiday she had taken since arriving back at her desk, on three hours' sleep, on 15 April.

'It's a funny story that people like to hold on to because they think it just emphasises the dedication and commitment,' Dorrington explains. 'It's part of the narrative, that they want to believe, but it's not true. We never did. My husband Mark read that on Ceefax …. I got home that night and he was like, "What the hell are you doing?" I think people hang on to that because it's part of that deliver-at-all-costs narrative.'

*****

The inaugural Women's Rugby World Cup was certainly delivered successfully, that much is evident in the speed with which people began planning the next one. At 'The Way Forward' conference, which was held during the tournament, it had been decided to stage the second edition of the women's World Cup in 1994. Griffin drew up hosting criteria, and interested parties were instructed to submit their applications to WRFU secretary Rosie Golby ahead of a second meeting in Madrid in September.

All 12 competing nations were invited to draw up proposals for the tournament, which Griffin admitted to the *South Wales Echo* 'may mean we come back to Wales again'. In the end, though, it was the Netherlands, the setting of the first-ever women's international match, who were selected as hosts for the second World Cup. However, two years later, on 29 December 1993, the Dutch organising committee announced that the 1994 Women's Rugby World Cup had been cancelled. In subsequent correspondence with the WRFU, sent via fax naturally, they cited 'the enormous negative and unsympathetic international pressure' they had faced.

Two months earlier, the IRFB had delayed its decision on whether to sanction member unions who wished to take part in the tournament, a move which Dr Lydia Furse has discovered was only communicated to the Dutch at a FIRA meeting in Paris in December. As the IRFB were not scheduled to meet again until March, and the World Cup was due to take place in April, the deferral effectively amounted to a ban by stealth. The Dutch union itself would not have known whether it was able to compete at its own tournament until a matter of weeks before it was supposed to kick-off.

Not willing to let the tournament disappear completely, a group of Scottish women, led by Sue Brodie, managed to stage a 12-team competition in Edinburgh and its surrounding area at just 90 days' notice. The Netherlands did not send a team, while New Zealand, Italy and Spain (countries in which the women's game was overseen by the men's union) were also notable absentees. Spain's withdrawal came so late that their place had to be taken by a team of Scottish students.

On the pitch, there was revenge for Steve Dowling and England. With Karen Almond's post-final words ringing in their ears, the squad had made it their mission to usurp the USA as the premier team in international women's rugby by the time the next World Cup rolled round. In the end, they managed it a year ahead of schedule, beating the women's Eagles 17–6 in Canada in June 1993.

The American backs were no less fearsome when the teams met in the World Cup final at Raeburn Place in Edinburgh ten months later, but England's players backed themselves and their game plan to get the job done. With Carol Isherwood, who had hung up her international boots due to injury, cheering on her former teammates as part of Dowling's coaching staff, they did exactly that. Jane Mitchell, Jacquie Edwards and Gill Burns each crossed the whitewash, while two penalty tries and Karen Almond's boot helped England to a 38–23 win.

'[It was] amazing, absolutely amazing. Hard to describe it, really. It was huge,' Almond says. 'I went back to England in 2010 and watched when New Zealand won that final. And their cup was presented to them on the pitch, and they had fireworks and a big crowd, and it was amazing. But I remember thinking it was just the same feeling when we were given the World Cup. We didn't even stand on a podium, we just walked through, and someone gave us the cup, and there was about a few thousand people there. It was totally different, but the feeling was exactly the same.'

One member of the England squad who wasn't in quite the same mood for celebration was Dorrington. Having captained the side in the pool-stage win against Scotland, the 1991 World Cup organiser found herself on the bench, an unused replacement as Nicky Ponsford started the final. 'I wasn't happy about that, and never will be,' Dorrington admits. 'I know it sounds really self-focused and self-centred, but I felt a little detached from the team win despite having captained England against Scotland up there. But when we actually won and beat the USA, I felt a little detached from it.'

Cooper had spent the previous two weeks in Edinburgh covering the tournament as a freelance journalist, but both Griffin and Forsyth had stepped back from administration of the women's game after the inaugural World Cup. Griffin's second child, son Lawrence, was born the day before that second final, while Forsyth remained treasurer of Richmond's men's club and would head down to watch her old team at the Athletic Ground. 'Our club was very special,' she says. 'I used to go down and watch Richmond women play until my Anna, who's our third daughter, fell and cut her head and I thought, "I can't do this. I have two hands and three children!"'

Griffin would later return to administration and was a director of Women's Rugby World Cup 2010, which was held in England. By that time, the tournament was overseen by the International Rugby Board (IRB), which had assumed responsibility for the tournament ahead of the 1998 edition, Keith Rowlands taking his place on the organising committee. Did his experience at the 1991 final pave the way for IRB acceptance of the women's game? 'People do change their views, and I suspect when I was talking to him, he'd probably never watched women play,' Griffin says.

'Men of that generation thought that we were just taking the piss out of them, and we weren't, of course. You know, we wanted to play the game because we loved the game, and that was it. And we also weren't trying to replicate them. We were trying to do our own thing, and I think when they realised that and they look at the game and they go, "Actually, these guys really want to play", they can turn their minds around to supporting it.

'You see 3,000 or 4,000 people who've come to watch the game and they're enjoying themselves and the quality of the rugby is good. You've got to go, "Why am I objecting to this? There isn't a good reason to object to it, is there?"'

The 2010 World Cup bore a striking resemblance to Griffin's earliest sketch of what a women's World Cup could look like. It featured pool matches played at a provincial location, Guildford, with the semi-finals and final played at a major club ground – Harlequins' Stoop. The group-stage matches were the first to be fully ticketed, and the showpiece match between the hosts and New Zealand (who had a link to 1991 in 45-year-old fly half

Anna Richards) was a sell-out. That is a trick Griffin hopes can be repeated across the road at Twickenham in 2025, when the country again hosts the tournament. It goes without saying that the original organising committee chair, by then an RFU board and World Rugby council member,[iii] was part of the successful bid team.

'We've fought so long for this,' Griffin says, referring to the work she does with the RFU and World Rugby. 'People involved now haven't been involved all along, and that's not a criticism, but I don't want them to destroy what we have done. I want the game to move forward. I want the game to grow. I want more people playing. I want the teams to be more professional in all sorts of ways. But you know, decisions you make now are really, really important for what happens in five, ten years' time. And it's making sure that we make the right decisions to keep that growth going.'

Women attempting to play the sport they love still face myriad obstacles. However, countless female rugby players, including those who will line up at Rugby World Cup 2021 in New Zealand in October 2022, are grateful for the difficult decisions that Griffin, Cooper, Dorrington and Forsyth made at the beginning of the 1990s. Without their hard work, dedication and sacrifice, it is impossible to know how long it would have taken for the dream of a women's World Cup to become a reality.

'What's important to me is that women want to play. They want to coach. They want to referee. And they want to do it to the best of their ability and, you know, go forward and move forward,' Griffin concludes. 'What happened in the past is nice, it's historical and it's interesting. But I'm not one to think that they should thank us or be grateful because, you know, they'd do the same thing now.'

[iii] The IRB became known as World Rugby in 2014.

EPILOGUE

BY THE TIME the cheque signed by Dudley Wood was pushed through the letterbox of 224A Camden Road, the world of women's rugby had moved on from events in South Wales. A new rugby season was about to begin and bids to host the second Women's Rugby World Cup had been submitted. Deborah Griffin had scrambled to plug the hole in the tournament's finances, but work and life commitments dictated that she was not able to meet with Alice Cooper, Sue Dorrington and Mary Forsyth to celebrate or decompress. There was no time for a tournament debrief following the inaugural women's World Cup.

'I don't think there was a proper sit down, to say, "Shit, what just happened?"' Dorrington recalled. 'Because we were all so busy getting on with our lives.' Of the four members of the organising committee, only Cooper remained involved in the day-to-day running of the women's game heading into the 1991/92 campaign. Cooper had been voted in to serve as the WRFU's press and publicity officer for the upcoming campaign, building on the work she had done before and during the World Cup.

Given the toll the previous 18 months had taken on the organising committee, it is no surprise that Griffin, Dorrington and Forsyth should decide to take a back seat. Now that the tournament's accounts had been balanced, Griffin could focus more time on her young family and in time would return to Richmond as a player. She dusted off her boots for one final season the following year, before putting them back in storage when she became pregnant with her son, Lawrence.

Forsyth remained involved with Richmond as treasurer of the men's club, a role she held for a couple more years until managing her own growing family made it impractical. Having been born into a large family, she always hoped to replicate the loving, boisterous environment that she had experienced as a child in Pittsburgh. Mary and Piers would become parents six times, although tragedy struck in 1992 when their second child, a son, died suddenly. Forsyth approached her kids' education and activities with the same gusto as she had the World Cup, putting her energy and organisational skills to use in the wider community.

She was left in no doubt of the esteem in which her children hold her following a chance encounter with England great Sue Day at a Red Roses match in 2022. When Carol Isherwood introduced her to England's record try scorer, Forsyth initially queried her name as Daisy Day. 'She's such a legend,' Forsyth said, embarrassed as she relayed the story to her son. 'Mum, you're a legend in your own right,' he replied. 'Don't you know that?'

Cooper and Dorrington both continued to represent Richmond on the Athletic Ground's pitches beyond the conclusion of the first World Cup. A broken leg suffered towards the end of the 1992/93 season curtailed Cooper's involvement with the first team and precipitated a change in position. However, she had been good enough to receive an invite to a Scotland trial in January 1993, ahead of the country's first international against Ireland.

International honours might have eluded Cooper, but she recovered sufficiently from her leg injury to enjoy one final season as a player, shifting from the second row to become a winger on the Richmond second team. 'It was great because you didn't have to be that fit,' she remembered. 'You just had to do a bit of sprinting and then you had hours to get your breath back.'

Perhaps driven by the hurt of the World Cup final loss, Dorrington was determined to keep her place as starting hooker for both Richmond and England. Following the break-up of her marriage, she bought her own flat close to the club and her change in circumstances meant that she was no longer able to afford personal sessions with sports psychologist Alma Thomas. She continued to work with her trainer David Crottie, a sporting relationship that survives to this day, but had to cut back on the regularity of their sessions.

Her new, and by necessity more frugal, approach did not initially appear to have any impact on her hopes of keeping the England number two jersey on the road to the 1994 women's World Cup. She started the victories over Wales and the Netherlands at the beginning of 1992 and a year later, Dorrington also lined up in the middle of the front row as England exacted revenge on the USA with a 17–6 win at the Canada Cup in Brampton. By the time the rescued global tournament took place in Scotland, however, it was her great rival Nicky Ponsford who was back in favour. Unperturbed, Dorrington continued to push for a recall. She remained a member of the England squad until 1997, when she was 39, and would excel for Richmond into the next millennium.

The world in which Dorrington ended her playing career was a very different one for female rugby players than existed when she first headed down to training in Minnesota two decades previously. There had been many steps taken on that journey, from the moment Emily Valentine joined her brothers on a pitch in Enniskillen, however, none had quite the impact on the future direction of the women's game as the inaugural women's World Cup.

In taking the tournament to the rugby heartland of South Wales, setting ambitious standards in terms of venues and referees, and engaging with the WRU, RFU and IRFB, the organising committee legitimised the World Cup and put women's rugby on the radar of many who appeared predisposed to ignore it. Griffin and co. did not need the approval of the IRFB to stage their event and in seeking it they only opened themselves up to fraught meetings and legal threats. Crucially, though, in doing so, the organising committee started a dialogue that ultimately led the global governing body to take steps to become truly inclusive.

That first World Cup showcased to those watching on, including IRFB secretary Keith Rowlands, not only the talent of the best players and teams but the spirit and resolve that existed among the female playing community. If that was what could be achieved when the organisers were fighting prejudice, what could those women accomplish if they had the backing of those in positions of power?

Moreover, and contrary to the worst fears of many male club members, women who laced up a pair of boots were not driven to do so by a desire to burn the clubhouse to the ground. As Cooper had so pithily told Paul Wade in Llanharan, most women wanted to play rugby for exactly the same reasons as men. They relished the physical contact and enjoyed the post-match opportunities for singing and socialising. If society determined that women who enjoyed playing collision sports were in some way radical or counter-cultural then that was a problem for society. It should not have been an issue for the women who discovered a freedom when running with ball in hand, or the men whose clubhouses they chose to drink in on a Sunday afternoon.

'I think part of what we had was that thing [of saying], "You know what? It's OK to want to play what would have been perceived then as a non-female sport,"' Sarah Wenn, who lined up in England's second-row in the first World Cup final, said in an interview for this book. 'It's not so odd for us to want to make it into a woman's sport as well as a man's sport. I remember for a long time when I was playing, most people would say to me, "What's it like to play a man's sport?" I was like, "But it's not a man's sport!" We don't play like men, we're not physically built like men. Yes, we follow the same laws, and we have the same referees, but we play within our physical capability.'

Having given the participants an opportunity to experience life as a full-time rugby player for ten days, meeting like-minded women from across the globe while free of the sexism that may have marked their previous endeavours, it is logical that the World Cup would quickly flourish independently of those who initially organised it. Regardless of the many challenges faced before, during and after the event. Indeed, the tournament was seen as such a success by those taking part that planning for a second one began before the semi-final line-up had even been decided.

The IRFB was slow to wake up to the potential of the women's game, even after Rowlands had enjoyed the hospitality of the first World Cup final, almost derailing the second edition entirely as it stalled on making a decision about allowing member unions to take part. However, the board could not ignore the spirit contained within the female game for much longer. In 1995, a year after a group of inspirational Scottish women saved that second tournament on three months' notice, the IRFB began the process of becoming inclusive when it formed its first women's advisory committee. Tasked with producing a five-year women's development plan, the committee was a significant step in the right direction. It was also one that would have seemed inconceivable only five years before, when Griffin and co. set about planning the first women's World Cup.

*****

It was a chance phone call that pulled Griffin back into the world of rugby administration. In February 2002, Australian Rosie Williams began life as the managing director of the Rugby Football Union for Women (RFUW), the body that oversaw female participation in England following the disbandment of the WRFU in 1994, and soon discovered that she had inherited a mess. 'Sport England had given the RFUW a report that they were not fit for purpose,' Griffin recalled two decades later. 'There was a lot of shenanigans going on with the committee at the time.'

Williams had been alerted to Griffin's financial expertise and faced with a 'big VAT bill' and few records, convinced her to help dig the organisation out of a hole. 'I had to recreate the VAT records for about three years. I mean, it was just horrendous,' Griffin added. 'I spent hours doing that. At that time, I was working four days a week and my fifth day was always doing the RFUW accounts and trying to get them sorted. So that's when I got back involved ... and sorted it!'

Energised by being involved in the women's game again, Griffin put herself forward as chair of the RFUW when the role became available in 2005. It was a position she would hold until 2012, when the RFU belatedly took on official responsibility for female participation. 'In 2005, 2006, we had some meetings with a lovely, lovely guy called Budge Rogers, who was Sussex council member and subsequently became the president of the RFU in 2006 and we wrote a paper,' she said.

'[It was] about why the RFU should merge with the RFUW... It was a really well-written paper and he wrote it, but we worked together on that and he wanted it to happen before his presidency or for his presidency. But the main reason they always said that they couldn't do it was because we were largely funded by UK Sport and Sport England. And what they were worried about was that if they took it over, that money would cease. And yeah, I think they were probably right, some of it may well have done. That was their main issue, but it was also probably a little bit of ...'

When the RFU offered the RFUW a seat on its council in 2010, Griffin was the obvious choice. In that year, she also helped Williams organise the biggest and best Women's Rugby World Cup yet as sold-out signs went up during the pool stage at Surrey Sports Park in Guildford and again at the Stoop for the final. That match again ended in defeat for hosts England, as New Zealand edged to their fourth successive World Cup triumph winning 13–10 in South-West London. That tournament proved more than any other up until that point that there was a market for women's rugby and was vindication for Griffin's decision to charge for tickets to the preliminary rounds and price the showpiece match at a competitive rate.

'We put forward a plan for the final to have tickets at about £15 and £10 and things like that,' she recalled. 'They (the IRB[i]) were adamant that this was far too high, and we wouldn't sell, and we should have them at £5. And they sent all these examples like, you know, England women cricket played in Taunton and the cost of the tickets was £5, you know, and I said, "No." The main reason, I said, was we will sell out ... please! We'll sell out at that price. I said, "If you do that, you're devaluing the game because you're saying it's only a £5 game."'

Griffin served as the women and girls' representative on the RFU council until 2018, when she became one of the English union's representatives on the World Rugby council, the biggest decision-making body in the global game. The organisation that

---

[i] The IRFB became known as the IRB in 1997, before changing its name again to World Rugby in 2014.

Griffin joined four years ago was very different to the one she had dealt with almost three decades previously. World Rugby had assumed responsibility for the women's game 20 years previously. As Ali Donnelly notes in her excellent book, *Scrum Queens*, the development plan devised by the first women's advisory committee set out three principle aims:

1. To encourage the participation of women in playing, coaching, refereeing and administration
2. To promote women's rugby nationally and internationally
3. To integrate women's rugby into all relevant aspects of the IRFB's operation

More than a quarter of a century on and World Rugby is still wrestling with at least two of those initial goals. Women who pick up an oval ball still have to overcome more barriers to do so than men. There remain fewer opportunities for women and girls to play and in turn fewer pathways for those female players to become coaches, referees and leaders. Women's teams and tournaments, meanwhile, are still not seen as attractive commercially, or from a broadcast perspective, as men's. On the pitch, moreover, the drive to professionalise the international game has skewed results in favour of those, primarily England, with money.

World Rugby, though, can no longer be accused of ignoring its female playing base or being deaf to their concerns. Following the most recent women's World Cup, in 2017, it published an eight-year strategic plan for the women's game that was designed to help dismantle obstacles to female participation at all levels of the game. Central to that was the decision to expand the council by a third and add 17 female members, Griffin included, thus finally giving women a voice when it came to making decisions.

In 2019, Griffin lined up as one of 15 'Unstoppable' ambassadors whose stories were used to launch the 'Try And

Stop Us' marketing campaign and a new brand identity for the women's game. I have written for the World Rugby websites since 2018 and have seen the impact the governing body's initiatives have had globally in creating opportunities for women in coaching, refereeing and administration. At the end of 2021, at around the time the Women in Rugby plan was updated, World Rugby also set up a dedicated women's player welfare working group, funding much-needed research in that area.

As those initiatives have been rolled out, World Rugby has tapped into the knowledge of several women who participated in the inaugural World Cup, including Isherwood, Anna Richards and Nicky Ponsford. Former Wales captain Liza Burgess, meanwhile, joined Griffin on the council as one of the WRU's representatives in 2021, and it is not only World Rugby whose plans for the future have been infused by the ideas of those pioneers who were around in 1991. Ponsford, for example, joined the global governing body in July 2021 on a two-year sabbatical from the RFU.

*****

One of the challenges facing the women's game today is how best to communicate inspirational stories from the past to current and future generations. World Rugby has relatively recently begun to celebrate the trailblazers of an era it could have chosen to conveniently overlook. In 2009, the decision was taken to officially recognise the first two women's World Cups. Five years later, following a campaign on scrumqueens. com, six women were inducted into the World Rugby Hall of Fame, five of whom – Patty Jervey, Nathalie Amiel, Gill Burns, Isherwood and Richards – excelled in South Wales across those eight days in 1991. Burgess took her place in the exclusive club four years later.

The World Rugby Museum, which despite its name is based at Twickenham and does not have any link to the body formerly known as the IRFB, meanwhile, launched the brilliant Rugby World Cup: In Her Own Words exhibition in March 2022. Curated by Donnelly and Dr Lydia Furse, with help from a number of prominent former players, including Dorrington, it lets visitors follow the path the women's World Cup has taken from the first edition in South Wales all the way to the present day.

Burns, England's goal-kicking number eight in 1991, spoke at the launch event for the exhibition and she has done a brilliant job in fostering a community among British players from the 1980s, '90s and '00s. The former Lancashire RFU president organised for commemorative caps to be made and distributed to those women who played for England, Great Britain and regional sides when there was no money to produce official mementos of those achievements. Cooper, Dorrington and Forsyth were all grateful and proud recipients of their ornate headwear.

Backed by the RFU, Burns has visited the current England squad with former players to talk to them about their experiences. In October 2021, she travelled to the Red Roses' base in Berkshire with a group including Dorrington, on the same day that she had taken possession of the trophy that had been competed for at Cardiff Arms Park more than 30 years previously – and which had been assumed lost. The antique silver trophy was taken along to Bisham Abbey, and it seems the young players were transfixed by the tales of those who had gone before them.

'The girls were genuinely, totally engaged and interested,' Burns told me for an article that appeared on the World Rugby website. 'Ellie Kildunne said to me afterwards, "I was at school, I was a rugby player, I was good at it and now I'm paid for doing it, and I never once thought about that not being possible for people who've been international players before." She just opened her eyes to the fact that it had been a struggle for a while for us, and it was lovely to hear that.'

Kildunne looks set to be part of the England squad that will compete in the pandemic-delayed Rugby World Cup 2021[ii], which is due to kick off at the iconic Eden Park in Auckland on 8 October 2022. The ninth edition of the women's tournament, it will be the first to be played in the southern hemisphere and New Zealand. Billed by organisers as a family reunion following the impact of covid, the event offers the women's game its latest opportunity to take another step forward.

It could well be a reunion of sorts for those four women who set the women's World Cup on its journey to Aotearoa. Griffin, who was re-elected as one of the RFU's representatives on World Rugby council in June 2022, is hoping to start her retirement at the tournament. She is scheduled to step down from her role as bursar at Homerton College, Cambridge University at the end of September and her plan is to 'fly straight off to New Zealand for the World Cup'. If Cooper, Dorrington and Forsyth are able to join her at Eden Park then maybe, finally the four pioneers can have that debrief.

[ii] World Rugby adopted gender neutral naming for its competitions in 2019.

ACKNOWLEDGEMENTS

IT GOES WITHOUT saying that this book would not have seen the light of day had it not been for the support of the four amazing pioneers who poured so much of themselves into that first Women's Rugby World Cup: Deborah Griffin, Alice Cooper, Sue Dorrington and Mary Forsyth.

The seed of the idea for this book was planted during my first meeting with Deborah, for an interview for World Rugby, at Twickenham in April 2019. Since I started work on the project properly at the start of the following year, she has given up hours of her time and also entrusted me with boxes of meticulously kept documents from her personal archive. Alice, Sue and Mary have been equally generous with their time, welcoming me into their homes or meeting for coffee and on Zoom to discuss their memories of those events three-plus decades ago. I am indebted not only to their recollections but also for the trust they have placed in me to help tell the story of that inaugural World Cup.

I have received nothing but encouragement from the women in rugby who I approached to be interviewed for this book. It was impossible to quote everyone who I spoke to, but you each gave me something that has gone into the final book. Carol Isherwood, Emma Mitchell, Sam Robson, Gill Burns, Jami Jordan, Krista McFarren, Liza Burgess, Amanda Bennett and Anna Richards were particularly helpful in sharing contacts as well as insight.

It was a pleasure to chat to Rosie Golby, Karen Almond, Steve Dowling, Cheryl Stennett, Giselle Mather, Nicky Ponsford, Sarah Wenn, Barb Bond, Tara Flanagan, Tam Breckenridge, Candi Orsini, Kevin O'Brien, MA Sorenson, Chris Leach, Dawn Barnett, Belinda Davies, Jackie Morgan, Kate Eaves, Helen Littleworth, Natasha Wong, Jeannette Toxopeus, Sue Eakers, Isla Meek and Fiona Reynolds. Lauren O'Reilly, meanwhile, gave invaluable insight into the early days of the women's game in New Zealand and a heartfelt account of life with her late father, Laurie. Eileen Langsley provided a different viewpoint on the Soviet squad, having travelled through the USSR as a sports photographer. Erika Morri kindly provided photos of the Italian squad in South Wales. Chris Jones, Stephen Jones and David Hands were all gracious with their time, as were David Crottie, Brian Moore, Peter Owens and John Taylor.

Kathy Flores has sadly passed away since we chatted over Zoom in May 2020. She could not have been more forthcoming with her time or recollections. Speaking to Kathy about rugby was invigorating and inspiring in equal measure and I hope the sections of this book in which she features do justice to her incredible legacy.

As I told her when we first discussed the foreword for this book, there is no one I would rather have written it than Sarah Hunter. I am extremely grateful that she was able to find the time in her incredibly busy pre-Rugby World Cup schedule to deliver such fitting prose. Thanks too to Emily Liles at the RFU, one of the most accommodating communications managers I have had the privilege of working with.

Philippa Sitters, my agent, was the driving force who helped shape the book into what it became. Without her input and support it would not be here, and I hope this is the start of a fruitful working relationship. Pete Burns at Polaris has done a brilliant job of pulling everything together in such a short amount of time and has been a dream to work with. I am grateful too to Alan McIntosh, who edited the finished manuscript with care.

To my great mate, Laura Forker, thank you for reading the very first draft of the potential manuscript, for putting me in touch with Philippa and for helping to convince her that this was a book she wanted to work on. Steven Saunders, my old boss at *ESPN*, also read those early chapters and gave me some invaluable advice. I would also like to thank Ali Donnelly for the tips and guidance she has offered in recent months. *Scrumqueens*, the website she runs with John Birch, has of course also been an invaluable resource. In terms of research, I could not have finished the book had it not been for frequent visits to the World Rugby Museum at Twickenham. Thanks to Niamh Field, Phil McGowan and Dr Lydia Furse, all of whom contributed to the finished work.

Truthfully, I cannot say whether I would have even had the idea for this book had I not started working with World Rugby in 2018. So, thanks to Dom Rumbles for putting early work my way and to Karen Bond who continued to commission me and ultimately asked me to concentrate more on women in rugby. Both Karen and Ben Sillis allowed me to write about the first women's World Cup for the governing body's website, which helped theories that appear in the book to ferment. Sarah Mockford at *Rugby World* also took an article on the USA's success in Cardiff on the 30th anniversary of the tournament, enabling me to live out a childhood dream and see my name on a byline in the magazine.

I would like to thank my parents, Keith and Sian, and my brother, Gareth and his partner, Tarin for their support. For a couple of hours at the beginning of December 2021 I feared my dad would not be around to read this book but watching him attack his recovery from a serious spinal injury has been inspirational. It has certainly put any stress or anxiety I felt in the course of this project into perspective. Finally, I owe a huge debt of gratitude to my wonderful partner, Clare. Polaris' offer came through on the day that she gave birth to our first child, Romy, and she has been this book's biggest supporter through what any new parent will know is an incredibly difficult, and tiring, time. Clare was the first person to read anything written for it and I could not have hoped for a better editor. Thank you, and sorry that I didn't accept *all* your suggestions.

POLARIS
PUBLISHING